Teaching
children
to think

2ND EDITION

Robert Fisher

Nelson Thornes
a Wolters Kluwer business

First published in 1990 by:
Basil Blackwell Ltd

Second edition published in 2005 by:
Nelson Thornes Ltd
Delta Place
27 Bath Road
CHELTENHAM
GL53 7TH
United Kingdom

06 07 08 09 / 10 9 8 7 6 5 4 3 2

A catalogue record for this book is available from the British Library

ISBN 0 7487 9441 7

Page make-up by Northern Phototypesetting Co. Ltd, Bolton

Cover photograph: Image 100 EE (NT)

Printed and bound in Spain by GraphyCems

Acknowledgements

I wish to thank the following individuals, organisations and publishers for their generous permission to use copyright material in this book: John Kitching for the poem 'Why' first published in *A Second Book of Poetry* compiled by John Foster, published by Oxford University Press, 1980; The National Association for Gifted Children for permission to reproduce the 'Mother and Baby' drawing; Extract from Darwin's notebook reproduced by permission of the Syndics of Cambridge University Library.

My thanks go to the many colleagues, teachers and children who have helped develop my understanding of thinking and learning and have granted permission to quote from their work in schools. I also wish to thank the many people who have contributed to the first edition including my sons Jake and Tom, and those who have helped prepare the second edition, in particular Lizann O'Conor and Julie Winyard for their helpful comments. My debt is to all who have helped to improve this book; the flaws and shortcomings that remain are my own.

Every effort has been made to contact the copyright holders but if any have been inadvertently overlooked, the publishers will be pleased to make the necessary arrangement at the first opportunity.

Contents

Preface

'Your first thoughts are not always your best thoughts,' said a child, when explaining the need to revise his work, 'but you don't always get the chance to change them.' It is a pleasure to have the chance to update and amend this book in its second edition. Approaches to teaching and learning have moved on considerably since the first edition of this book. This is reflected in the text, with revisions to existing chapters and a new end chapter, 'Thinking schools', giving updates on resources and approaches to teaching thinking. Also included is a new bibliography and glossary.

The need to put the teaching of thinking at the heart of education has become a common vision in schools, educational communities and organisations. The principles enshrined in this book became the basis for the 'thinking skills' element in the National Curriculum for England and Wales (1999) and are reflected in many other curriculum guidelines developed in recent years. There have been huge changes in education during this time, including the use of new information technology, changes in curriculum content, tests and examinations, and in home and school environments. With so many new initiatives in recent years, it is easy to forget what is really important in education. What is heartening and a cause for optimism is the new focus on thinking and creativity in education in countries across the world. A huge amount of effort has gone into finding ways of helping teach children to think more creatively and effectively. And there is good reason for this.

Teaching for thinking is essential if we are to improve the functioning and development of society and of schools. Teaching for thinking is developed through intellectual engagement, purpose, energy and interactive tension with others. It results in children better able to communicate what they think, to benefit from the thinking of others, and to be resourceful in solving problems and flexible in the face of new challenges. These positive, creative attributes are essential to citizens living in an increasingly complex, changing and challenging social environment. A true democracy requires critical and creative citizens. The moral life requires imagination. Thoughtfulness should not only be the intellectual but also the moral aim of education. We have good reason, therefore, to invest in the development of children's thinking at individual, social and national levels.

This book is about finding ways to help children fulfil their potential in learning and in life. Although primarily directed at teachers, it aims to be of use to other professionals, to parents and other carers, in providing a vision of the thinking child and practical ways to develop in children the habits of intelligent behaviour. This book has its focus on strategies to develop thinking. A companion book, *Teaching Children to Learn*, looks at ways of helping children to learn how to learn.

In this book I hope you will share in the excitement, adventure and challenge that I have had in trying to find out what children think and helping them to share their thinking with others. As Kirandeep, aged 8, said: 'Thinking is what we are here for.'

Robert Fisher

Introduction

All lessons are lessons in thinking.
Gilbert Ryle

This book is written for anyone interested in teaching children how to think, to reason and to solve problems. It reviews the main concepts, methods and research findings in the teaching of thinking skills that have been developed in recent years. The aim is to present a survey of current approaches and ways of teaching children to think for themselves both at home and school. The teaching of thinking skills is potentially one of the most valuable areas of educational research and development today.

Much of education is focused on the achievement of certain basic skills, rather than on the potential that might be achieved. Perhaps our present mental and intuitive capacities are only a shadow of what might be. Perhaps it is possible to teach people to be more effective thinkers, to be more intelligent. The movement to teach children thinking skills stems from the belief that thinking can be learned and taught, and that it is possible to raise the general level of intelligence of any child through the mediation of teacher or parent.

What can be done beyond teaching children the basic skills of literacy and numeracy and giving them some knowledge of the world to help them use their skills and knowledge for effective problem solving, reasoning and thinking? One approach is to look for specific ways of raising individual levels of intelligence, of accelerating cognitive development and enhancing a child's capacity for thinking and learning. Part of this initiative arises from:

- the development of programmes aimed at teaching thinking
- research into the study of intelligence
- a response to the problem of *passive knowledge* – the teaching of inert ideas that do not stimulate effective thinking and learning
- a search for ways to develop the key skills in learning that will transfer out of the classroom and the textbook into real life situations.

Past theories tended to focus on simpler forms of learning. They were successful in generating many improvements in the teaching of basic skills. Today there is a greater emphasis on the *process* of learning, on investigation and problem solving, on reading for meaning, on the use of reasoning in writing, on study skills and on developing autonomous ways of learning. Reasons for this lie in our changing view of children, of schools and of society.

Part of the need to teach thinking skills has come from a growing awareness that society has changed. Skills that were appropriate 20 years ago no longer prepare children for the world beyond school. Technological change has both created and destroyed jobs. Many clerical and middle-management positions are being phased out by hi-tech replacements. Jobs grow in areas where technology opens new work opportunities. Changes in society are accelerating so rapidly that it is difficult to assess what factual knowledge will be needed for the future. The educational implications of this are that we should focus on teaching skills essential to the gaining, organising and using of information. To be prepared for the challenge of the future, children will need

skills that will give them control over their lives and their learning, for of their learning there will be no end. They will need knowledge, but more importantly they will
need the capacity to gain new knowledge, their own knowledge. They will need an
attitude of open-mindedness to the future, not our future but their future.

The foundation for thinking skills needs to be laid early in life, for open-mindedness
begins in the formative years when a child's identity as a thinking person is being
established. As children become adults there is an increasing tendency to closed-
mindedness where beliefs are ego-centred (where what '*I* believe' becomes more
essential than what 'I *believe*'), where those who disagree are regarded as biased and as
not having the capacity to enter into a reasoned and open-ended discussion. This need
not be the case. Children can be taught to value their capacity for thinking, they can
be taught the principles of reasoning, how to use reason as a tool for learning, how to
learn from others and how to play their part in the shared enterprise of enquiry. For
this they need to be given the opportunity to work out their own thoughts, to put their
ideas into words, to advance theories and to justify their beliefs. They need to discover
themselves as thinking, feeling, whole people. How these skills are nurtured in home
and school is crucial to their development.

Traditionally schools have been places where children receive rather than give information and thoughts. Generally teachers have expected children to learn and to
reproduce the accepted wisdom, a 'learn this because I tell you' approach. The following exchange was overheard in one such classroom:

Gary was sitting at his desk, leaning on his hand as still as a Rodin statue.

Teacher	Gary what are you doing?
Gary	Thinking.
Teacher	Well stop thinking and listen to me!

Another child when asked about thinking remarked, 'I think in the playground when
I go out to play.'

There were various reasons for the neglect of thinking in schools, including misconceptions about the nature of reasoning and intelligence.

One misconception about reasoning is the belief that thinking is just one of the so-
called basic skills, like reading, writing or arithmetic. Reasoning is not simply a 'fourth
R'. It is the foundation skill of all learning, and fundamental to the development of all
the other skills. All human action is embedded in human thought, though much of this
thinking may be subconscious or functioning on an automatic and non-rational level.
Even the simple acts of speaking, listening, reading, writing or computation entail a
vast number of highly diversified cognitive skills and mental acts. There is no doing
without some form of thinking; it is the primary process of human life.

A second misconception about reasoning is that reasoning skills are natural functions,
like breathing, walking, talking, seeing and hearing, skills that necessarily improve
with age and experience. This may be partly true, but as adults we retain the basic
repertoire of reasoning skills that we had as children. The higher order skills that we
use when we engage in elaborate and sophisticated thinking are not different skills but
the same skills used in more sophisticated combinations. An analogy used by Matthew
Lipman[1] is of the car mechanic, who has certain primary skills to do with the individual tools in his toolkit, skills with screwdriver, wrench and pliers that we might share.
What we do not know, in what he does, is how to organise and sequence the use of

these tools to repair the engine. He uses the tools in a certain calculating and strategic way to solve a mechanical problem. The skills he uses together with knowledge of the engine provide his understanding of the mechanical problem that makes the difference between him and us. The task is how to give children experiences in using their thinking that will develop their higher-order skills.

Another misconception is the idea that the teaching of reasoning must entail ignoring the emotional side of life. There is no necessary dichotomy between thinking and feeling. Teaching children to think does not mean impoverishing their emotional development. They will not be turned into unfeeling robots, knowing the price of everything and the value of nothing. Thinking does not flourish in an emotional vacuum. Thinking is an activity that requires a purpose and a driving force. Emotions, feelings and passions of some kind or other lie at the heart of human behaviour. What we need to free ourselves and our children from is not feeling or emotion but prejudice and other irrational emotions and beliefs. It is the linking of reason with emotion that provides the prime motivation for learning, and for the development of intelligence.

Throughout the last century the study of intelligence was dominated by the question of whether intelligence is primarily determined by heredity (biological/genetic factors) or environment (social/cultural influences), that is, the nature versus nurture debate. Psychologists were preoccupied with the question 'How can we measure intelligence?' and largely neglected the more important question 'What is intelligence?' Intelligence has often been defined as what is measured by intelligence tests. However, although IQ tests permeate the education system, there is no general agreement on what it is they actually measure. The old idea that intelligence is a fixed commodity given to all children in differing amounts has been challenged by many researchers. Attention turned to ways of raising intelligence through 'teaching for thinking'. We teach children many skills, physical skills, social skills, expressive skills, linguistic and mathematical skills, why not thinking skills?

The implications of recent research into intelligence are discussed in Chapter 1, 'What is thinking?' It is an intriguing subject, the source of human capability, and key to human survival. It is an inherently human capacity, which differentiates us from animals (and from computers). Yet even among experts the definitions of what we call thinking vary greatly. There is much in the concept that is still in the process of being uncovered, and much still to be learned. Research on the nature of thinking does, however, offer answers to such questions as:

- What are the characteristics of intelligent behaviour?
- What strategies identify mature and successful thinkers?
- What are the common weaknesses of human thinking – how can we help children to avoid them?
- Is intelligence a unitary factor or is it a group of aptitudes?
- If there are separate functions can they be improved by practice?
- How do children's elementary forms of thinking convert into higher order skills?

One perennial question put by parents and teachers to children is, 'Why don't you think?' There now exists a major international movement aimed at promoting intellectual development and thinking skills in children. Many different programmes and approaches are geared towards the teaching of thinking. Each section of this book will consider one of the following aspects of teaching thinking.

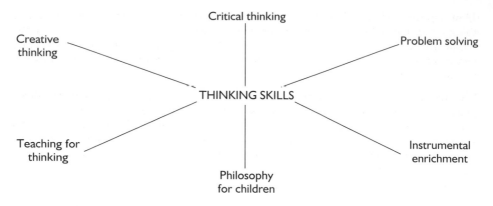

If not encouraged at an early age children will stop speculating and playing with ideas. They need to learn to think creatively to prepare themselves for a fast-changing world. What is creative thinking and how can it be encouraged? Creativity consists largely of rearranging what we know in order to find out what we do not know.... Hence to think creatively we must be able to look afresh at what we usually take for granted. Ways of looking afresh at things are explored in Chapter 2, 'Creative thinking'.

Creative thinking supplies the context of discovery, the generation of hypotheses. Critical thinking provides the context of justification, testing the acceptability of reason and proof.

The term 'critical thinking' used here does not mean thinking that is negative or primarily fault finding, but rather the thinking that evaluates reason. It highlights the ideal of the 'reasonable person' who is capable of independent autonomous thinking. The child as critical thinker does not simply accept or reject reasons and beliefs without applying some form of judgement or evaluation. Chapter 3, 'Critical thinking', addresses the questions: What are the identifiable skills of critical thinking? How can they be taught?

Human life is a problem-solving process. Chapter 4, 'Problem solving', shows how problem solving can provide an effective way of practising skills in finding and using facts, relevant both to school and to life situations. Thinking is what happens when a person solves a problem. How do we help children to be more effective problem solvers?

All children face problems but not all children achieve success in tackling them. One of the pioneers of the 'thinking skills' movement was Reuven Feuerstein. His programme, discussed in Chapter 5, 'Instrumental enrichment', was devised to overcome the causes of failure in thinking and learning. It aimed to transform children's thinking, learning and ability to solve problems through special instruments of learning. Feuerstein stresses the key role adults can play in overcoming a child's cognitive deficiencies and thereby raising his general level of intelligence.

Another pioneer was Matthew Lipman, whose ambitious curriculum for teaching thinking skills and more is the Philosophy for Children programme. Lipman's objective was to get children to think for themselves instead of learning by rote, or simply accepting the authority of the teacher. Lipman's approach, discussed in Chapter 6,

'Philosophy for children', was to adapt philosophy to the needs of children, whatever their age. Philosophy for Children has developed into a worldwide movement, with a growing interest being shown in Britain. The Philosophy for Children approach offers ways to transform the way children think through establishing a real community of enquiry in the classroom.

Chapters 7, 'Teaching for thinking', and 8, 'Teaching thinking across the curriculum', present ways of teaching children to think across the curriculum. The premise of these chapters is that the quality of teaching rather than the content of the curriculum is the key to realising a child's potential. The quality of teaching is reflected in the way it helps children to remember, to build on the concepts they have learned and to process new ideas into their own patterns of thinking. Various ways in which this can be achieved are explored in this chapter, including activities that can be used to develop the child's self concept as a thinker and stimulate his unique capacities for thought and action. Chapter 9, 'Thinking schools', discusses recent developments and approaches in teaching thinking.

The philosopher Martin Heidegger wrote:

It is one thing to have heard and read something, that is merely to take notice; it is another thing to understand what we have heard and read, that is to ponder.

This book looks in detail at ways in which we can help children to ponder and to gain power over the inner forces that affect their lives.

1 What is thinking?

Our present-day knowledge of the child's mind is comparable to a fifteenth century map of the world – a mixture of truth and error . . . vast areas remain to be explored.
　　Arnold L. Gesell

Imagine a child sitting in a room. As she looks round she can see objects and people. She is able to categorise these objects as 'table', 'chair', 'picture', 'book'. She may notice the bird flying past the window or the fly settling on the table. She can communicate with people in the room, and can draw some meaning from the page of an open book. She may look at and make sense of the picture on the wall, listen to sounds and realise they are a piece of music. She may be aware that some time ago she had breakfast and that soon it will be lunchtime. We take such behaviour from our children very much for granted. But if the child was born brain damaged, or blind or deaf, or if she became ill or injured, these cognitive processes would be much more difficult, if not impossible. How is it that children can so successfully make meaning from the world?

To understand the world the child must first perceive, attend to or take in the visual and auditory stimuli around him. He must hold these in his mind while he decides what they are and how to respond. What was that dark shape moving across the window? Does it need thinking about and storing in the memory or is it a fleeting impression to be ignored? The fact that he can recognise a bird means that he has previously stored memories, has developed the concept of a 'bird' and has some idea of the process of 'flight'. He has developed some of the tools of language to communicate this experience. He has learnt to translate the shapes and symbols in the book or the picture on the wall. These processes of perception, memory, concept formation, language and symbolisation are the basic cognitive skills that underlie the ability to reason, to learn and to solve problems. To study thinking is to study these structures and processes through which we as humans experience and make sense of the world. As one child put it, 'If we didn't think there'd be no us.'

All humans subject to normal development have the capacity and ability to think, although these capacities vary widely between (and perhaps within) individuals. It may be that young children have the same cognitive processes as adults. They can perceive, remember, form concepts and communicate, although their thinking is not as effective as that of most adults and the uses to which they put these processes are often different from those of adults. Much of what adults see and do is familiar and recognisable. They automatically process information that for a child would seem strange and novel. The adult has probably seen that bird many times before and can automatically classify it as a blackbird or seagull. The child, however, is presented with a continual array of totally new stimuli. While the adult knows her way around the world, and can employ her cognitive powers as she chooses, the child needs to use his powers to make sense of a strange and novel environment. Children are travellers in a largely unknown land, and we are their guides.

As frail creatures in a hostile environment humans have needed to develop their cognitive capacities to ensure survival. The most effective strategy (for adults or children)
is to attend to those aspects of the environment most essential for survival at any one
time. Most adults today are relatively free from threats to their survival. There is little
need for heightened cognitive awareness. They can exist quite happily and successfully
with low levels of cognitive activity. As one woman was overheard saying, 'It's best to
be philosophical, Ada, don't think about it.' Children may also learn to ignore stimuli
that pose no immediate threat. They too can live lives with relatively little thought.
They have, however, a need to understand the world and a natural curiosity about the
stimuli that surround them. But to make sense of the world they need help in responding to and processing information they have gathered about their experiences. In order
to help the child we need to try to understand what these sense-making processes are.
What is thinking? What *is* thinking?

To find out about the mysterious process of thinking, where better to start than to ask
a child? The following is part of a conversation with Tom, aged 6.

RF	What do you think with?
Tom	What do you mean?
RF	When you think, where do your thoughts come from?
Tom	I don't know – everywhere, I suppose.
RF	When you think of something, what do you think with?
Tom	I know ... your brain.
RF	How do you know?
Tom	I've seen brains.
RF	What brains?
Tom	In a book. The brains of animals ... like guinea pigs.
RF	Can you see thoughts?
Tom	No, they were dead. But you think with your brain, I know that.
RF	Is a thought something you can see?
Tom	Yes.
RF	What thought?
Tom	An ice cream.
RF	You can see a thought of an ice cream?
Tom	Yes. I'll show you. (Fetches paper and pencil. Draws a man with a bubble coming out of his head, containing an ice cream.)

Tom's view reflects many of the intuitive assumptions that are held about thinking:
thinking is closely associated with what goes on in the brain, thoughts (when they
are correct) correspond with facts in the world, thoughts (with the inner eye) can be
visualised, thoughts (when they are expressed) can be observed and shared. We have
evidence here of one clear factor that differentiates us from other animals, or from
robots: we are species who not only think but we can think about and control our
own thinking. This introspection may give us no clear or accurate account of what
we do when we think, but it gives us the capacity to study, to know more and hope-
fully to improve the processes involved. We have been helped in our understanding
by those who have, over the centuries, made a study of the mind, what mental
faculties are and how they can be improved. We are given no final answers but the
continuing research may broaden our knowledge of what thinking is and how it can
be developed in our children.

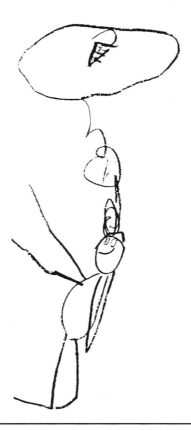

Figure 1.1

Our knowledge of thinking

Our knowledge of thinking derives largely from two distinct traditions, philosophy and psychology. Philosophers have long regarded the mind as the seat of reason and the cultivation of reason to be the ideal of education. Philosophy has emphasised the study of critical thinking, through analysis of argument and the application of logic. Psychologists have studied the mechanism of mind. Cognitive psychologists have, in particular, tended to emphasise creative thinking, how ideas may be generated in the mind.

Thinking involves critical and creative aspects of the mind, both the use of reason and the generation of ideas. Thinking is involved in any mental activity that helps to formulate or solve a problem, to make a decision or to seek understanding. It is through thinking that we make meaning out of life. In the main this activity is conscious, but it does not exclude unconscious processes. This activity is personal and individual but it is not done in isolation. It is mediated by others. We are not solitary individuals wrapped in a world of our own thinking, isolated beings as in the image of Rodin's 'Thinker'. Thinking takes place in a social context, is influenced and moulded by our culture and our environment. Learning to think is not achieved in isolation from others. The thinking child is a social child.

More fundamental than the social dimension is the physical context. Our thinking is made possible by our physiological make-up and much has been learnt from the study of the brain in recent years. The modern discipline of neurosurgery has made a major contribution to our understanding of the physiology of thought and has raised interesting speculations about the nature of human intelligence. The more we know about the biology of the brain the better prepared we will be for the task of developing its powers and its potential.

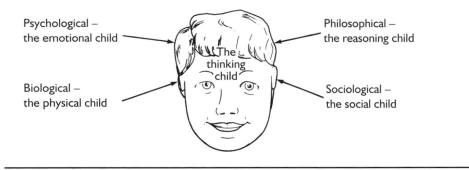

Figure 1.2 Aspects of the thinking child.

Thinking and intelligence

The early psychologists tended to look for general laws about mental faculties, rather like the great philosophers had looked for the general laws that governed logic, reason, argument and ethics. They looked for a universal pattern in cognitive growth and human knowing. One of these pioneers, Francis Galton (1822–1911),[1] had a particular interest in genius and he devised statistical methods for ranking all human beings in terms of physical and intellectual powers. Through this he was able to forge a link between genealogy and superior minds. From this two principles emerged: genius was hereditary and superior minds would be superior in every capacity. These principles, much modified by later psychologists, became the basis of the traditional view that intelligence is a property of the brain as a whole and that this general factor is largely inherited.

If intelligence is largely inherited is there any point in trying to improve intellectual performance? Can you hope to improve children's thinking if they have not got the innate ability? One who thought you could was Alfred Binet (1857–1911). Binet devised the first mental tests in France, later to be known as IQ tests. Binet viewed such tests as practical instruments that would enable him to identify mentally backward children and so be able to offer them appropriate teaching. He would have been disappointed to see IQ testing become a tool that reinforced belief in the traditional view of intelligence. He was critical of the claim that a person's intelligence is a fixed quantity and cannot be improved. We ought to protest against this brutal pessimism, he said, and he tried to show that it had no foundation.[2]

Binet was particularly critical of the view held by some psychologists such as Charles Spearman (1863–1945)[3] that our thinking derives from a single function called intelligence. Rather, he argued, it is made up of many smaller functions, such as attention, observation, discrimination, memory, judgement, etc. These can be improved by training so that we can become literally more intelligent than before. What is important is not the mental faculties that we are born with but how they are used and developed. What children need to do is *to learn how to learn*. To achieve this Binet proposed a system of training he called 'mental orthopaedics' – a kind of mental PE. This involved special exercises for strengthening attention, memory, perception, invention, analysis, judgement and will.

An example of Binet's method was his attempt to improve the short-term memory of a group of mentally retarded children. Binet was able to get two-thirds of his class to remember a group of nine different objects, which they were allowed to see for only a few seconds. A party of visiting French dignitaries was so impressed when they saw this that they tried the memory test for themselves and failed. What of course they had not taken into account was the intensive training that the children had previously undergone, as well as a hidden factor that Binet regarded as crucial to the teaching of children, i.e. motivation. He believed that given adequate motivation children could be trained to become more intelligent in their thinking. It is ironic that the founder of mental testing should also be a forerunner of programmes that aim to improve children's thinking skills. The debate begun by Binet continues to this day.

One of the main arguments against any special attempts to improve children's performance in thinking is that intelligence is largely inherited and has little chance of being modified. Hans Eysenck,[4] for example, believed that intelligence is the result of factors 80% of which are hereditary and 20% due to environment and upbringing. Arthur Jensen[5] also believes that low intellectual performance is largely determined by inherited genes and can be modified only a few points at most on the IQ scale. The close correlation between IQ test scores and accurate prediction of school success seems to support this view.

However IQ tests have relatively little predictive power outside the context of school. IQ tests do not show how the mind works, *how* one goes about solving a problem, only whether one gets the right answer. They provide a shotgun approach to assessment and feature tasks often unrelated to any real-life situation. They rarely assess skill in what is important in the real world, such as assimilating new information or solving problems. Two individuals may receive the same IQ score, one being at a peak of thinking power, the other capable of a huge spurt of intellectual attainment. A low IQ score may be more a danger signal than an incontrovertible fact about a child's intelligence. The IQ test does not recognise potential, it does not assess a child's learning experiences, it cannot judge key qualities like imagination, creativity or perseverance. Behaviourists such as Hans Eysenck, however, continue to have faith in IQ tests and adhere to the traditional view of intelligence as a fixed entity.

Opposing this genetic view, many psychologists have emphasised the part played by the social environment.[6] The Russian psychologist Vygotsky (1897–1934)[7] argued that all psychological processes are the result of social and cultural interaction. A child's thinking develops essentially through social experience, particularly in the interactions between child and adult. 'All the higher functions originate as actual relations between human individuals.' Vygotsky claimed that 'elementary' mental functions such as native cunning are part of our genetic endowment, which culture and education convert into the higher functions such as speech and writing. It is through the use of language that children take control of their thinking and make meaning from the world. Intelligence for Vygotsky is a dynamic and not a static force. All children have a potential for development in collaboration with others. 'What the child can do in co-operation today, he will do alone tomorrow.' The vital role of a child's social experience in developing thinking will be explored more fully in Chapter 5.

What seems clear is that our intellectual abilities derive from our biological inheritance and are activated by our social experience, our educational, social, family and cultural environment. Today psychologists have moved away from simply assessing what children know, the model of the old IQ tests, to finding out why and how something is known or acquired. A pioneer of this approach was Piaget (1896–1980). Piaget was brought up in the IQ tradition (starting in Binet's laboratory by studying the wrong answers children gave in Binet's tests). He came to believe that it was not the accuracy of the child's response that was important but rather the lines of reasoning involved. For example, he found that most 4-year-olds think a hammer is more like a nail than a screwdriver. What is revealing for Piaget is why they think so. He asked them and they told him, because hammers are found close to nails (not because they are in the same category of tool). He found that young children thought in physical rather than abstract terms and concluded they could *only* think that way.

For Piaget human thought is aimed at making sense of the world. Piaget was not interested in forms of knowledge that are simply memorised (like word definitions). What was important for him was the child's understanding of concepts that philosophers through the centuries have regarded as central to the human intellect – ideas of time, space, number, cause and effect. Piaget took logical reasoning to be the central factor of intelligence but in stressing this aspect of thinking he ignored the kinds of competence shown by artists, engineers, politicians and athletes. As a biologist Piaget looked for stages of mental growth that would mirror the patterns of physical growth. He regarded learning as an activity with different stages of development that are biologically programmed and cannot be changed. However, many researchers looking at Piaget's 'stages' have found that they occur in a far more irregular fashion than he claimed.[8] We now know that instead of related abilities emerging at about the same time or stage, closely related abilities can emerge at very different points in time. There is no one pattern of cognitive growth that all children pass through. The pattern of development for each individual child is unique, and research shows that the way children are taught can have a profound effect on their progress.[9]

There are realms of human creativity and potential untouched by Piaget's theory. However his research does highlight some important factors in teaching children how to think, which will recur through the book, such as:

- the need to look at the reasons why the child is thinking in such a way
- the need to remember that thinking is doing and not just being told, that it is an active not a passive process
- the need for children to explore certain key concepts, which help unlock their potential.

What Piaget failed to emphasise was the central role that language has to play in developing a child's understanding and the essential role of adults in providing what Bruner called 'cognitive scaffolding' for a child. To find ways of providing such scaffolding we need to look beyond the theories of Piaget.

Let us begin by looking at what children imagine to be going on inside their heads when they are thinking. 'What goes on inside your head?' is a question that can elicit interesting answers at any age. Often it helps to make thinking visible through a drawing or diagram. One 6 year old drew the following sketch to explain what went on inside his head.

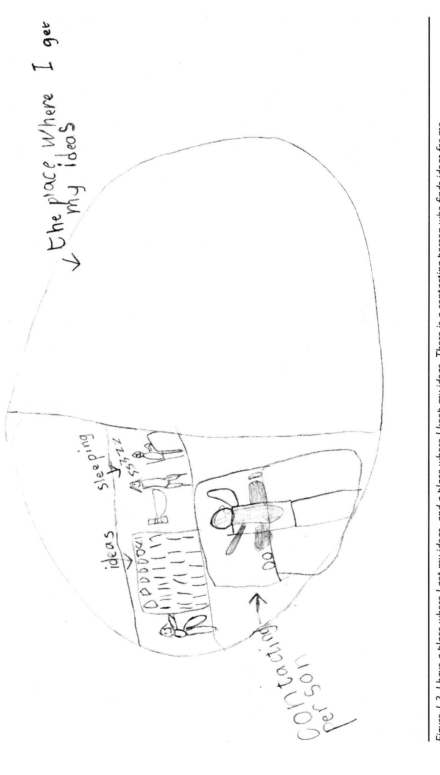

The place where I get my ideas

↓ the place where my ideas

sleeping ↗ zzzz

ideas

contacting person

Figure 1.3 I have a place where I get my ideas, and a place where I keep my ideas. There is a contacting person who finds ideas for me.

Explanations tend to be more sophisticated as children get older. One 9 year old drew the working brain as follows:

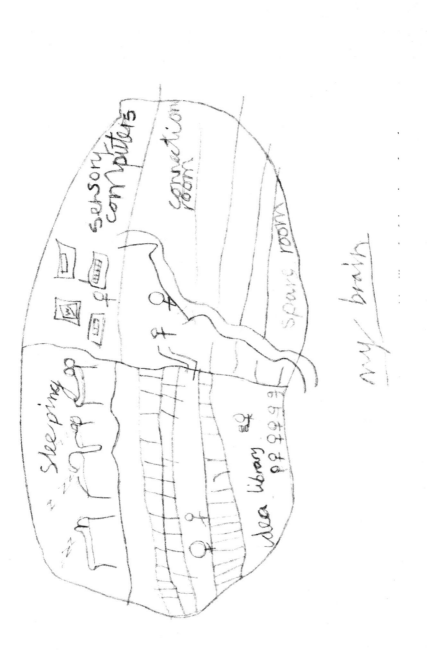

Figure 1.4 There are kind of sensory computers which control the senses, anything like a shock is registered on the computer. There is an idea library where ideas are stored. Ideas are kept there like books. Sometimes they are hard to find. The connection room is where ideas connect up to the mouth. There's a spare room for more ideas and knowledge. The sleeping part is the part of the brain which works at night. It's where dreams come from.

Common to these descriptions is a view of the brain as a place for information or idea processing. Ideas come in, they are stored. There is some sort of 'contacting person' or 'sensory computer' that controls the input and output. The brain also has spare capacity, a 'spare room' or 'place where I get my ideas'. Children often suggest that there is something in the brain, what philosophers have dubbed 'a ghost in the machine', that controls thinking. This dynamic view of the brain as a centre of information-processing activity is one shared by many psychologists in their efforts to explain the workshop of intelligence. There seems to be something unique about human thinking, but what is it?

Some psychologists maintain that the one factor unique to human thinking is metacognition, which is the ability we have to reflect on our own thinking processes. Human intelligence, they suggest, derives from the information-processing capacity of the brain. Sternberg[10] identifies three component elements involved in our capacity to process information. They are metacomponents, performance components and knowledge acquisition components.

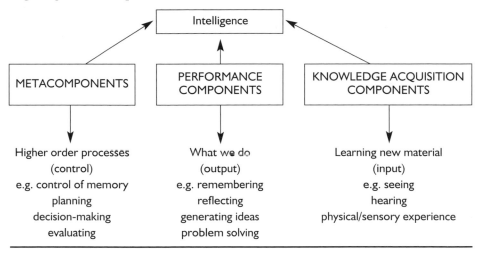

Figure 1.5 The brain as information processor.

According to this analysis, success in thinking is determined by efficiency in the three operations of

1 acquiring knowledge: *input*
2 strategies for using knowledge and solving problems: *output*
3 metacognition and decision making: *executive control*.

All the underlying processes and components of intelligence, reception of knowledge, activation of ideas and control over thinking can be trained and developed. The various thinking skills programmes[11] that have been pioneered over recent years aim to improve one or more of these information-processing abilities. Intelligence has traditionally been viewed as a property of the brain as a whole, either a general factor (Spearman), general structure (Piaget) or information-processing centre (Sternberg). Others have argued that intelligence has no unitary character, the mind is a community of separate intelligences. Howard Gardner,[12] a powerful exponent of this view, calls these intelligences 'frames of mind'. The exact number and nature of these intelligences, he says, have not been finally established. In daily life these intelligences usually work in harmony so that their separateness and special characteristics seem invisible. In teaching children to think our task is to develop each one of the many forms of a child's intelligence. This need to divide intelligence into different forms is not just a conceptual convenience. Evidence of the nature of these separate intelligences has come from the study of neurobiology.

In the late nineteenth century it was discovered that mental functions might be localised in different parts of the brain. Surgeons found that damage to the left hemisphere of the brain impaired linguistic ability and they could predict which lesion of the brain would impair reading and which would impair memory. Since then neurosurgeons have located many separate and individual functions in different areas of the brain. Psychologists studying the expression of these functions have sought to classify the different areas of intelligence. Thurstone (1887–1955)[13] identified seven factors as the 'primary abilities': verbal comprehension, word fluency, number, visual/spatial skills, memory, perception and reasoning. Instead of one general factor, intelligence was made up of several factors. To Marvin Minsky[14] the mind is a 'society' made up of many small processes or agents that are themselves mindless. Each mental agent does its own thing and only when they are combined, he argues, do we have true intelligence.

Many efforts have been made to detail the basic elements of intelligence. Philosopher Paul Hirst[15] has argued that there are seven distinct and separate 'forms of knowledge': scientific, aesthetic, mathematical, ethical, religious, philosophical and interpersonal understanding. However, what appear as separable forms of knowledge may really be differing forms or modules of human intelligence. In addition to these separate modules there is a central information processor, which has access to the different modules, receives data from various inputs, controls decisions and activates the solving of problems.[16] This central information processor is the coordinator (sometimes like a contacting person when thinking is planned, sometimes like a computer when it is automatic know-how) of the various forms and functions of intelligence.

Forms of intelligence

The mind has a central information-processing capacity that controls functions like memory, perception, learning, etc. and can apply these functions to the following forms of intelligence:

- Linguistic intelligence
- Logico-mathematical intelligence
- Scientific intelligence
- Visual/spatial intelligence
- Musical intelligence
- Bodily–kinaesthetic intelligence
- Interpersonal intelligence
- Metacognitive intelligence.

Linguistic intelligence

Language is the mirror of the mind. – Noam Chomsky

From birth the brain is poised to learn speech. The left hemisphere of the brain is naturally sensitive to the structured forms of speech sounds. Linguistic intelligence is a miracle still shrouded in mystery. How is it a child can learn from the hubbub of sound the pattern of a language? The child's brain is programmed to scan the environment for patterns of meaning. This ability is of crucial importance not only for language development but also for maths, science, music, art and many other areas of a child's experience.

Noam Chomsky[17] has argued that linguistic mastery is only possible because children are born with a considerable 'innate knowledge' about the grammatical rules and forms of language. It is this that enables the young child to decode and speak their own or any other 'natural language'. How else, Chomsky asks, could children acquire language so rapidly and accurately simply learning from some erratic samples of speech? The normal child is able to master the complex problems of speech acquisition long before other problem-solving skills are developed.

The ability to use sounds to convey a point of view and to convince others into a course of action begins at the baby stage. It is an ability that will influence happiness and success throughout a child's life. It needs to be nurtured from the earliest years. There is only one necessary condition for a normal child to learn speech: she must have lengthy lessons from a competent speaker, usually the mother. No wonder our language is called the *mother* tongue. It is one of the characteristics of the brain that nerve cells repeat their patterns of activity. A characteristic of good parents, and of good teachers of the very young, is to repeat the same phrases, songs and rhymes for the child to learn to model and to develop. The child looks for meaning in its interactions with its mother (or teacher) and similarly the mother/ teacher will look for meaning in the cues and signals given by the child. This 'looking for meaning' is a two-way process and is a key element in the child's linguistic and creative development.

One of the keys to linguistic intelligence is memory. Astounding feats of verbal memory have been recorded in different cultures, for example Arab children who have memorised all 114 suras of the Koran. What accounts for this amazing information-processing skill is the meaningfulness of the pattern of words being learnt and the cultural value given to the task. This power to recall cultural knowledge was often tested during rites of passage (e.g. initiation ceremonies, confirmation services in church, exams). Social and political power have been reserved for those whose advantage of birth has been allied to superior linguistic skills. From Greek times superior memory and verbal skill have been identified with intelligence. However in our modern society greater emphasis is placed on the second stage of symbolisation, which begins developing between the ages of 4 and 6, the written word.

Literacy, the ability to read and write, encourages a more abstract form of thinking, it brings greater precision to the definition of terms, it allows us to refer back, to think about our thinking, to weigh arguments, to supplement memory, to organise future activities, to communicate with others and to learn in autonomous ways. No wonder such a powerful form of intelligence provides the key to success in school and beyond.

While the psychological processes that facilitate linguistic intelligence are common to all normal children, there are vast individual differences in the rapidity and skill of learning, as well as in the style of learning. Linguistic intelligence, like the physical body, needs daily exercising. Ways of helping children develop and use this family of skills, the inter-related modes of speaking, listening, reading and writing and inner speech (communication with self), will be explored in subsequent chapters.

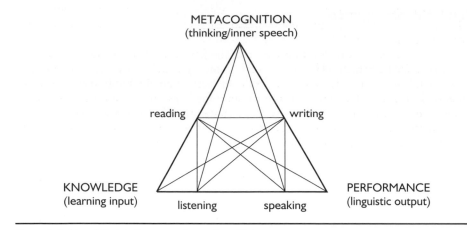

Figure 1.6 Linguistic intelligence – the modes of language.

Logico-mathematical intelligence

Piaget took logical reasoning to be the central factor of intelligence. He regarded the development of logical intelligence as occurring in certain key stages through the child's operation on the world. Such development begins from birth, with the young infant exploring all sorts of objects, rattles, mobiles, fingers, through touch and sight. In the early months the child's knowledge of objects is related to his moment-to-moment experience with them. When they disappear from sight, for example the doll is put behind a cushion, they are lost from consciousness. Only after about 18 months does the child come to realise, after much trial and error experience, that objects continue to exist even when hidden from view. This principle of object permanence, that objects exist independent of our actions or perceptions, is a key stage in mental development.*

The next stage is a recognition of the qualities of objects, their similarities and differences, their continuities and transformations and the concept of change. Children become able to group objects of a similar kind together, for example cups or red buttons, and to recognise a class or set. The next stage of logical abstraction will be to relate the elements of a set to a number.

* This belief reflects a real philosophical problem: does an object exist when no-one is aware of it? A limerick from nineteenth-century Oxford proposes the problem:

> There was once a man who said 'God
> Must think it exceedingly odd
> If he finds that this tree
> Continues to be
> When there's no-one about in the Quad.'

The following was written in reply:

> Dear Sir, Your astonishment's odd
> I am always about in the Quad.
> And that's why the tree
> Will continue to be,
> Since observed by Yours faithfully, God.

Children can often count from an early age. At this stage it is a linguistic rather than a mathematical skill. Not until the child can abstract from a group of objects the number they represent can this skill be called mathematical. Piaget[18] describes a boy aged 5 playing with his collection of pebbles. First he laid them in a line and counted along the line from left to right. There were 10. Then he counted them from right to left and 'to his great astonishment' the total was again 10. He put them in a circle, counting them clockwise then anti-clockwise, 'full of enthusiasm': he found that there were always 10. Whatever way he counted, the sum of objects was always the same. The boy grew up to be a professional mathematician, attributing the choice of his career to the excitement and delight at achieving this new cognitive control of the world at the age of five.

Around the age of six or seven the child can count and compare two sets of objects and begin the more complex operations of adding the sets, then subtracting, multiplying and dividing.

Logico-mathematical skills begin with the handling of real objects. Through classifying objects children learn numerical equivalence and become able to transfer their abstract operations to the tasks of daily life, for example shopping, playing games, following recipes. Numerical operations gradually become internalised but for children from seven to 10 they remain essentially related to physical objects. This is what Piaget calls the period of 'concrete operations'. For Piaget the final stage of logical development occurs in early adolescence when the normal child becomes capable of 'formal operations', using words or symbols (like equations) to stand for objects. The child can now work with hypothetical statements and explore logical relationships between statements. Many believe that this stage can be reached long before puberty and that young children are capable of abstract reasoning, given the appropriate stimulus, far earlier than Piaget believed possible.[19]

Maths and logic

There is a close link between logic and maths, because underlying the most complex of mathematical equations are simple logical principles. Every correct sum is an exercise in logic. As Wittgenstein said 'In logic (mathematics), process and result are equivalent. Hence no surprises.' Many practical real-world maths problems involve logical combinations and permutations. For example 'If six friends met and all shook hands with each other, how many handshakes would there be?' The power of mathematical logic is that once a logical procedure (or algorithm) has been found it can be used to pattern an indefinite number of results. How many handshakes if there were 10 friends, 100, 1000?[20] The application of logic is not, however, the whole of maths. For example, 'How could you drop an egg 1 metre on to a hard pavement without breaking the shell? *Answer:* Drop it from a height of 1.5 metres, it will drop 1 metre without breaking!' Mathematical thinking also involves the processes of:

- creative thinking – creating hypotheses, using insight and inspiration
- critical thinking – applying logical chains of reasoning
- problem solving.

Some children will show a selective weakness in logico-mathematical understanding, just as some show specific difficulties in the realm of language, either in reading/writing (dyslexics) or listening/speaking (dysphasics). All need to have this form of intelligence strengthened and developed. The skilled mathematician is not necessarily able at rapid calculation, this is merely an incidental advantage; what s/he is good at is applying mathematical processes to the investigation of problems. In posing and solving problems there is a close link between the logic of maths and science.

Scientific intelligence

Scientific intelligence is the human capacity to enquire about and to investigate the natural world. Successful scientific investigation requires the application of maths and logic but also requires the use of many other mental processes such as imagination, observation, pattern-seeking, communication and hypothesising. When Piaget asked nursery-age children 'What makes the wind?' one child replied 'The trees made the wind by waving their branches.'

From an early age children can think up their own scientific theories. Scientific methods and procedures, such as experimenting and fair testing, will be needed to test theories. Part of this process will involve the logical planning, the step-by-step approach of systematic enquiry and will also involve mathematical processes such as classification into sets and precise measurement. As George Santayana wrote, 'all the sciences aspire to the condition of mathematics'. All science seeks the certainty of logic, and logico-mathematical intelligence is needed to judge how far it falls short of this. It also requires creativity in thinking, for, as Blake observed, 'what is now proved was once imagined'.

Visual/spatial intelligence

To develop a complete mind, (a) study the science of art, (b) study the art of science, (c) learn how to see *(use your senses)*.
    Leonardo da Vinci

Visual or spatial intelligence comprises the capacity to perceive the visual world accurately and to recreate visual experience in the mind's eye. To fully understand we need to 'see' first; seeing in this sense comes before words. It is through seeing that the child comes to know and to recognise his place in the world. Rudolf Arnheim argues that the most important operations of thinking come directly from our perception of the world. For him spatial imagery is the primary source of thought. He claims that unless we can conjure up an image of some process or concept we will be unable to think clearly about it. This visual thinking is also a key tool for problem solving.

Consider these problems:

1 Which tap controls the hot water, left or right?
2 If a piece of paper is folded in half, then folded twice again, how many folded shapes are there?
3 What is the quickest route from home to the nearest library?

The first problem can be solved by visualising taps, for example in the bathroom but also through other ways such as the bodily response of the left or right hand. The second problem can be tackled by visualising the process in the mind's eye, or by logico-mathematical means, i.e. 2×2. The third problem can be visualised, drawn or described in words but the use of visual/spatial intelligence will be essential for its solution.

To the old question 'Can there be thought without words?' the answer is yes, via the perceptual cognition of visual stimuli. Leonardo da Vinci[21] referred to the power of 'confused shapes', such as clouds or muddy water, to create in the mind new images.

> *You should look at certain walls stained with damp, or at stones of uneven colour ... you will be able to see in these the likeness of divine landscapes ... and then again you will see there battles and strange figures in violent action ... and an infinity of things.*

The use of visual intelligence can help the child see more, for example in these precise but paradoxical images:

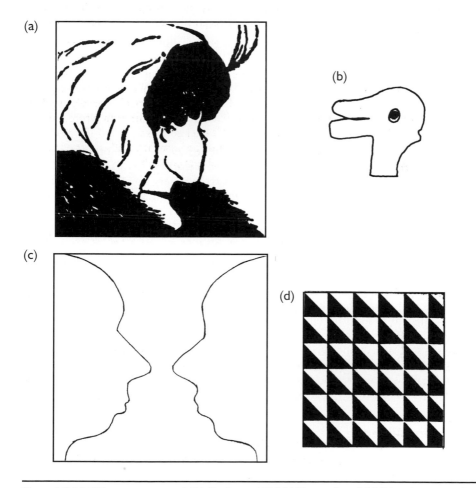

Figure 1.7 (a) Old or young woman? (b) Duck or rabbit? (c) Vase or faces? (d) Triangles, pyramids or boxes?

Piaget[22] divided visual thinking into 'figurative' knowledge, i.e. a static mental image of an object, and 'operative' knowledge, the active ability to visualise, manipulate and transform the image of an object in the mind. Young children have the ability to remember and retrace routes but find it very difficult to describe their routes in words or to draw maps. What they find difficult is abstracting and symbolising spatial layouts, coordinating their piecemeal knowledge into an overall pattern. Children's spatial understanding develops much faster than the symbolic codes of their linguistic or logico-mathematical intelligence and provides a powerful means of early learning. Children can 'read' pictures much earlier than they can read words.

Confronted with a problem we tend to encode it either in words or spatial images. This may be partly due to the fact that spatial intelligence is mainly centred in the right hemisphere of the brain, while the faculties of language are located largely in the left hemisphere. It may also be due to the fact that one area has been relatively neglected in a child's educational experience. Children vary greatly in their ability to solve the types of visual problem that often occur in IQ tests, for example choosing identical pictures from a closely related series or spotting subtle differences in patterns. Some adults too are poor visualisers. In a pioneering study at the turn of the century Francis Galton was amazed to discover eminent scientists who could not accurately recall the scene of that morning's breakfast while individuals of modest intellect could recall most detailed images. There are also many examples of persons with high artistic abilities producing low scores on non-spatial IQ tests. Visual thinking is an intelligence as variable as any other and as important.

The success of the human species seems closely linked to the development of spatial skills, both as primitive hunters and as sophisticated scientists. To this day the Bedouin of the desert and the Inuit of the Arctic display extraordinary abilities in finding their way across apparently featureless terrain. Children too need visual thinking to find their way around the world. Much of the information they will need to process is of a visual kind: words, numbers, pictures, images, patterns, signs and symbols. They are visual animals living in a visual world.

Visual knowledge is valuable as an aid to thinking, not only for potential artists, scientists, architects and engineers but for all children. Visualising can help in the expression of information and ideas. Visual expression provides a means of formulating and solving problems. Though a necessary and arguably neglected area of education, it is not sufficient in itself for effective problem solving. We need to abstract, encode and symbolise the patterns of our visual experience. We need an abstract memory as well as a visual one. Napoleon regarded individuals who only thought in concrete mental images as unfit to command. What he wanted were leaders who were able to think in flexible strategies, who were able to modify plans and who could look beneath the surface to see the underlying patterns.

Musical intelligence

Music is in the air – you simply take as much of it as you want.
    Edward Elgar

As babies, normal children sing as well as babble. By 4 months infants can match the rhythms and simple melodies of their mothers' songs. By the middle of the second year children are inventing their own rhythms and melodies in spontaneous songs. Before long they are able to reproduce snatches of songs and nursery rhymes. From the age of 3 this spontaneous exploration of song is usually on the wane. However the child's intuitive *feel* for music, his musical intelligence, remains part of his mental make-up for the rest of his life.

Musical ability derives from a core talent plus training but all children, including musical prodigies, begin in the intuitive mode of appreciation and improvisation. Later it becomes important to develop this intuitive understanding with systematic instruction, conceptualising the experience through a symbolic code such as the dots and squiggles of modern musical notation. Relatively few musicians can remain in the intuitive mode 'playing by ear' rather than through formal musical knowledge. Evidence from a wide range of cultures shows how susceptible musical intelligence is to cultural training and stimulation. In Japan, Suzuki has shown how large numbers of young children can learn the violin to a high (Western) standard. In Hungary, children trained in the Kodaly method are expected to reach a high standard of singing and instrumental playing. Children in Bali and in parts of Africa learn their culture through developing skills in singing, dancing and percussion playing. Across cultures there is a wide variation in the musical experience of children.

The sense of rhythm that we all have in differing respects is located primarily in the right hemisphere of the brain (for right-handed people) but musical intelligence shows some interesting links with other forms of intelligence. In learning musical notation children are drawing on skills related to linguistic abilities (this may be why early learning of musical notation has been associated with accelerated reading ability). Since Pythagoras the close association between music and maths has been noted through shared concepts of proportion, ratio and pattern. Composer Claude Debussy called music 'the arithmetic of sounds'. Music is also closely linked to bodily movement, both in the physical performance of playing an instrument and in bodily responses to rhythm and melody. The close relationship between music and dance also shows the link between musical and bodily/ kinaesthetic intelligence.

Bodily-kinaesthetic intelligence

'Why' said the Dodo, 'the best way to explain it is to do it.'

Lewis Carroll, *Alice in Wonderland*

The Greek ideal was a sound mind in a healthy body. A mind trained to use the body properly and a body trained to respond to the expressive powers of the mind. The aim was beauty, balance and grace, inspired by virtue and wisdom, a physical and mental harmony of human powers. But it is not only in the athleticism of the Greeks that we see bodily intelligence at work. It is involved in fine motor skills like writing and painting, in movement and gesture and in mastery of physical performance.

Between the ages of 5 and 12 most children make great progress in developing physical coordination, muscular control and manipulative skill. The various skills that relate to physical intelligence can be classified as follows:

- skills of manipulation – cutting, holding, guiding, writing, drawing
- skills of construction – building, assembling, arranging, adjusting, carrying, placing
- skills of projection – throwing, catching, grasping, striking, kicking
- skills of agility – running, jumping, rolling, climbing, balancing, gymnastics, swimming
- skills of communication – non-verbal communication, gesture, touch, voice control.

Physical skills are more accurately called psycho-motor skills, as in humans there is no purely physical skill; all involve some mental processing. Skills come through the gaining of 'know-how' and often this know-how cannot be expressed in language. It is a form of knowledge learned slowly and through repeating patterns of action. After becoming established this skill or patterning of activity becomes unique to that person. No one swims, draws, rides a bike or mends a car in exactly the same way. Bodily skills may seem identical in action but they are the product of an individual intelligence, a personally distinct patterning. Once learned, such skills become pro-grammed as a series of sensorimotor responses. They become natural and durable, so that dormant skills such as the ability to cycle can be quickly re-established after a gap.

Mental and physical skills are closely linked in that they both require the processing of information, a sense of timing and a sense of direction. The need to remember and to imitate physical actions is common to many skills, such as dancing, acting, making and doing. Success in these activities will also depend on other intellectual skills such as con-centration, judgement and close observation. The ability to create and manipulate and transform objects is needed in a diverse range of skills such as writing, drawing, craft-work, cookery and engineering. All require the combination of several forms of intelli-gence, not only bodily–kinaesthetic intelligence but also visual–spatial intelligence, to conceptualise the tasks involved, as well as logical abilities in patterning of objects and relations and linguistic competence to learn from and with others. A child needs bodily intelligence to make the most of the physical world of which he is a part. Since the Greeks, Western philosophical tradition has tended to divorce the mental from the physical. The body came to be regarded as a machine inhabited by a ghostly presence, the mind.[23] The body is not simply a machine but is the vehicle of the child's sense of self and self-worth. The uniqueness of the child's body is a reflection of his uniqueness as an individual. It is the repository of his personal and interpersonal intelligence.

Interpersonal intelligence

They can swim under the sea like fishes, they can fly in the air like birds, but they have not learnt to walk hand in hand like brothers.
   Martin Luther King

The child has a growing understanding of herself as a person and of her relationships with others. This interpersonal or social intelligence manifests itself in two ways. First in the developing sense of self, of being a person with feelings and emotions that guide behaviour; second in the capacity to understand and empathise with the feelings and emotions of others.

The growth of interpersonal intelligence is a gradual process that passes through several stages. The initial social experience is between baby and mother. Lack of this attachment can have damaging effects on an individual's capacity to relate to others, as the research of John Bowlby and others have shown. From birth the infant shows signs of empathy, responding to the facial expressions and behaviour of others. The first evidence of self-knowledge comes around the age of 2 when the child realises she is a separate entity, that the person looking at her in the mirror is herself. The child recog-nises her own name and becomes her own person, the miracle of 'me'!

Many theorists have argued that children (and adults) are dominated by impulses towards selfish pleasure. Piaget regarded early childhood as a period of egocentrism. Dawkins argues that there is a 'selfish gene' in all of us. Research,[24] however, has shown that children as young as 14 months can begin to show awareness of the emotional experience of parents and siblings. In the face of family distress young children may try to comfort others and/or themselves. As they get older, children begin to explore social roles and behaviour through play. The child gradually comes to know himself through coming to know others, personal and social intelligence grow together.

In the pre-adolescent years the child shows a growing ability to decentre, to see the viewpoints of others, to appreciate jokes and to understand complicated social interactions such as 'I think that she thinks that I think . . .' Their descriptions of others become more realistic and perceptive, moving from predominantly external characteristics such as clothes, age and occupation to a growing ability to assess personal characteristics and capacities. Risks at this age include making premature judgements and unrealistic assessments of others and themselves. They may grow in a sense of confidence and self-worth, or develop a sense of helplessness that they cannot do certain things, for example girls thinking that they 'cannot do' maths and entering a vicious cycle of diminishing expectation and achievement. The education of the emotions and the growth of a moral sense involve thinking processes. The less the child understands her own feelings the more she will become a prey to them. The less she understands the feelings of others the more likely it is that her social relationships will be unsuccessful. Several factors exist to help in the growth of understanding. These include the prolonged period of childhood, the social nature of family life, the urge for exploratory and problem-solving play and the role of language as the facilitator of interpersonal communication.

Within a domain of intelligence a person's development in any activity can be shown as a series of stages which lead from novice to apprentice to expert. Child prodigies can pass rapidly through these steps. To do this they need:

- high levels of natural aptitude
- great amounts of stimulation from parents and teachers
- a culture or society in which aptitudes can flower.

Studies of child prodigies show that precocity is often in one area of development, characteristically in symbolic domains like maths and music, and that they can pass through stages of development at a rapid pace. Such studies can teach us a lot about the tremendous flexibility and potential of the human brain. Just as we know more about the factors that guide and enhance human growth, so we are learning more about the factors that may retard development. Just as some children are born with a huge potential, others are born 'at risk'. They may be at risk because of genetic factors, for example diseases such as haemophilia, or neurological conditions such as severe retardation. Other factors, such as accidents of environment or special treatment, will influence the 'at risk' condition, as will the amount of stimulation they receive and the amount of support society gives for them to fulfil their potential.

All children, including the naturally gifted and the at risk, are born 'at promise'. All have the potential, given the right stimulation and support, to realise their particular talents. Even children with seemingly very modest aptitude can achieve remarkable success in a chosen field of activity. The reasons for this tremendous human flexibility lie in the structure of the brain.

Metacognitive intelligence

Metacognitive knowledge is knowing how you know things and the processes by which you think. Asking a child what thinking is, how and where it takes place, may elicit some interesting answers:

> 'It just happens, like going to the toilet' (7-year-old)
> 'It's like a television, you have to switch it on and find the right channel; sometimes the picture is clear, sometimes it's fuzzy' (11-year-old)
> 'You ask your brain and your brain tells you the answers, if it knows – sometimes it doesn't' (9-year-old).

Metacognitive skills help us to acquire, control and regulate our knowledge and thinking. The skills involve reflecting on ourselves as thinkers, for example on our feeling of knowing or not knowing, our mental abilities and limitations. Important questions that relate to metacognition include:

- What are our strengths and weaknesses?
- How do we build on our strengths and overcome our weaknesses?

Research into medical practice has suggested that it is not doctors with the most knowledge of medicine that make the best practitioners; it is those who know how and when to apply their knowledge. Children are often prone to the sorts of error that, if they used their knowledge, they could correct. A child may have produced a wrong answer in an arithmetical sum, for example $602 - 25 = 477$, yet know, if asked, that subtracting 25 from 602 should produce an answer closer to 600 than 500. In following an abstract problem children are not necessarily influenced by their semantic knowledge. They need to be encouraged to verbalise what they are doing, to exercise their linguistic intelligence in monitoring their actions and to explain to themselves (or others) what they are doing. In gaining more control over their attempts to perform intellectually challenging tasks a child is developing metacognition and learning how to learn.

Questions to help children gain metacognitive control include:

- Have I thought it through? – Stop and think! Think before you ink!
- Have I made a plan? – PLAN: Prepare Learning Actions Now.
- Do I know what to do? – Re-read/re-tell. Check–double-check.
- Is there anything more I need? – What else do I need?
- What do I know that will help me? – What is this *like*?

Helping children to cultivate their introspective self-monitoring abilities provides some defence against blissful ignorance. What strategies does the child adopt when she does not understand the meaning of something? Does the child feel in control of the process of learning? Does the child see the purpose of what she is doing? Being in control means knowing *why* you are doing something as well as how to set about it. It means knowing about your own thinking and how *your* brain works.

Your amazing brain

It is estimated that within the brain there are 10 billion nerve cells (neurons), each of which conducts impulses on to other nerve cells.[25] Between two neurons is a microscopic gap called the synapse, which acts as a filter for the nerve impulses and messages. These impulses, which depend on chemical and electrical energy, travel from neuron to neuron along connecting branches of fibres called axons and dendrites. There are up to 10 000 connection points for each neuron.

Neurons, rather like silicon chips in a computer, can be used to store and process all sorts of information. Like a computer, the brain must be programmed before it can operate successfully. The child's brain is programmed by means of stimuli sent along the nerve pathways, from his senses or from his own thinking. These make connections within the cerebral cortex, which is the information-processing part of the brain, the seat of thinking and consciousness. When the nerve cells repeat patterns of information-processing activity, learning takes place. On the basis of these simple patterns more elaborate response patterns can be built so the child moves in stages from novice to apprentice, towards expert. The more stimulus a child experiences to activate his patterns of learning the greater will be the capacity of his brain to function intelligently.

stimulus (internal or external) → *connections* → *patterns* → *learning*

The cerebral cortex is the thick layer of grey matter that forms the outer surface of the brain. Parts of the human cortex, like other portions of the brain, have a fixed function even at birth. But parts have no fixed function: they remain undeveloped and uncommitted, part of the tremendous potential, the natural flexibility and adaptability of the brain. This flexibility is at its greatest in young children. A child with cerebral brain damage may activate uncommitted areas of the brain and learn to speak, whereas with an adolescent or an adult this capacity may be only partially recovered. Some adults do, however, recover the ability to talk despite massive injury to the left or dominant hemisphere of the brain. There are limits to the adaptability of the brain but we rarely know for sure what these limits are.

The brain, and therefore the cerebral cortex, is divided into two interlinked hemispheres. It has been accepted for some time that one hemisphere is dominant. The dominant hemisphere, normally the 'logical left', is largely responsible for language, logic, number, sequence and analysis, while the 'creative right' deals with space, colour, musical rhythm, daydreams and imagination.

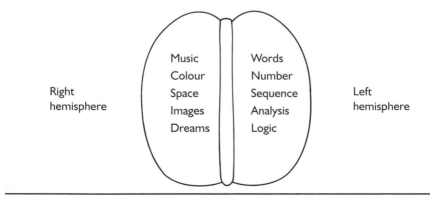

Figure 1.8 The hemispheres of the brain.

These priorities, also called the 'artistic right' and the 'scientific left' are reversed in those (normally left-handed) people whose right hemisphere, rather than the left, is dominant.

This orthodox view of the two hemispheres has been challenged by research[26] that suggests that the division is not as clear-cut as was once supposed. Most types of thinking involve both hemispheres: indeed, one of the keys of successful thinking lies in linking the faculties of the two hemispheres. Different mental skills do tend to predominate in either the right or left hemisphere, as may be judged by the following experiment. Ask a person a numerical question, such as an addition or multiplication sum, and watch their eyes. These may well look to the right (possibly to prevent the left hemisphere from being too distracted by processing unnecessary visual information). Ask a spatial question, such as describe what is behind you at this present moment, and see if the person's eyes look to the left (if they have a dominant right hemisphere). Of course the person may close both eyes, to concentrate more effectively, or to confound the experiment!

The period from birth to puberty is the time of most rapid growth of the brain and the time when the human being is most ready to learn. At the age of five the brain will be 90% of its adult weight. The child's sensory organs, her eyes, ears, sense of touch, taste and smell are highly developed, ready for absorbing the experiences that will be the raw material for thinking and learning. The quality of the thinking/learning environment in these years is therefore vital. It is not a quick process. The long period of childhood is necessary for the patterning of thought processes to be established. Nor will progress be steady. The pattern of growth tends to come in fits and starts. Sensitive periods exist in the life of every child for specific types of learning. And children cannot learn alone. They need the mediation, the necessary help of others (peers and adults), together with the appropriate stimulation, if they are to be given the chance of developing to their full potential.

Many aspects of the brain's functioning remain a mystery. Every time a child learns something there must be changes in the brain but we still do not know what these involve. We are still in the foothills of understanding and only have clues to the mechanisms of the mind. Research indicates that there are certain principles of learning and an attempt will be made in subsequent chapters to give these principles practical application. What research cannot show and what we will also need to consider in teaching children to think is what will *motivate* their thinking. As Binet reminds us:

> *Our examination of intelligence cannot take account of all those qualities – attention, will, popularity, perseverance, teachableness and courage – which play so important a part in school work, and also in after life, for life is not so much a conflict of intelligence as a struggle between characters.*[27]

Summary

Thinking is involved in any mental activity that helps us to process information and solve problems. Our intellectual abilities derive from our biological inheritance, but are activated by social, educational and emotional experience. The thinking child is an intellectual, emotional, physical and social child. The stages of development through which children move are not fixed. The way children are taught can influence the growth of intelligence (the information-processing capacity of the brain). Intelligence may take many forms, including linguistic, mathematical, scientific, visual, musical, physical, philosophical, interpersonal and metacognitive intelligence. Children need the help of others for their thinking and intelligence to reach their full potential.

2 Creative thinking

The principal goal of education is to create men who are capable of doing new things, not simply repeating what other generations have done – men who are creative, inventive and discoverers. The second goal of education is to form minds which can be critical, can verify, and not accept everything they are offered.

Jean Piaget

A father was out with his son, aged 3. Suddenly the son saw his first horse. 'Look, Daddy,' he said, 'There is a big dog!' His father laughed and replied, 'No, Tommy, that is a horse.' Later, thinking it over, the father wished he had dealt with his son's observation quite differently. Perhaps by saying, 'It has four legs like a dog. What else is like a dog?' or 'This is a horse. You've not seen one before. How is it different from a dog?' What the father had failed to do was to extend the child's powers of speculation.

Telling a child produces a two-way connection between concept in question and concept given in answer.

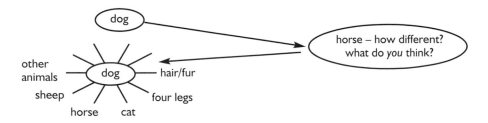

Figure 2.1 Encouraging a child to speculate opens up the possibility for many more connections.

A damaging change in the learning process often happens around the age of three or four, which can last a lifetime. The child learns to stop guessing and inventing answers when his efforts are rejected. After many rejections the child stops speculating. Instead he asks questions like 'Daddy, what is that?' He learns that answers lie not in what the child thinks but what the parent/teacher thinks. Instead of continually practising making connections, guessing and inventing, the focus of learning shifts subtly away from learner to teacher. Instead of steadily increasing her skill in retrieving, connecting, comparing and transforming information the child reacts passively and comes to rely on the authority of others. If she does not know the precise answer, or does not fully understand an observation, she waits for others to explain.

It was once sufficient to regard learning as an inheritance from the past. What sufficed was reproductive learning, the acquisition of a fixed body of cultural knowledge, accepted skills, fixed outlooks, methods and rules necessary for dealing with known and recurring situations. Reproductive learning was geared to a fixed pattern of society. It was a type of learning designed to maintain an existing system and to reproduce an established way of life. It enhanced problem-solving ability for a fixed and given range of problems. Reproductive learning answered the survival needs of individuals and societies in the past. It continues to be necessary today, but it is no longer enough.[1] What is needed for future survival is innovative learning. If our children are to anticipate and cope with the turbulence of change both at an individual and social level they need to learn not simply how to accommodate to the future but how to shape it. If one of the challenges of education is to prepare children for a fast-changing world, then teaching children to think creatively becomes a clear need.

The call for creative thinking comes in the face not only of the demands of the future, but also of the needs of the present. Those who investigate achievement in schools report the failure of some schools to stimulate and extend creative thinking in children, particularly more able children. Good schools are characterised by intellectually challenging teaching.[2] Good homes are also places of intellectual stimulation. Schools and homes often succeed in providing their children with the technical aids for learning. But the use of TV/video, computers, calculators and other hardware does not take the place of thinking. It is only through thinking that these aids have any meaning. They do not replace the mind, though some, like TV, can remove the need for thinking. They are like pencils, pens and rubbers, simply tools of the mind, tools for learning.

What is creative thinking?

Creativity has been regarded as a special and rather mysterious attribute. Researchers have related this quality to one or more of four aspects of creativity:

- the idea or product created
- the process of creating
- the person of the creator
- the creative environment.

Creativity is something creative persons use to make creative products. A creative idea or product is usually defined as original and appropriate. Creative products would include works of art and scientific theories and also less tangible products such as inventive conversations or imaginative ideas. A reproduced or stereotyped product does not count as creative, no matter how fine it is in terms of craftsmanship.

Creativity is also a collection of attitudes and abilities that lead a person to produce creative thoughts, ideas or images. Part of this creative process lies in the use of intuition, the chance connections that bear fruit. Intuition or insight is the ability to reach sound conclusions from minimal evidence. Albert Einstein knew the value of making 'mental leaps' in the formulation of hypotheses. He wrote:

> *I believe in intuition and inspiration .... At times I feel certain that I am right while not knowing the reason .... Imagination is more important than knowledge. For knowledge is limited, whereas imagination embraces the entire world.*

Intuition and other aspects of creativity seem so mysterious because they draw upon the subconscious. In many ways the mind is like an iceberg: we are aware only of the visible, conscious part while submerged lie great areas of unconscious activity, hidden patterns and forgotten knowledge. There seem to be two kinds of human thought process, one voluntary, effortful and conscious, the other automatic, effortless and unconscious. This can be related to the left/right hemispheres of thinking as follows:

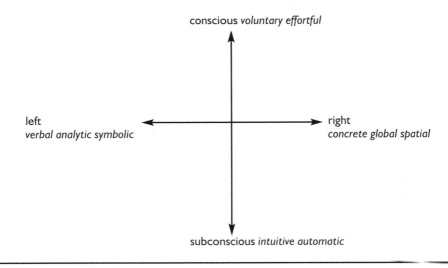

Figure 2.2

Thinking something new usually takes effort, which is one reason why 'it is harder to teach an old dog new tricks'. We prefer to rely on our automatic processes – they take less thought, less effort – but they have two major weaknesses. They tend to make thought stimulus bound and they tend to make it habit bound. As with children, we tend to respond only to what we see, hear, feel and sense: out of sight is usually out of mind. 'Bringing to mind' is a service that mediating adults can offer to children, not only by telling but by prompting, suggesting and questioning. It involves looking beyond the surface of things, seeking hidden patterns, expanding in the mind the boundaries of space and time.

According to Thurstone,[3] a key aspect of intelligence in each of its manifest forms is that it can control impulsiveness. Impulsive behaviour aims at the immediate satisfaction of a want, desire or impulse; it fails to consider alternative solutions that may in the longer run bring more satisfying results. Intelligence, for Thurstone, lies in the ability to consider and evaluate possible courses of action without actually engaging in them. The value of creative thinking is that it leads to flexibility of choice. What it lacks in speed it gains in quality of decision. It is able to break the bonds of accustomed perceptions and habits, and to bend the mind to new ideas and possibilities.

Many writers have contrasted two types of thinking. The distinctions they draw are not identical but they generally reflect a division between creative or exploratory thinking and critical or logically analytical reasoning:

Creative _____ Critical
Exploratory_____ Analytical
Inductive _____ Deductive
Hypothesis-forming _____ Hypothesis-testing
Informal thinking_____ Formal thinking
Adventurous thinking _____ Closed thinking (Bartlett)
Left-handed thinking_____ Right-handed thinking (Bruner)
Divergent thinking _____ Convergent thinking (Guilford)
Lateral thinking_____ Vertical thinking (de Bono).

There is a danger in all our thinking of a 'hardening of the categories' in which the labels we attach to clusters of ideas become limiting boundaries. Concepts become cordoned off and connections severed. One of the misconceptions that can arise about creativity is that it is something quite unrelated to critical thinking.

Misconceptions about creativity

1 That creativity is unrelated to critical thinking

The partitioning of thinking into two types is an oversimplification. It reflects to some extent the physical division of functions between the hemispheres of the brain. It also reflects the conceptual difference between analysing the elements of a problem in a logical fashion (the critical approach) and adding to the elements, re-combining them or looking at the problem from a fresh angle (the creative approach). It is mistaken, however, to think of these approaches to thinking as radically different or unconnected. Most problems require both types of thinking. Creativity is not just a question of creating new solutions to problems but of creating better solutions, and this requires critical judgement. To find an original solution to a logically complex problem can require creative powers of invention. An education that focused on only one type of thinking would be incomplete and unbalanced.

2 That creativity is found in some subjects but not in others

We have traditionally thought of creativity as a function of the arts but not of maths and science. But any activity that involves imagination and originality can be regarded as creative. Abraham Maslow[4] argued that 'a first-rate soup is more creative than a second-rate painting'. Karl Popper[5] wrote that every scientific discovery contains an 'irrational element' or 'creative intuition'. Einstein maintained that 'the most beautiful thing we can experience is the mysterious. It is the source of all true art and science'. Works of art and scientific enquiry are both explorations, looking at different aspects of nature, both require imagination, reason and emotional involvement. They ultimately have roots in the intuitive faculty, the 'Ah!' of the educated guess, when what we have done seems right.

3 That creativity is simply 'doing your own thing'

Experts at work in some creative field often seem to create with an effortless skill. Their seeming mindlessness may spring from either of two causes: a reliance on subconscious inspiration or the deployment of a skill refined through long practice. When Whistler was challenged about the price of one of his paintings, 'For two days' labour you ask 200 guineas?' he replied, 'No, I ask it for the knowledge of a lifetime.' A characteristic of expert performance in widely differing fields is the care, effort and length of time that goes into the preparation of a creative act. The astronomer Kepler was seven years working out his laws of planetary motion. Brahms began sketching his first symphony when in his twenties, but he did not finish it until he was 43. Ian Fleming was 43 when he wrote his first book after years of apprenticeship in journalism. Thomas Edison worked up to 20 hours per day for 13 years before achieving a breakthrough with the invention of the phonograph. In searching for the right filament for the first electric light bulb he experimented with over 1800 substances; no wonder he said 'Genius is 99% perspiration and 1% inspiration'. Creativity requires resilience in the face of possible failure.

Creative thinking requires high motivation and persistence, taking place over a considerable period of time (either continuously or intermittently) or with high-intensity effort. One virtue of our long childhood is that we have the time to practise a wide range of creative activities. The child has time to learn the value of practice and perseverance, to learn that in any chosen field making an effort will make a creative difference.

4 That creativity requires a high IQ

Creativity levels show little correlation with scores on IQ tests. As Thurstone pointed out, the confusion between intelligence and creative talent is common. For example, quiz kids are often referred to as geniuses. They would undoubtedly score high in memory functions .... However, it is doubtful whether they are also fluent in producing original ideas. All children can be creative at different levels and it is important to develop this creativity at a young age. It may be that the creative attitude – being inventive and adaptable, finding the unknown, challenging and offering unique and original solutions to problems – is established early in life and that once established it tends to continue. All children need is the right conditions for their creativity to flourish.

The creative climate

All children are born with creative ability but it is up to us to provide a climate to support the child's creative efforts. Psychologist Carl Rogers[6] says that human beings require two conditions if they are to function creatively, psychological safety and psychological freedom. The child's sense of psychological safety, he says, may result from three related processes:

- accepting the child as an individual of unconditional worth and having a faith in the child no matter what his/her present state
- avoiding external evaluation and encouraging self-evaluation
- empathising with the child, trying to see the world from the child's point of view, understanding and accepting him.

The guiding adult should feel free to express reactions such as 'I don't like your behaviour' but not to evaluate the child as a person by for example saying 'You are bad/naughty/wrong/lazy'. The difference is subtle but can be crucial to the climate of creativity. A child's creativity is nurtured by warmth and the positive approval of significant adults in her life. Children, like all of us, will tend to create for those they love.

Psychological freedom fosters creativity by permitting children freedom of expression. Children's behaviour needs to have limits and be moulded to the needs of society but their symbolic expression need not be so circumscribed. Children should feel secure enough to try out new things and be given the freedom to do so, within bounds. Their freedom of expression should not inhibit the freedom of others. In a creative climate adults and children value originality rather than conformity, not the sameness but the difference of ideas. We need to support the experimental rather than the safeguarding self.

I sense within me these two selves. They are not real selves but metaphors for the debate that goes on in my head over possible courses of action. Sometimes it is the safeguarding voice that dominates, 'I wouldn't bother ..., It's too risky ..., You're doing fine as you are ..., Stick to what you know will work...' and sometimes it is the experimental, 'Let's try it this way ..., What does it remind me of ...?, It might be interesting ..., I'll take a chance ....' The ideal is to have the two selves cooperate fully. With children (and transactional analysts would say there is a child in every adult) we need to strengthen their rational safeguarding selves in a world of threat and dangers but we also need to foster the expressive and experimental self, which can so easily be inhibited. The following are some of the approximate characteristics of these two selves:

Table 2.1 The safeguarding self and the experimental self

Safeguarding self	Experimental self
Suspicious of the new	Open to experience
Cautious	Curious
Sticks to known ways	Speculates
Likes to follow rules	Is intuitive
Conventional	Unconventional
Relies on others	Shows independence
Punishes mistakes	Does not mind being wrong
Avoids risks	Takes risks
Alert to possible dangers	Seeks new patterns
Avoids being wrong	Makes hopeful connections
Fearful of consequences	Likes to play
Is serious	Sees the fun of things
Avoids surprises	Likes surprises
Seeks reassurance	Uses own imagination
Keeps feelings private	Shares dreams

The creative climate is maintained by communication and communication is rarely neutral. Everything that is said can make a difference. Either it helps create an atmosphere where it is safe to share thinking and speculation or it damages that climate. It is not always what you say but the way you say it that is important. We slip easily into familiar phrases. Some verbal habits can unwittingly sap a child's confidence. Examples of demeaning comments include:

Where did you get that silly idea?
Don't ask such stupid questions!
Can't you ever do anything right?
Try to act your age.
It's not going to be as easy as you think.
Why don't you ever think?
Is that all you can do/say/think about?
How many times do I have to tell you?
Whoever heard of doing it like that?
Why don't you think before you speak?

An overdose of such statements can damage self-esteem and do little to elicit and support creative thinking. How much better to use, where possible, such encouraging comments as:

That's an interesting idea.
Tell me about it.
How did you reach that conclusion?
It's nice you can think it out for yourself.
Have you thought of some alternatives?
Whatever you decide is fine with me.
Try it yourself first – if you need help, tell me.
That's an imaginative idea.
That's a good question.
I'm sure you can get it right.

We should approach children with a generosity of understanding, aiming to minimise their mistakes and to praise their efforts. Research studies[7] have also shown the importance of having high expectations of children. Adult expectations, whether positive or negative, will affect a child's responses to thinking and learning. There is a need to provide stimulus, also to allow the child his areas of success. Nothing succeeds like success. This is important to remember, because creative thinking involves risk taking. As Torrance[8] reminds us: 'It takes courage to be creative. Just as soon as you have a new idea, you are a minority of one.' A willingness to stand up for one's own ideas and feelings requires a sound basis of self-esteem. This basis is built up not only by the confidence we instil by word and deed but by the model we present as parents and teachers. We need to raise our own self-esteem and to have confidence in our own creativity, for we may teach more by what we are than what we say.

No printed word, nor spoken plea
Can teach young minds what they should be
Not all the books on all the shelves –
But what the teachers are themselves.
    Anon

Figure 2.3 summarises some of the actions that can encourage or inhibit the climate for creative thinking and speculation:

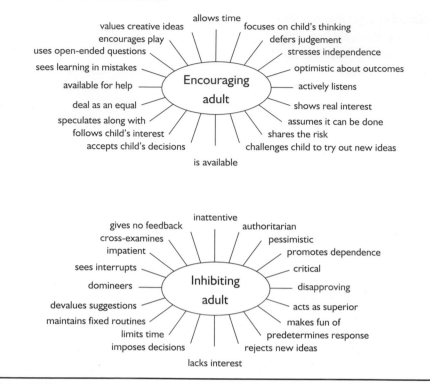

Figure 2.3 The encouraging and inhibiting adult.

The blocks to creativity may be internal and established as habits, feelings, experience, the inhibitions of a safeguarding personality, or they may be external and determined by the environment or other people such as peers/parents/teachers. It is not easy to get the balance of the creative climate right for any individual. Indeed, establishing the conditions for creative thinking can be more difficult than the creating itself. And once you have the right soil and a creative climate you need the seed of stimulus before the creative process can begin.

The creative process

Creative thinking is a way of generating ideas that can in some way be applied to the world. This often involves problem solving utilising particular aspects of intelligence, for example linguistic, mathematical and interpersonal intelligence. The process is often more important in encouraging creativity than the solution or end product. Products may be short-lived things but training in the process can be of lifelong value.

Since creativity is a way of thinking and ways of thinking mould attitudes, creativity is also a process of developing attitudes. It is the attitude, alongside the uses of the process, that can stimulate countless creative ideas through a child's lifetime. Various steps have been identified in the working of the creative process. These can be summarised as five stages:

1 stimulus
2 exploration
3 planning
4 activity
5 review.

The steps may overlap and the child can enter or leave the process at any stage. The child may get no further than an original stimulus, may stay in an exploration stage (as in a lot of creative play) or may get bogged down in planning and never execute a creative scheme (many would-be artists know this stage well). Some children may produce but never get round to reviewing and evaluating their creative work (often done by others).

These five main stages are as follows.

1 Stimulus

Creative thinking does not occur in a vacuum: it needs some stimulus, some content to work on. As the ancient Greeks used to say, nothing comes from nothing. There needs to be a fertile ground for growth to take place. Sometimes this growth can be sudden and unexpected, the incubation of a long-dormant idea, the thought that drifts into the mind from the subconscious. But:

> *the unconscious, though one cannot force it, will not produce new ideas unless it has been painstakingly stuffed full of facts, impressions, concepts and an endless series of conscious ruminations and attempted solutions.*[9]

The paradox of creativity is that in order to think creatively we need to be stimulated by the thinking of others. There is an impulse to create within each child ready to be wakened. It derives from the disposition to be curious, to wonder and to question. As Rudyard Kipling wrote:

> *I keep six honest serving men*
> *(They taught me all I knew)*
> *Their names are What and Why and When*
> *And How and Where and Who.*

The following are the sorts of question that may arise in a child's mind to act as a stimulus for investigation.

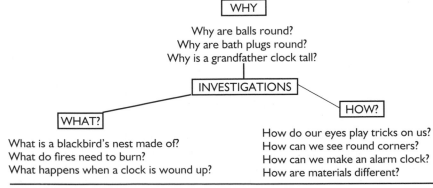

Figure 2.4

The initial stimulus may be prompted by an awareness that there is a problem to be solved, or a vague feeling that there is an idea that is not quite grasped or fully realised. Often this state will be triggered by a challenge to the child's thinking offered by parent or teacher. The task of teaching is to spark off the creative impulse within the child and to support the process of exploration.

2 Exploration

Creativity has been said to consist largely of rearranging what we know in order to find out what we do not know. Many children fall short of their creative potential because they grab at the first idea or solution that presents itself. First ideas can be trite and commonplace. Children can be helped to move beyond their first ideas and to consider alternatives before making a decision. To think creatively they need to be able to investigate further and to look afresh at what they normally take for granted.

Certain principles or techniques can be applied to improve the range and quality of ideas gathered. As Bruner says, 'We move, perceive and think in a fashion that depends on techniques rather than wired-in arrangements in our nervous system.'[10] Such techniques include:

- *Divergent thinking* – the kind of thinking that generates many different answers, not being restricted to convergent thinking, which seeks one absolute or correct answer.
- *Deferring judgement* – the principle of 'think now, judge later', removing the anxiety of having to be right and preventing imagination being hampered by judgement. Useful when children are working alone, thinking up ideas, or brainstorming with a group.
- *Extending effort* – providing the opportunity of quantity breeding quality. As Nobel prizewinner Linus Pauling put it, 'The best way to have a good idea is to have lots of ideas.' To extend effort children need the support, interest, questioning and stimulus of adults.
- *Allowing time* – there is an Irish saying, 'When God made time he made plenty of it'. Allowing time for the incubation of ideas, the 'do nothing' stage is vital in the creative process. As with creative artists who work on several projects at a time, children may need minutes, hours or days to incubate a solution to a problem. They can learn that useful technique for any problem-solving activity, leave it for a while and return to it refreshed.
- *Encouraging play* – to see how far an idea extends, encourage playing with it, pull it about, apply it in novel situations, build on it, draw it, represent it with objects, act it out, test it in action. According to Huizinga,[11] it is man's ability to play that has provided the creative impulse for civilisation.

3 Planning

When analysing the differences between novices and experts, in any creative field, one key element stands out. Experts tend to spend more time in planning. This stage usually involves three parts, which often overlap.

- *Defining the problem or task* – what is the purpose of our thinking, what are we trying to achieve? Children often get bogged down, sidetracked or confused because they are not clear about the task or problem. Asking them to define what they are doing can often help them to clarify ideas – or reveal their confusion.
- *Gathering information* – facts and observations are an aid to thinking. 'We can have facts without thinking, but we cannot have thinking without facts' (John Dewey). The child's mind is like a kaleidoscope. The more facts and sensory impressions the child has, the more intricate can be his patterning of ideas. Adult help is often needed in this gathering of data, the raw materials of thinking, and often these new data will alter the nature of the problem or open up new avenues of enquiry.
- *Making thinking visible* – some children simply wait for the penny to drop, the answer to come, the illumination to happen. They do not realise that thinking is an active process, that all productive effort from cookery to car maintenance requires planning. They can be helped to become aware of their thinking process through thinking aloud, using images, drawing or writing. Thinking can be improved by sharing it or recording it. Leonardo da Vinci's notebooks, Beethoven's sketchbooks, a poet's drafts or an architect's plans are all ways of expressing thinking and showing thought in process. Making thoughts concrete pins ideas to the reality of paper and prevents them from shifting or fading from memory. Internal concreteness helps too, thinking aloud and forming mental images. The page from Darwin's notebook in Figure 2.5 shows how he gathered information and made thinking visible in his study of finches in the Galapagos Islands. He worked in an unstructured way, like many creative people, scribbling notes haphazardly as he gathered information from around the world. It took him years of concentrated study, note taking, sketching and playing with ideas to arrive at his theory of evolution.

4 Activity

The creative process begins with an idea or a set of ideas. It is doing something with one's ideas that counts in life. 'What can we make of this idea?', 'Where does it lead?', 'How can it be put into action?' are all questions thathelp to focus on the productivity of ideas. We need to give children the opportunity of realising their creative thinking in action. See below for suggestions of activities for children of all ages.

5 Review

Once an idea has been realised, a problem solved, an investigation concluded, what then? Often before the goal has been achieved or the task accomplished new challenges will initiate the creative process all over again. Some time, however, should be set aside for evaluation and review. What have we done? How successful was it? How might it be improved? Did we achieve our objective? What have we learned? Even the very young

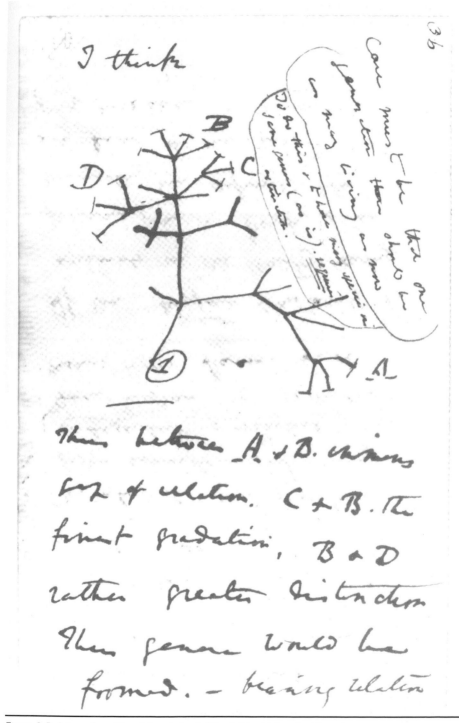

Figure 2.5 A page from Darwin's notebook (Cambridge University Library).

can be trained to use their judgement and imagination to evaluate their ideas. This is where creative process becomes subject to critical thinking and where Piaget's second goal of education 'to form minds which can be critical, can verify, and not accept everything they are offered' becomes so important. In helping children to reflect on their own creative efforts they will also be encouraged to be more active in assessing the ready-made slogans, opinions and the 'hidden persuaders' that form part of their environment.

Creativity in practice

Creativity in practice requires a response involving both feeling and thinking, creative attitudes combined with cognitive skills. Creative attitudes, or affective traits, will encourage the child to be curious, take risks, use complex ideas and exercise the imagination. Cognitive skills will allow the child to generate, process and play with ideas. Researchers have suggested there are four aspects to divergent or creative thinking skills – fluency, flexibility, originality and elaboration.[12]

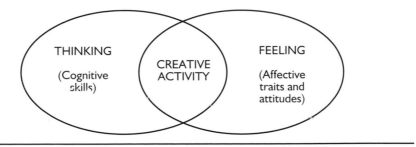

Figure 2.6 The creative response.

Fluency

Fluency of thinking is the ease with which we use stored information when we need it. As Michael Polyani has suggested 'We know more than we know.' The mind like a muscle develops with use, the more we stimulate and challenge its resources the more will be its information-processing power. The more a child generates ideas in play and informal settings the more fluent he will be in generating solutions to the real and important problems of life. Examples of activities to stimulate fluency could include:

- How many things can you think of that are: yellow/round/miniscule/transparent/ striped, etc.?
- How many words can you think of that are similar to, or rhyme with another?
- How many words can you think of that begin with a certain letter? (Put some of these together to make your own tongue twister.)
- Make up a sentence using a group of letters, for example the letters of your name, or egbdf (every good boy deserves favours/each girl buys duty frees).
- Name acrostics – write down the initials of your name, create words that describe you with each letter, or write down the names of places, flowers, colours with each letter.

These and other word games are a valuable way of developing fluency of ideas and words in children.

Flexibility

Flexibility is the ability the child has to overcome mental blocks, to alter his approach to a problem. Children may get stuck by assuming rules and conditions that do not apply to a problem. Many puzzles such as these require flexibility of thinking.

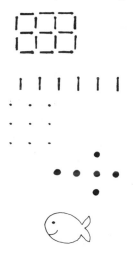

- Remove 4 matches to leave 3 squares. (Clue: the squares do not have to be the same size.)
- Use 6 matches to create 4 triangles. (Clue: the triangles can be three dimensional.)
- Draw 4 straight lines to pass through these 9 points without taking the pencil off the paper. (Clue: the straight lines can extend beyond the points.)
- Move one coin so there are 4 coins vertically and horizontally. (Clue: you can move one coin on top of another.)
- Draw this fish keeping your pencil on the paper. (Clue: You can fold the paper and continue part of the drawing on the reverse.)

Originality

Originality or novelty is shown by an unusual or rare response. Typical of questions that test this ability is the call for interesting uses of common objects:

- Think of as many things as possible that you could use a blanket for.
- How many uses for a brick, or a paper clip?
- How many uses can you list for a matchbox? (Try them out.)
- How many different items can you get into a matchbox? (A cub scout managed 150.)
- What could you add to a familiar everyday object, for example a coffee cup, to improve it?

Originality can also be assessed by the game of Consequences and thinking about the future can also stimulate original ideas, for example ask children to try to visualise what life will be like 160 years from now, in particular how life at home would be different. Design a dream house of the future.

Elaboration

Elaboration is shown by the number of additions that can be made to some simple stimulus to make it more complex. For example:

- Make a drawing based on a squiggle, as in Figure 2.8.
- Elaborate on a magazine picture or newspaper photo by drawing pictorial additions or speech bubbles (adding creatively apt comments!).
- Write a story by filling a bag with words written on separate pieces of paper, pick out some words and weave a story using the words.
- Invent different drawings all based on the same circle, as in Figure 2.9.
- Choose a toy and think of ways to change it to make it more fun to play with.

Drawing by C. Barsotti; © 1977
The New Yorker Magazine, Inc.

Figure 2.7 Ten ways to improve a coffee cup (a creative exercise).

Figure 2.8 The squiggle drawing shown here was produced in a competition run by the National Association for Gifted Children.

face

sun

tadpole

ice cream

watch

sign

jet fighter

moon

Spider's web

pig

petrol tanker

snake

Figure 2.9 Drawings all based on the same circle.

Elaboration can be on the ideas of others, for example in 'Pass Along Pictures' a child draws anything of her choice for a minute before passing the paper to the next child to add interesting details. After about six 'passes along', the child must tell a story about the picture. Then return the picture to the original child to see how her idea has been elaborated by others.

Various checklists have been devised to help children, parents and teachers to generate ideas. The best known of these is the list of idea-spurring questions devised by Alex Osborn.[13] Table 2.2 adapts Osborn's questions into a Scamper checklist of idea-generating questions that can be applied to thought, things, themes and much more.

Table 2.2

Scamper checklist for creating ideas

Substitute	Who else instead? What else instead? Other place? Other time? Other material? Other approach?
Combine	Bring together? Unite with another? Combine purposes? Combine ideas?
Adapt	What else is like this? What ideas does it suggest? Can it be adjusted for a purpose?
Modify	Magnify? Minify? Multiply? What to alter? To add? Change – colour, form, shape, motion? Other changes?
Put to other uses	New ways to use? Other uses if modified?
Eliminate	What to remove, omit or get rid of? Part or whole?
Rearrange	Try different pattern, layout or scheme? Turn it round, upside down, inside out? Try opposites?

Children can try out the Scamper techniques on simple objects, like a toy, and apply the idea-generating questions to it. Get them to collect *objets trouvés* or pictures from magazines to question and create ideas from. Share ideas but keep in mind the principle of deferred judgement. The focus is on generating ideas, not rushing to judgement. The more experience children have of looking at things in new and thoughtful ways the more likely they are to apply this approach to other aspects of learning and life.

Strategies for generating ideas have also been devised by Edward de Bono[14] in his *CoRT Thinking Programme* and books on lateral thinking. He calls them 'attention-directing tools'. Just as a parent teaches a child to cross the road safely not just by telling children of possible dangers but by showing them how to look left and right before crossing the street, so there is a need for procedures that direct the child's attention to aspects of a situation that might otherwise be neglected.

One such tool is PMI, which stands for:

Plus – the good things about an idea, why you like it.
Minus – the bad things, why you don't like it.
Interesting – what you find interesting about an idea.

Instead of saying you like or don't like an idea, do a PMI. De Bono illustrated PMI in action in a classroom in Sydney, Australia.[15] The teacher asked his class of 10 year olds whether they would like to be paid 5 dollars a week for attending school. All 30 raised their hands in agreement, and eagerly gave their reasons:

We would use the money to buy candy.
Having money is more grown-up.
We wouldn't have to ask our parents for money.

The teacher told the children about PMI and put them into small groups to list the plus, minus and interesting (not easily classifiable) points. After only four minutes' work the teacher asked for reactions. The good points were repeated but now some drawbacks are noted:

> *Our parents would stop giving us pocket money.*
> *The bigger boys might beat up the smaller ones to take their money.*
> *Adults might not give us presents.*

After listing the plus, minus and interesting points on the board, the teacher again asked how many were in favour of being paid. This time only one child raised his hand. The rest had changed their minds.

Other techniques suggested by de Bono include:

- *CAF: Consider All Factors* – When you have to choose or make a decision there are always many factors to consider. Unless the child is careful some factors will escape notice and decisions that seemed right at the time may well turn out to be wrong. PMI was concerned with judging good, bad or other points. CAF simply notes all possible factors so none are left out of consideration. For example, do a CAF on the factors to consider in buying a new house, a second-hand bicycle, a teddy bear or a toy.

- *C & S: Consequences and Sequel* – In thinking about an action we should think of the consequences. Children need training in thinking about consequences not only to themselves but to others. What might happen if . . . the world runs out of oil and petrol . . . children could go out to work instead of going to school . . . you won a million pounds . . . animals could speak . . . you went blind, etc.

- *AGO: Aims Goals Objectives* – Children often do things out of habit, because everyone else is doing it or as a reaction to a situation. Sometimes they do something in order to achieve a purpose, aim or goal. They need to be aware that human actions often have a purpose; the human world is not a random one. For example, do an AGO for the police, put their aims in order of priority. Everyone has to eat to live – do an AGO for a homemaker, cook, shopkeeper, food manufacturer, farmer and the government.

- *FIP: First Important Priorities* – After generating a number of ideas children need to decide which are the most important. For example, what makes a TV programme interesting? In running a school, what do you think the priorities should be? What do you want from your next holiday?

- *APC: Alternatives, Possibilities, Choices* – Often there are more alternatives in taking a decision than you first thought. Sometimes the most obvious choice is not the best one. What alternatives do you have if your best friend is a thief? A strange hole appears in your garden, what might have caused it? You find a £5 note, what choices do you have?

- *OPV: Other Point of View* – People look at the same situation from different and personal points of view. Everyone thinks differently, and children need help in that most difficult of tasks: seeing from other points of view. Imagine that a child gets into trouble for shouting at a parent or teacher. What might the point of view of the child, parents, teacher and other children be?

The aim of these and other CoRT techniques is to improve planning and decision making. To do so a child needs to practise considering all the factors and consequences and to rehearse mentally all the arguments for and against an action before carrying it out. De Bono also advocates a technique called lateral thinking, which he takes to be the basis of insight or creativity. The following activities can help children to develop lateral thinking, the habit of looking for alternatives and not simply accepting the most obvious approach.

Pictures

Pictures can provide opportunities for looking closely and attending, not just 'seeing'. The child needs a stimulus to focus her thinking, show selectivity and gain insight. Colour magazines provide a rich pictorial resource. With a chosen picture a child might:

- describe what is happening – whether there could be different interpretations
- describe three or more different things that are happening
- visualise the picture and describe it without looking at it, guess causes and consequences for what is happening in the picture
- think of a title to it, alternative titles, best title
- generate questions about a picture for others to answer
- imagine what might be hidden from view within the picture or beyond the picture frame.

When showing pictures to children, try altering the pictures by covering parts of them. As you slowly, stage by stage, reveal the picture, can the child guess what the hidden parts will show? How would you describe the picture to someone who couldn't see it? Describe a hidden picture and see if the child can draw it. Try not describing a hidden picture, but let the child ask questions to find out how to draw it. Children can try these activities with each other, or describe picture details for you to draw. To the enquiring mind every picture tells a story, and provides opportunities for creative visualisation. Reproductions of abstract paintings can be used to stir the imagination, as can ink or paint blots on folded paper. The nineteenth-century German romantic poet Justinus Kerner used symmetrical ink-blots to inspire poetic thoughts and images. Figure 2.10 is an example of one of his ink-blots. Children can create their own ink-blot stimuli for creative thinking, writing or stories.

Stories

Stories can provide a rich stimulus for divergent thinking.[16] All stories to some extent require thinking about and recreating in the listener's or reader's mind. Some traditional stories, such as the fables of Aesop, the tales of Nasruddin or religious parables, have been specifically created to stimulate thought. Poems and nursery rhymes too can provide a lively stimulus if thinking can be extended by the use of open-ended questions. For example, in the nursery rhyme 'Jack and Jill':

Why did they go up the hill to fetch water?
Where might they be getting it from?
Why did Jack fall down? Why did Jill fall down?
Did they fall down on the way up or the way down?
Was Jill hurt? What happened next?

Figure 2.10 An ink blot created by Justinus Kerner to inspire poetic thoughts and images.

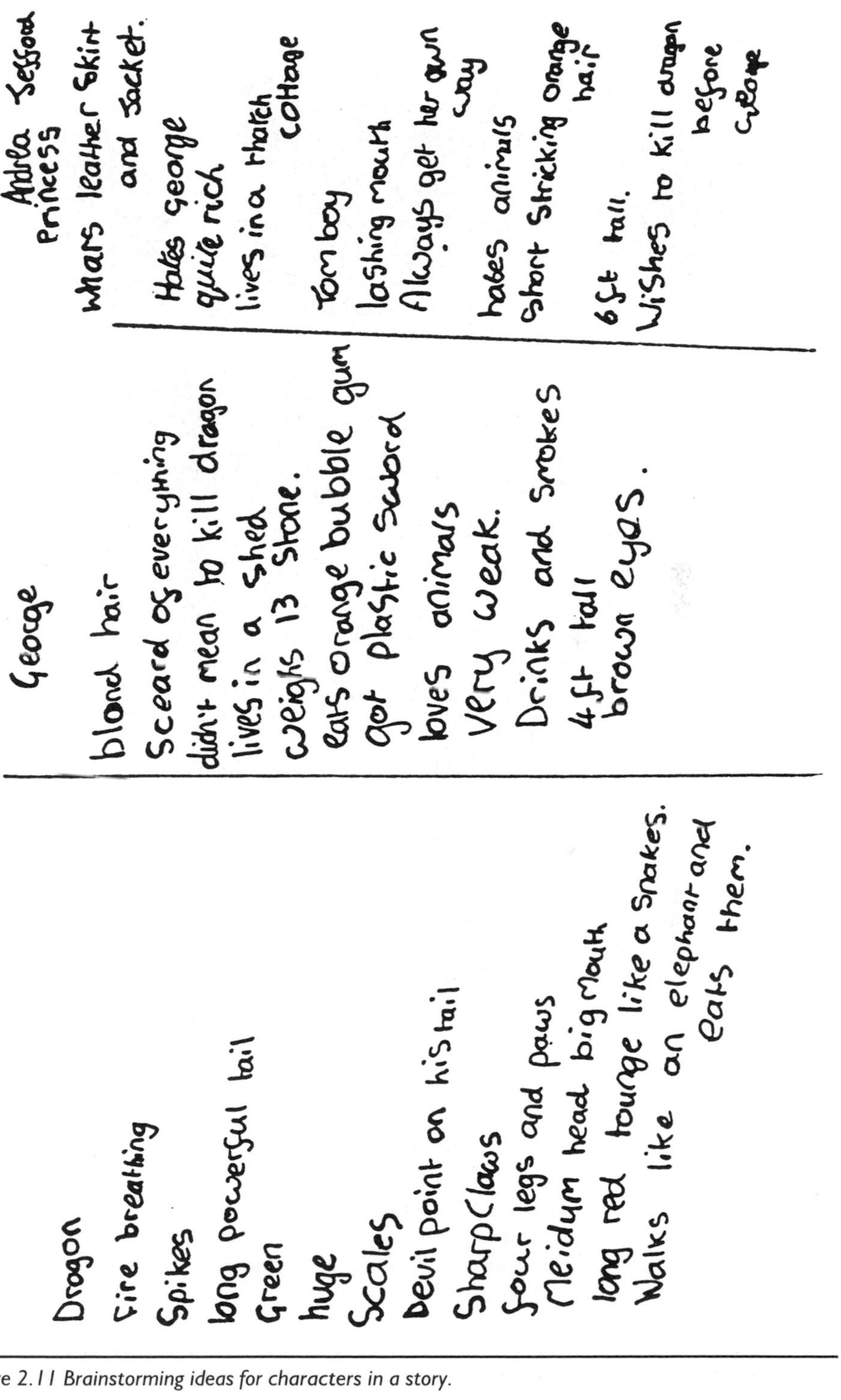

Andrea Sefford
princess
whars leather skirt
and Jacket.
Hates george
quite rich
lives in a thatch
cottage
Tom boy
lashing mouth
Always get her own
say
hates animals
short stricking orange
hair
6ft tall.
wishes to kill dragon
before
George

George

blond hair
Sceard of everything
didn't mean to kill dragon
lives in a shed
weighs 13 stone.
eats orange bubble gum
got plastic sword
loves animals
very weak.
Drinks and smokes
4ft tall
brown eyes.

Dragon
fire breathing
spikes
long powerful tail
green
huge
scales
Devil point on his tail
sharp claws
four legs and paws
Meidum head big mouth
long red tounge like a snakes.
walks like an elephant and
eats them.

Figure 2.11 Brainstorming ideas for characters in a story.

The question, 'What happened next?' is one that can be used at any point of any story to generate thinking about alternatives. 'What do you think were the different points of view of the characters?' 'How might it have ended?' After hearing the story of George and the Dragon and talking about it, some 7-year-old children decided to write their own version of the story. In Figure 2.11, Andrea brainstorms her ideas for the main characters.

Brainstorming

Brainstorming is a useful strategy for generating ideas with children of all ages. A trigger word is offered and the children are asked to catch any thoughts, ideas, information or memories that arise in association with the word. It is very useful in the exploration stage of a creative activity. Brainstorming helps children to reveal and share the fund of knowledge they bring to the learning situation. Often the greatest obstacle to creative thinking is the critical attitude of others. Brainstorming was devised as a way of overcoming the criticism of others and encouraging children to build on one another's ideas. Children often need help in building up ideas. The process involves

1 listing as many ideas as possible
2 withholding comments on the ideas proposed
3 building on the ideas suggested
4 choosing the best ideas.

Brainstorming also involves the useful practice of paraphrasing ideas into a few key words. For example, before being given the challenge of finding out as many uses as they can for a matchbox, a group of children brainstormed the special qualities of a matchbox. The suggestions they came up with:

It has two parts, it can float, it can hold things, it is very light, you can cut holes in it, you can fit several together, it has a rough side

helped them to think of unusual uses, for example as 'wish boats':

You could use the matchbox tray as a boat, put a small candle in it, light it, then float it down a river. Make a wish, and if your boat gets washed up on the shore your wish will come true.

The words and phrases that are jotted down in a brainstorming session can be developed by classifying them, reorganising them or adding further ideas, which can be used as starting points for stories or research (what do I need to find out?). In response to the question 'What do you know about food?' one 8 year old classifies her information as she brainstorms it (Figure 2.12).

Children can be encouraged to trap their ideas before they are lost, in a notebook or a 'think book'.

Designing

Drawing is a wonderful way of making thinking visible. A child may not find it easy to express thinking in words but can always attempt to express it visually and find it easier to understand something in visual terms. We are primarily visual animals: over half the brain's capacity is taken up with processing visual stimuli (beware any book on thinking or learning that is expressed only in words). The work of Edward de Bono[17] has illustrated the considerable ability of young children to generate ideas through drawing. Posed such intriguing problems as designing 'a dog-exercising machine, a

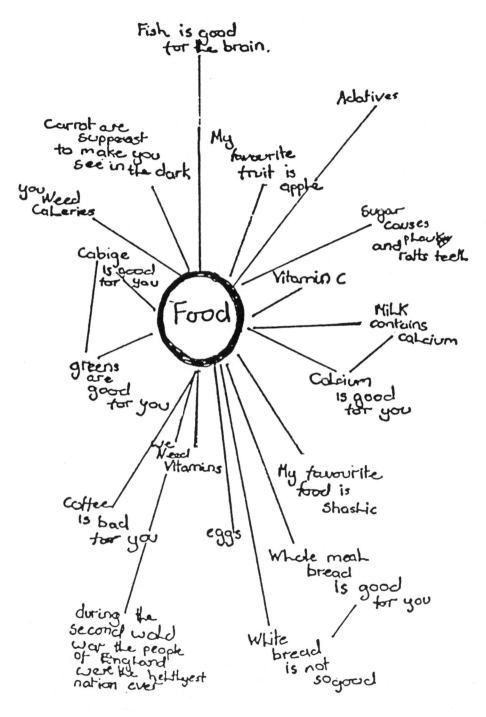

Fish is good
for the brain.

Carrot are
suppeast
to make you
see in the dark

Adatives

My
favourite
fruit is
apple

you
Weed
CaLeries

Sugar
couses
and plauty
ratts teeth

Cabige
Is good
for you

Vitamin c

Food

MiLK
contains
caLcium

greens
are
good
for you

Calcium
Is good
for you

We
Need
Vitamins

My favourite
food is
Shaslic

Coffee
Is bad
for you

eggs

Whole meal
bread
Is good
for you

during the
second wold
war the people
of England
were the helthyest
nation ever

White
bread
is not
sogood

Figure 2.12

machine to weigh an elephant, how to improve the human body, stop a cat and dog fighting, invent a sleep machine ...' children of all ages responded with lively and inventive drawings (Figure 2.13).

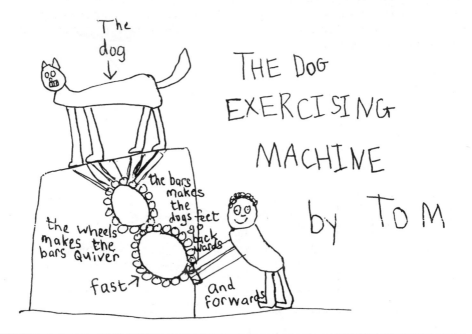

Figure 2.13

Other design topics could include:

- a machine to cut hair
- a machine to dig tunnels
- a fruit-picking machine
- a money (or egg)-sorting machine
- a secret den
- a pet's home
- a device for watering house plants while you're away
- a bird scarer
- a climbing frame
- a litter bin.

Speculative design is a valuable preparation for practical designing where the creative idea is actually constructed in suitable materials. It is in practical design that children learn the need to compromise between an ideal solution on paper and what can actually be achieved within the constraints of time, money, materials, facilities and technical ability.

The beauty of a young child's thinking is that it is unconstrained. They will quite happily redesign the human body, the family car or the local school. Offer children a random arrangement of lines and they will soon start to pick out significant patterns and pictorial possibilities. Ask children to draw a number of dots on a piece of paper and see how they create a design or picture by connecting the dots or incorporating them in some overall scheme. A generous supply of felt-tip pens or crayons can offer a wealth of creative opportunities.

Drawing

Try drawing some droodles. To droodle, as defined by American humorist Roger Price, means 'to drool with pleasure over a few scribbles on paper'. To encourage creative effort, ask children to draw a squiggly line on a piece of paper, put them in a box and draw one out. The game is to convert the squiggle into a drawing. Marks or votes may be given for the best creative effort, or for the most inventive title. For example what title might you give these?

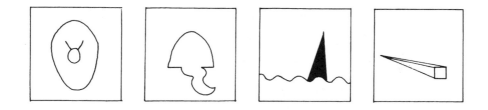

Figure 2.14

Warm up by creating titles for minimal pictures:

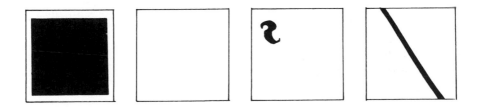

Figure 2.15

Can you think of five or more possible titles for each?

A variation for older children is to think of new titles for famous paintings. This game can help to liven up a visit to the art gallery.

As the Chinese proverb says, a picture can be worth a thousand words. But words too can be drawn by children in ways that illustrate their meanings as visual puns. For example:

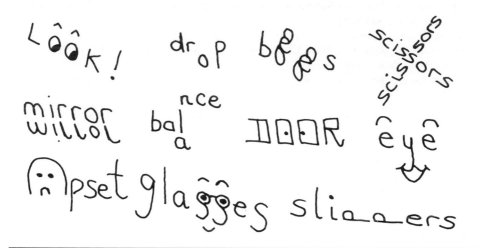

Figure 2.16 Visual puns.

Word play

Words are the principal vehicle for the expression of creative thinking and what more typical way for children to express themselves than through humour? Humans are the only animals that laugh. Jokes can be seen as a form of creative thinking,[18] testing and expanding a child's imagination, guessing powers and memory. Jokes create vivid pictorial images that can fire a child's imagination. Riddles, either joke-riddles or true riddles, stimulate divergent thinking and critical response. Riddles highlight the contrast between appearance and reality, between that which has to be guessed and that which appears at first sight. They stimulate by being enigmatic and puzzling: 'What is it that grows bigger the more you take away? *Answer:* a hole.' There is usually a twist in the tale, as in the following child's joke-riddle:

> *There was a donkey on one side of the river and on the other there were some beautiful carrots. The river was very wide, so the donkey couldn't jump over it, and it was so long he couldn't walk round it. There was no boat and he couldn't fly and he couldn't swim. So how did he get across? How? Do you give up? So did the donkey.*

To remember the joke and retell it again increases the power of memory. Once joke and riddling sessions begin the child must quickly recall the joke, organise it in his mind and tell it with all the smoothness and verbal skill he can muster. The aim is to perform well, often, as is the way with children, in competition with others to convince everyone of your story and its truth. The accent is on quick thinking and slickness of verbal delivery. It is a skill top comedians are paid a fortune for. Descartes wrote 'I think, therefore I am', but a more apt comment on the human condition might be 'I think, therefore I laugh'.[19] Wittgenstein said that 'a good and serious philosophical work could be written that would consist entirely of jokes'. Certainly a verbal fluency and comprehension test could be devised for children consisting of riddles and jokes. Children's humour often depends on verbal trickery and in this older children have the advantage over younger ones, as in the following exchange overheard in the playground.

10-year-old	Pete and Repeat were walking down the street. Pete fell down. Who was left?
7-year-old	Repeat.
10-year-old	Pete and Repeat were walking down the street. Pete fell down. Who was left?
7-year-old	Repeat.

etc.

Some favourite children's jokes rely on ambiguity of meaning combined with a vision of the absurd. The following is a favourite joke of a 9 year old. 'A woman walks into a butcher's shop and asks "Have you got a sheep's head?" '"No Madam, it's only the way I part my hair."' What are the favourite jokes of your children? Can you add to their store? People develop their own style of reportage, in speech and writing, and retelling jokes gives a child the chance to try a variety of styles and forms. For some children jokes will never become a chosen way of communicating with people, for others this early form of rhetorical training and re-creative thinking, will stay with them throughout their life.

Jokes and riddles rely for their impact on making unexpected connections between events and ideas. In teaching children to be creative we should make use of their chance interests and discoveries and help them to make connections between facts, ideas and experiences. A key feature of creative thinking is the ability to make *connections* between ideas and to see likenesses in the features of the world. Researching into creativity Bronowski[20]

> *found the act of creation to lie in the discovery of a hidden likeness. The scientist or artist takes two facts or experiences which are separate; he finds in them a likeness which had not been seen before; and he creates a unity by showing the likeness.*

An analogy can act as a model to enrich our understanding, for example in science, thinking of gas as a swarm of small elastic balls, the atom as a miniature solar system. Gordon[21] coined the word 'synectics' to describe this connection making. 'Synectics' is derived from the Greek word for joining together and has the aim of achieving a new way of looking at the old world of people, ideas, feelings and things. When an 8 year old was asked what it would be like to be the only person on earth, he replied, 'It would be like being the only star in the sky.' He had pointed out a similarity or connection in the form of an analogical relationship. Children can be helped to make connections by playing analogy games, such as:

1 Write names of things on slips of paper. Put them into a box or bag. Child draws two slips, for example, 'Horse', 'piano' and must think of a connection between the two, for example, 'has four legs'. Others may add their own connections, turns are taken and points awarded. The list of objects to be connected can be endless, for example, 'potato', 'toothbrush', 'book', 'window', 'cup', 'typewriter', 'basket'.

2 Children take turns to say any random word, for example, 'egg', 'book', 'clock', 'train', 'light', 'summer' and the aim is for others to spot a connection between a word spoken and the previous word, for example, 'during summer time there is more light'. Discussion in these games may ensue as to whether a real connection has been made and differences of opinion resolved by majority decision, or impartial umpire.

The following game encourages children to make creative conceptual links between ideas. Any number of players may take part. One player thinks of a thing or a person and asks the others, 'What is my thought like?' Each in turn makes a guess as to the object of thought. No clues are given so the guessing is random. Once all players have made a guess they are told the object in mind and are given a short while to think of a link or relationship between the object and their guess. If, for example, the object was a lion and the player had guessed a steam train, he might go on to explain that a lion is like a train because both make a powerful roar. Players may discuss the relevance of explanations. Those that can link their guess with the original thought win, any explanation not considered relevant loses. Each round of 'what is my thought like?' begins with a different questioner.

Opportunities for children to think creatively may occur at unexpected moments, and be extended through informal talk and discussion. Such occasions might include:

- *Seeing/reading the news* – How might the latest disaster have been averted?
- *Finding a strange object* – What might it be a part of/used for? What uses could you put it to?
- *Responding to the weather* – If it rains, what could you do indoors? What could you do in the rain?
- *Out and about* – What could you do if you got lost? If you lost something?
- *Responding to an unusual question* – A young child once asked 'Where do dreams come from?' and was read Roald Dahl's story *The BFG* about a giant who kept dreams in bottles. Later when he saw a drunk reeling down the street he remarked, 'He must have been drinking the wrong dreams.'
- *Extending everyday play* – What might Teddy be thinking? What adventures might a battered old toy have had?
- *Seeing shapes in nature* – Can you see figures, faces, shapes in the clouds? What does that gnarled piece of wood, or strange stone remind you of?

Creative thinking depends on the exercise of the imagination. To be creative, imagination must be active. Stories will spark the imagination and so will illustrations that hold the attention. The child's imagination will respond to a challenge.

Questions can stir the imagination into creative thinking:

- Which would you rather be, a door, a window or a hole in the roof? Why?
- In what ways could you use the pattern of a cobweb to create new or unusual products?
- The answer is London. What are the questions? The answer is . . . . What are the questions?
- What would happen if there were no hills, trees, rivers, etc.?
- How many how or why questions can you ask about the story you have just heard or read?

In the story of Hansel and Gretel, how would you stop yourself getting lost in a strange wood? If you were a Robinson Crusoe how would you survive on a desert island? The ancient Greeks thought of seven wonders in their world, what would be the seven wonders in your world, people, places, activities, feelings, smells? What would be the seven horrors in your world? Choose one of the horrors and think of ways of changing it for the better.

We create not only through words and pictures but also through movement and touch. Physical intelligence is shown through movement and gesture, for example through mime (can you guess the person, activity or occupation being mimed?). Kinaesthetic intelligence is shown through the sense of touch. It is touch that gives us our sense of reality. Some things cannot be touched. Ask children what they are. Examples are rainbows, reflections and sunbeams. These things puzzle children. Their whole conception of what exists outside themselves is largely based on their sense of touch. Children can be helped to be 'in touch' with themselves and to develop a sense of creative control over the physical world, for example through moulding, junk modelling and craftwork, thinking with their hands.

Visual intelligence can be developed through creative games with shapes, such as tangrams, the ancient Chinese seven-piece puzzle. Creating with tangrams was the favourite pastime of Napoleon in exile on St Helena. What can you or your children make with tangrams, a rabbit, a face, a boat, a swan, a church, a chair, a person, a teapot, a table, a candlestick – something beginning with every letter of the alphabet?

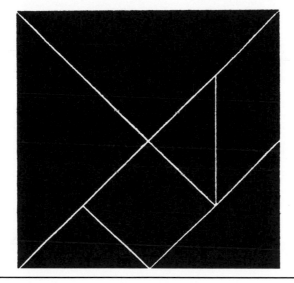

Figure 2.17 Chinese tangram.

Creative thinking is imaginative, inventive and involves the generation of new ideas. Every creative activity that seeks the solution to a problem requires the use of critical judgement, for creative ideas should not simply be novel but be of value. Creativity is not merely a question of generating new solutions to problems but of creating *better* solutions. True creativity requires therefore the use of critical thinking. A.N. Whitehead wrote

> *The probability is that nine hundred and ninety nine of our ideas will come to nothing... but we had better entertain them all, however sceptically, for the thousandth idea may be the one that will change the world.*[22]

It is through the use of critical thinking that children will learn to identify their most powerful ideas.

Summary

Children need creative rather than reproductive thinking to face the challenges of the present and future. Creativity is about bending the mind to new ideas and possibilities. It relates to critical thinking, can be applied to all subjects and developed in any child. All children are born with creative ability but need a creative climate and practice in creative processes to develop creative potential. The creative process requires stimulus, opportunities for exploration, planning, activity and review. Creative outcomes can be judge in terms of fluency, flexibility, originality and elaboration. Stimulus for creativity includes stories, brainstorming, designing, drawing, word play, games and puzzles.

3 Critical thinking

The first key to wisdom is constant questioning .... By doubting we are led to enquiry, and by enquiry we discern the truth.
　　Peter Abelard (1079–1142)

Michel, a 9-year-old, was once questioned by Piaget about his attitude to foreigners. When asked who foreigners are Michel mentions the French, Americans, Russians and English. Piaget asks first about the French..

Michel	The French are very serious and they don't worry about anything, and it's dirty there.
Piaget	And what do you think about the Americans?
Michel	They're ever so rich and clever. They've discovered the atom bomb.
Piaget	And what do you think of the Russians?
Michel	They're bad, they're always wanting to make war.
Piaget	And what's your opinion of the English?
Michel	I don't know ... they're nice ....
Piaget	Now look, how did you come to know all you've told me?
Michel	I don't know ... I've heard it ... that's what people say.[1]

Children often absorb the attitudes and opinions of the significant adults in their lives. The belief structures of adults can, in effect, be imposed on children. And children can learn to become dependent on the thinking of others. They can be condemned to closed mindedness or they can be encouraged to value the authority of their own reasoning capacities, to consider it natural that people may differ in their beliefs and points of view, to question their own reasoning and the reasoning of others. If a child is to become open-minded and critical, her thinking should not be left to chance. They need to be shown how to think critically.

Learning to think critically means:

1　Learning how to question, when to question and what questions to ask.
2　Learning how to reason, when to use reasoning and what reasoning methods to use.

The word 'reason' is derived from the word 'ratio', which means balance. A child can only think critically or reasonably to the extent that she is able carefully to examine experience, assess knowledge and ideas, and weigh arguments before reaching a balanced judgement. Being a critical thinker also consists in developing certain attitudes, such as a desire to reason, a willingness to challenge and a passion for truth.

A readiness to reason

Children have a need to find or create order and meaning out of their experience of life. They want to be able to reason well, or at least correctly, about what is important in their lives. They want their thinking to be right, and for this rightness to be confirmed by experience. There are also other dynamics at work. The child's natural egocentricity, which provides a growing sense of selfhood, promotes at a very deep level a different view of reasoning, 'What I think must be right' or, as expressed by Lewis Carroll, 'What I tell you three times is true.'[2] A related tendency, which we all share, is the blocking-out of information we do not want to see or hear, especially when it does not fit in with our basic beliefs and desires.

To encourage a child to make an effort in reasoning, you will need to demonstrate that right reasoning makes a difference and leads to success, that errors in reasoning lead to faulty solutions and to failure. The child will be more willing to make that effort if he has seen an adult model the intellectual curiosity and persistence required. So, for example, if you have a problem with a recipe, a DIY job or a crossword puzzle, show your child what efforts are involved, for example, 'Let me think this out, if I do x, then y will happen', 'What should I try first?', 'Why does it show/say that?' A readiness to reason is helped by a healthy attitude to argument. Many people confuse argument with quarrelling. Argument is the offering of reasons for a belief, whereas quarrelling can be seen as a verbal fight. A quarrel generates heat and indulges the ego, it involves the emotions, vents frustrations and 'lets off steam'. Argument aims at discovering the truth by exposing belief to the light of reason. Argument should be a challenge to reason, not an invitation to quarrel.

> What arguments are there for it?
> What arguments are there against it?
> Can you convince me with your arguments?
> Have I convinced you with my arguments?
> Which argument would convince you?

A willingness to challenge

The mark of a critical thinker is the readiness to challenge the ideas of others. This means that if we wish our children to be critical thinkers then we should try to encourage their challenges to our ideas and ways of thinking. A corollary of this is that the child should also be willing to submit her own ideas to scrutiny and to the challenge of reason. This, however, is difficult to achieve. We all have a tendency to think of our ideas as extensions of ourselves. To doubt one's own ideas seems close to doubting oneself. For children, whose identities are still in a fragile and developing state, this willingness is doubly difficult. One of the challenges of teaching children to think is to help them to discover that the process of evaluating, approving and disapproving of one's own ideas is natural and healthy; the confidence to be self-critical can strengthen the sense of self.

Open mindedness in children does not mean having no beliefs or convictions, or being indecisive. To be open minded means to be prepared to give new evidence a fair hearing, to be willing to alter beliefs if there are sufficient reasons. Being open minded means a willingness to:

- make decisions which are based on evidence and evaluation of evidence
- challenge one's own ideas and decisions
- be open to the challenge of others
- entertain the possibility of being wrong.

Children should be taught that being open-minded does not threaten their integrity but affirms their worth as human beings.

A desire for truth

We all want to be right. Most of us want to be right all the time (some of us think we are right all the time!). One of the difficult lessons children need to learn is that not all they think is true is true. All thinking minds contain errors of fact or belief. What helps stimulate the search for truth with children is the attitude 'I'm not sure, let's find out'. The search for truth can be helped by an attitude of doubt. One way of formalising doubt is the so-called 'devil's advocate'. When the Catholic Church is deciding whether an individual should be considered a saint, it appoints a person as Devil's Advocate to present the case against canonisation. It can be fun testing out ideas; for example, what evidence is there that the earth is flat, that there are such things as ghosts, or that beings from other planets have visited the earth? It takes time and effort. Einstein spent 20 years thinking about relativity, working out the pros and cons of several formulations of his theory, before publishing a paper on it. Being systematic in the search, knowing what methods to use and applying them diligently also helps. Success is not guaranteed but the time spent on stimulating a child's desire for truth is well worth the effort.

John Stuart Mill wrote of the value of being taught by his father from an early age to think for himself.

> Striving, even in an exaggerated degree, to call forth the activity of my faculties by making me find out everything for myself, he gave his explanations not before but after I had felt the full force of the difficulties; and not only gave me an accurate knowledge of these two great subjects (economics and philosophy) as far as they were understood; but made me a thinker in both. I thought for myself almost from the first and occasionally thought differently from him, though for a long time only on minor points, and making his opinion the ultimate standard. At a later period I even occasionally convinced him and altered his opinion on some points of detail; which I state to his honour, not my own. It at once exemplifies his perfect candour, and the real worth of his method of teaching.[3]

John Stuart Mill grew up to be one of the great critical thinkers of his age, but what exactly is critical thinking?

The skills of critical thinking

Many attempts have been made to specify the skills of critical thinking. One of the founding fathers of the critical thinking movement in North America, Robert Ennis,[4] has identified 12 aspects. These are given below, each with a related question that can help in the critical analysis of an idea:

1 *Grasping the meaning of a statement* – is it meaningful?
2 *Judging whether there is ambiguity in reasoning* – is it clear?
3 *Judging whether statements contradict each other* – is it consistent?

4 *Judging whether a conclusion follows necessarily* – is it logical?
5 *Judging whether a statement is specific enough* – is it precise?
6 *Judging whether a statement applies a principle* – is it following a rule?
7 *Judging whether an observation statement is reliable* – is it accurate?
8 *Judging whether an inductive conclusion is warranted* – is it justified?
9 *Judging whether the problem has been identified* – is it relevant?
10 *Judging whether something is an assumption* – is it taken for granted?
11 *Judging whether a definition is adequate* – is it well defined?
12 *Judging whether a statement taken on authority is acceptable* – is it true?

There may only be one way of being right but there are an infinite number of ways of being wrong. The 12 aspects show ways of avoiding some of the pitfalls of thinking. As principles they may not be of much practical use to children but in the form of questions they can help children to stop to consider and assess statements or ideas (with your child, try applying them to a tabloid newspaper headline). The questions can also introduce children to the vocabulary of analysis: do they know what it means to be 'meaningful', to be 'clear', to be 'consistent'? The analytical vocabulary of the English language, with such terms as 'relevant', 'accurate', 'precise', 'justified', 'well defined', 'distinguish', 'evidence', 'interpretation', 'point-of-view', 'conclusion', enables us to think more precisely about our thinking.

For Bloom[5] and his associates the term 'critical thinking' means the same as 'evaluation'. It is the highest of six thinking skills, which he calls the 'cognitive goals' of education.

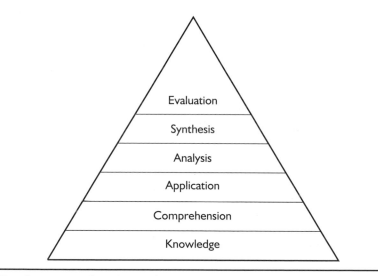

Figure 3.1 Bloom's taxonomy of cognitive goals.

Bloom's *Taxonomy of Educational Goals* has been one of the most influential books in curriculum development and has been used widely by American educators in planning their teaching programmes. Table 3.1 lists the various categories and processes involved in the various thinking levels.

Table 3.1

Category	Thinking process cues
1 Knowledge (remembering and retaining)	Say what you know, what you remember, describe, repeat, define, identify, tell who, when, which, where, what
2 Comprehension (interpreting and understanding)	Describe in your own words, tell how you feel about, say what it means, explain, compare, relate
3 Application (making use of)	How can you use it, where does it lead you, apply what you know, use it to solve problems, demonstrate
4 Analysis (taking apart)	What are the parts, the order, the reasons why, the causes, the problems, the solutions, the consequences
5 Synthesis (putting together)	How might it be different, how else, what if, suppose, develop, improve, create in your own way
6 Evaluation (judging and assessing)	How would you judge it, does it succeed, will it work, what would you prefer, why do you think so

Many learning activities can be organised or analysed in terms of the above categories. For example, when telling a story, such as 'Goldilocks and the Three Bears', a teacher might ask the following questions:

1 *Knowledge*   What happened in the story?
                         What did Goldilocks do in the Bears' home?
2 *Comprehension*   Why did it happen that way?
                         Why did Goldilocks like Little Bear's bed best?
3 *Application*   What would you have done?
                         What would have happened if Goldilocks had come to your house?
4 *Analysis*   Which part did you like best?
                         Which parts could not be true?
5 *Synthesis*   Can you think of a different ending?
                         What would you have done if you were Goldilocks?
6 *Evaluation*   What did you think of the story?
                         Was Goldilocks good or bad? Why?

Children need guidance in learning how to learn, particularly when planning a 'finding out' project. Teachers can help children to organise particular centres of interest in terms of levels of thinking. A useful approach is to plan for a topic on a series of cards, each one dealing with a different category of thinking.

A project on weather, for instance, could cover the following areas:

Knowledge
Facts to investigate: Definitions of weather, what is weather? Words to describe weather: rain, storm, shower, drizzle, hail, wind, gale. Terms to define: freezing, air pressure, forecast. Equipment and resources: chart, thermometer.

Comprehension
Questions to consider: Why do we need to know about the weather? Why do we need weather forecasts? Where can you find a weather forecast? Are the forecasts accurate? How could you find out about the weather?

Application
Problems to be solved: Is today's weather forecast correct? Can we make a weather chart? Can we measure the rain? Can we measure the temperature? Can we compare the weather in different countries?

Analysis
Concepts to explore: The way weather affects us. Weather statistics and records. Weather sayings: 'red sky at night'. Weather and safety, lightning, looking at sun, icy roads. Temperature, air pressure, water cycle.

Synthesis
Skills to develop: Devise your own weather forecast. Report on a weather disaster, flood, hurricane. Mime different weather conditions. Write a poem about the weather. Create your own book of weather.

Evaluation
Learning to review: What have you learnt about weather? What is bad weather? What are the good points about bad weather? What is weather like in different parts of the world? What do you still not understand about the weather?

Some educators have aims for their children that are little more than vague notions, such as teaching them to 'think for themselves' or 'to develop lively, enquiring minds',[6] with little sense of how these ideals can be achieved. Others think in terms of a laundry list of skills but lack a clear sense of how these skills can be realised. Richard Paul[7] of Sonoma State University (California) has attempted to overcome these problems by offering a set of basic critical thinking principles with suggested ways of developing these skills in the day-to-day practice of teaching. Paul's aim is to explain critical thinking by translating general theory into a set of possible teaching strategies. These strategies can be applied in the teacher's own way to any formal lesson material or to informal discussions with children. This approach does not teach critical thinking through 'recipe' lessons (although Paul does offer examples of these) but through teachers applying the strategies of critical thinking to their own lesson planning.

Paul divides critical thinking strategies into three types: affective strategies, macro-abilities and micro-skills. These strategies are interdependent. Specific skills relate to a child's general abilities and sense of self. Paul identifies critical thinking with fair mindedness. This involves not just thinking well but thinking fairly. He contrasts critical thinkers with two other kinds of thinker: uncritical thinkers, who have few intellectual skills and are easily manipulated and controlled by others, and what he calls 'weak sense' or selfish critical thinkers, who pursue only narrow, self-centred interests and who manipulate others. What he aims at is developing critical thinking in a 'strong sense' through strategies that encourage children to be reasonable, fair-minded and skilled thinkers.

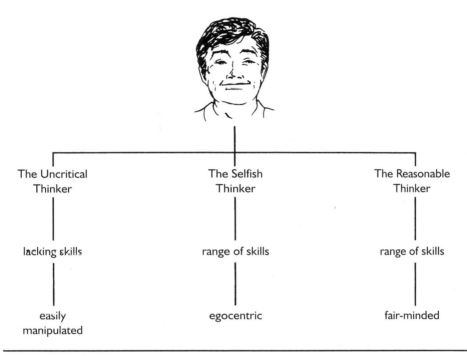

Figure 3.2 Three modes of thinking.

Affective strategies

Affective strategies aim to foster independent thinking, the 'I-can-work-this-out-for myself' attitude. Children should be encouraged to develop the habit of self questioning, 'What do I believe?', 'How did I come to believe it?', 'Do I really accept this belief?' To achieve this, children will need a role model in the parent or teacher. To develop intellectual independence children need to see people thinking independently. They need to be shown the way it is done. One of the dangers, however, of focusing on one's own thinking is egocentricity. One needs not only to be aware of one's own thinking but also the points of view of others. For example, 'How might two people describe a fight in the playground differently?' 'How might brothers or sisters explain a quarrel differently to their parents?' Think of personal examples, or examples from stories or TV shows. Write about an issue showing opposing points of view. Act out an argument on the telephone. Discuss a real argument that you were involved in. What did the other person think?

Macro-abilities

Macro-abilities are the processes involved in thinking, in organising separate elementary skills (such as defining meanings of words accurately) into an extended sequence of thought. The aim is to produce not a set of fragmentary and disjointed skills but an integrated and able thinking person. What we must guard against is the tendency to fragment, to focus on parts and ignore the whole, to emphasise micro-skills instead of global abilities.

These global thinking abilities include:

- giving reasons
- identifying purposes
- evaluating outcomes
- identifying criteria
- making judgements.

Giving reasons

An important cognitive strategy is the fostering of insight into mechanical skills. Rather than merely asking children to practise mechanical skills such as use of grammar or rules of arithmetic for their own sake, we should give a reason for using this skill, or ask the child why, for example, a standard unit of measurement is being used. Other questions to ask are 'Is this the only, or best way to solve a problem?' 'Can you think of another way to solve this problem?' 'Which way do you think is best?' 'Why?'

Identifying purposes

There is a purpose to our learning, there is a purpose to our thinking, there are purposes for rules, institutions and human activities. Exploring underlying purposes is another key strategy. For children things are often 'just there' as purposeless preordained packages they must learn about. But the world is not given, it must be created.[8] All human activity presupposes some purpose, reasons for doing things as well as ways of doing things. Often there is another way to do things and some ways that are better than others. The child who is able to understand the purposes of things will be in a better position at the appropriate time to judge and understand them. A child may have science lessons, but what is 'science'? They may know about scientists, but what do scientists do? What do they study? How do they find out? What questions might a scientist ask about, for example, a tree? What is the purpose of a particular science lesson? The question for the critical thinker is not just what are we doing but why are we doing it.

Evaluating outcomes

The ability to evaluate is fundamental to critical thinking, the evaluation of ideas, evidence, arguments, actions and solutions. The process of evaluation involves developing and using criteria of judgement. The child as critical thinker comes to realise that expressing a preference – 'I prefer it' – is only one criterion and not necessarily a reliable one for judging the rightness of outcomes. Test it, for example by asking the child to choose which number on a dice will come up. Roll the dice, does the child's preference affect the chances of the number coming up? Whenever children are judging something the teacher can ask what they are evaluating, the purpose of the evaluation and the criteria being used. For example, in judging a good breakfast food, the children could brainstorm examples, discuss why it is important to consider what we eat and consider criteria. Suggestions for criteria might include taste, texture, smell, food values such as vitamin, fibre and sugar content, an analysis of additives, cost, packaging and the need for preparation.

Identifying criteria

Children should also be encouraged to study the criteria that others use. What are the criteria an advertiser would use in judging a good advert? Choose an advert or television commercial – what ideas does it give you, what reasons for buying the product, what does the advertiser want you to feel? How else might it have been advertised? What would be your criteria for a good advert? Look at the news, on TV or in a newspaper – what were the criteria the editors used for judging the importance of stories? What other criteria might they have used? A different order, a different emphasis? What criteria would you have used in your reporting of the news?

Making judgements

Having distinguished criteria, children can be asked to judge between them. What are the most important criteria for judging which x is 'best'? Which facts relating to x are relevant to this conclusion? What are the consequences of this view? Where does it lead your thinking next? Children can be helped to evaluate any idea, object, action or event by a process of open-ended questioning. Only by exercising critical judgement will they learn to become critical and fair-minded thinkers.

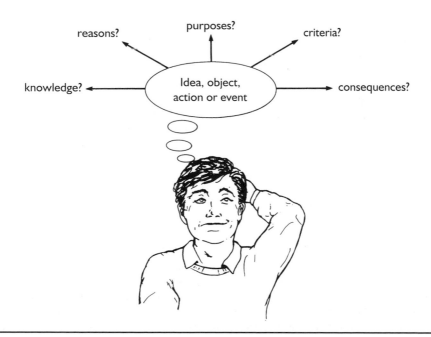

Figure 3.3 Questions related to the exercise of judgement.

Asking the right questions

Supposing no one asked a question. What would the answer be?
  Gertrude Stein

A teacher was beginning a maths lesson in which the children (a class of 7–8-year-olds) were to work in pairs. While assembling supplies for each pair the teacher asked 'How many pairs of children will we have?' The children seemed to have little idea so the teacher posed another question 'What do we need to know to figure this out?' The suggestion came that they needed to know how many children there were. Instead of saying how many the teacher asked, 'How can we find this out?' Different ways were suggested and the children were asked to discuss the problem in small groups. When sharing their answers the teacher prompted them some more, 'How did you figure that out?' 'Who did it another way?' 'Maria got another answer, can you convince her that yours is right?' The teacher's questions were giving the children the opportunity to connect what they knew with what they needed to examine and reflect on in their own thinking. It is this kind of skill in questioning that helps to stimulate and extend children's thinking.[9]

What is a good question? A good question is an invitation to think, or to do. It stimulates because it is open ended, with possibilities and problems. A good question is productive, it seeks a response. A good question will generate more questions. What forms, then, do good questions take?

Questions that focus attention

'Have you seen . . . ?', 'Do you notice . . . ?', 'What is it?' Such questions open up areas of investigation and help them to focus attention on particular details. Children are natural players of this game: 'What's that?,' 'Look at this', 'Come and see'. The first simple observations can lead to a spiral of questions that probe reasons, evidence and assumptions.

Questions that force comparison

Invite children to judge or assess for themselves by asking such questions as 'How many?' 'How long?', 'How often?', 'How much?'. Carefully phrased questions can help children to compare like with like, to classify more closely and to bring order to the variety of their experience.

Questions that seek clarification

Help children to focus on what they really mean by considering further the words that they use. 'What do you mean by . . . ?' 'Can you explain further?' 'Can you give me an example?' 'Can you show me?' 'Can you put it another way?' Such questions can help children to think about their thinking and to develop what they mean.

Questions that invite further enquiry

'What do we need to know?' 'How can we find out?' 'Can you find a way to?' 'What would happen if . . . ?'

Questions that seek reasons or explanation

'How did you know?' 'Why did you say that?' 'What are your reasons?' 'What is your evidence?' Reasoning questions help children to reflect on their own experience, their own answers. A reasoning question invites further elaboration, 'Why do you think that?' The answer 'to this question will always be right even if there is something wrong with the child's thinking. The child knows what she thinks, and to find this out we will often need to ask the child.

The questions children ask

Why?
Why are the leaves always green, Dad?
Why are there thorns on a rose?
Why do you want my neck clean, Dad?
Why do hairs grow from your nose?

Why can dogs hear what we can't, Dad?
Why has the engine just stalled?
Why are you rude about Aunt, Dad?
Why are you going all bald?

Why is Mum taller than you, Dad?
Why can't the dog stand the cat?
Why's Grandma got a moustache, Dad?
Why are you growing more fat?

Why don't you answer my questions?
You used to; you don't any more.
Why? Tell me why. Tell me why, Dad?
Do you think I am being a bore?

John Kitching

We cannot avoid the questions that young children ask. As they grow older children often grow out of the questioning habit. This may be due to inhibitions brought on by others such as the unresponsiveness of adults or the scorn of peers, or from a drying up of the natural curiosity that makes the young child such an avid learner. Whatever the reasons we need to fight this tendency to accept rather than to ask. We need to foster curiosity and encourage the questioning child.

Ways to foster questions

1 Ask questions yourself, 'I wonder why?' Share your curiosity, reveal your doubts, be open about the things you don't know. Be a model for the questioning mind.
2 Find books, objects and materials that stimulate curiosity. What you find interesting, of course, will not necessarily interest the child. Curiosity can, however, become infectious.
3 Encourage children to bring you objects of interest. Children's curiosity can be fired by the most ordinary and commonplace things. The tattiest piece of beach-combing debris can become an object of fascination and awe. Simple equipment like magnifiers and a microscope can extend and enrich a child's observations, adding exciting detail to the familiar and mundane. Help create a collection or 'cabinet of curiosities'.

4   Expose children to productive, provocative and open-ended questions. Teachers can include these questions on classroom displays for children to read, reflect on and explore further. A problem corner can be established where a question of the day or week can be on offer with materials or books to stimulate thought and action. Children can be asked to pose their own questions. But beware the danger of overkill, of being overly enthusiastic, overly demanding. As one child begged, 'Don't ask me another question, or I'll die.'

5   Use children's questions to generate further questions. Sometimes respond to a child's question by asking another back – as in this exchange overheard on a train:

Child: I wonder what would happen if a dinosaur stood on this train?
Mother: What do you think would happen?
Child: It would bend.
Mother: Why do you think it would bend?

Ways to respond to questions

'What does God do all day?'
'Where does your lap go when you stand up?'
'Why does life begin at forty?'[10]

Some questions are hard to answer, some have never been answered and some cannot be answered. Admitting 'I do not know' is a healthy lesson for children. Part of knowing what you know is monitoring what you don't know. When asked a difficult question the temptation is great for parents or teachers to bluff their way out with vague generalisations or hopeful guesses. But this does not help children. A positive response might be 'How can we find out?'

Questions are not always what they seem. Not only do questions vary in kind, requiring different sorts of answer, but children have different reasons for asking questions. A question might mean, 'I want to know the right answer', 'I've asked a question to show my interest and would like to discuss it further', 'I don't really mind what your answer is, I want your attention now!' The way we respond will depend on our relationship with the child and the needs of the moment. It may not be the right time to ask, the question may need deferring or it may be a welcome 'door opener' to an interesting conversation that ranges further than the original enquiry. It may be a question we need to say 'I don't know' to and explore some ways of finding out. Or a question we can turn back on the child to encourage productive thinking. What is required is a 'let's-see-what-we-can-make-of-this' approach, using one or more of the following monitoring strategies:

- *Analysing the question* – 'what do you mean by . . . ?'
- *Rephrasing the question* – 'are you saying . . . ?'
- *Turning the question back to the child* – 'what do you think?'
- *Asking a supporting question* – 'I wonder whether . . . ?'
- *Suggesting a line of enquiry* – 'perhaps we could . . . '

A question is an invitation to think and to respond, and this response should reflect as much concern for the child's thinking as it does to find the right answer.

Thinking time

Many teachers wait only one or two seconds after having asked a question before they call on another child or give the answer to the question themselves. It is easy to feel that unless someone is talking no one is learning. A short waiting time encourages short answers. If the adult waits for longer periods children tend to respond in whole sentences and complete thoughts. Periods of silence after asking a question may seem interminably long. But if children are being encouraged to do their own thinking and to reflect on the appropriateness of their answers, adults will need to allow them time. Even with questions that simply rely on the recall of facts it is useful to encourage children to check their answers before saying them:

Teacher   What is 8 times 7?
Child   64.
Teacher   *No response*
Child   No, it's 56. I was thinking of eight eights.

When the teacher remains silent it helps show the child that the responsibility for thinking is the child's, not the teacher's. It shows that trying takes time and effort. It allows the child the chance to continue thinking, to check his answer and possibly to reword the problem.

Teacher   What would happen if people didn't die?
Child 1   It would be great, you would live for ever.
Teacher   *No response*
Child 2   There'd be an awful lot of people in the world. It would be so crowded you wouldn't be able to breathe.
Teacher   *No response*
Child 3   You'd have to stop people having so many children. Then it would be all right.
Child 4   There wouldn't be enough food for everybody.

Research shows[11] that if a teacher waits after asking a question, or after a child gives an answer, children will tend to respond in more extended and thoughtful ways. The use of silence also communicates a teacher's expectations: not only is an answer expected but the teacher has faith that, given time, the child can find an answer.

The invitation to reason

Much of what children know, they have never learned: they have deduced it from other things they know. In one experiment[12] children were shown the following drawing:

Figure 3.4

They were told 'This is a wug'. They were then shown two of these creatures and asked to complete the sentence 'Here are two'. Most children aged 4 and over replied 'wugs'. In another experiment children were told, 'Today Arthur is glinging. He did the same yesterday.' They were then asked to complete the sentence, 'Yesterday Arthur . . .' Children from the age of 4 replied 'glinged' (adults were not sure whether Arthur 'glinged,' 'glang' or 'glung'). These studies show that young children can pick up the rules of grammar without being taught. Similarly children know that the River Nile contains water not necessarily because they have seen it or heard about it, but simply because it is a river. If we know a rule or have a mental model[13] we can apply it to different circumstances. We may not know how many hours are in a week but, given certain rules or models of procedure, we can work it out. Deductive reasoning works through the use of rules, models and definitions. Some of these we can work out for ourselves, some we need to be taught. What then are the key experiences children should have to develop their powers of logical reasoning?

Logical reasoning

Raymond Smullyan[14] was first introduced to the puzzles of logic at the age of six. As he lay sick in bed, his 15-year-old brother Emile said to him 'Today is April Fool's Day, and I will fool you as you have never been fooled before!' Young Raymond waited all day, but his brother didn't fool him. Late that night Emile said, 'So you expected me to fool you, didn't you?' Raymond replied, 'Yes.' 'But I didn't, did I?' 'No.' 'But you expected me to, didn't you?' 'Yes.' 'So I fooled you, didn't I?' For long after that Raymond wondered whether he had been fooled. (Years later he grew up to become a professor of mathematical logic.) The foundations for logical reasoning can be laid at a young age. The designers of the High Scope[15] pre-school programme have suggested the following key experiences for developing logical reasoning in the under fives:

- investigating and labelling the attributes of things
- comparing things, noticing similarities and differences
- using and describing something in different ways
- describing the characteristics something does not possess
- distinguishing *some* and *all*, classifying subgroups
- understanding *if . . . then*, causal and logical connections
- ordering things according to some dimension or relationship (e.g. longest/shortest).

Older children, too, can benefit greatly from this sort of experience, for example when they begin making collections of things like stamps, stones and labels; the skills of defining, ordering, classifying, sequencing and abstraction can be developed through open-ended questioning. Let us look at these elements of reasoning more closely to see how they can be developed.

Logic is often regarded as the science of reasoning, and logical thinking as the process of reasoning correctly. As Sherlock Holmes said, 'Crime is common, logic is rare.' Being logical involves many thinking processes. One of these is the deductive form of reasoning, sometimes known as pure logic. The logical deductions of Sherlock Holmes relied on a careful study of the facts. Pure logic is primarily based on the mathematical approach to knowledge (mathematical intelligence), it relies on translating an argument or line of reasoning into a set symbolic form. One traditional form of logical reasoning is the syllogism, which takes the form of two statements (assumed to be true), followed by a conclusion that is drawn from them. For example:

All children love sweets
Mary is a child
Therefore Mary loves sweets.

Children can be given practice in making similar deductions by supplying conclusions to examples set by a teacher. For example:

All fish can swim
The trout is a fish
Therefore ...

Examples of faulty reasoning can be shown:

All children love sweets
Peter loves sweets
Therefore Peter is a child.

Children can be shown how to test the validity of examples by drawing them in circles or sets.

All rabbits have ears
Flopsy is a rabbit
Therefore Flopsy has ears

All children love sweets
Peter loves sweets
Therefore Peter is a child

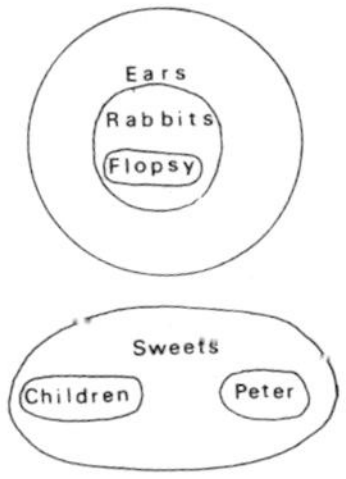

Figure 3.5

The drawing of circles or sets can help to show whether the relationship of one part to another is clear or whether it is ambiguous (and might be contained in another set, for example, Peter might be an adult or a horse). Examples such as these can generate much useful discussion on whether the evidence or information given is sufficient to reach definite conclusions. What else do we need to know?

Children can be asked to write, analyse (draw in sets) and discuss their own examples or to explore alternatives.

All teachers are ...
David is ...
Therefore David is ...

Encourage children to distinguish *some* from *all* in analysing arguments. For example, if most road accidents are caused by fast cars, what can we say about fast cars or any particular fast car?

Research suggests that there is a close resemblance between the reasoning of five-year-old children and that of older children and adults. Some logical problems handled correctly by young children are easier for older people. Other logical problems tend to be handled inefficiently by most people, young or old. From the age of five onwards children can draw the correct inference from the classic *modus ponens* problem:

If *p*, then *q*; *p*, therefore *q*
For example: If it is raining we get wet; it is raining, therefore . . . .

But both children and adults tend to draw incorrect conclusions from problems such as:

If *p*, then *q*; not *p*, therefore . . . ? ('not *q*' is wrong)
For example: If it is raining we get wet; it is not raining therefore . . . .
(no conclusion follows – we might get wet from another source).

Another common error is:

If *p* then *q*; *q*, therefore . . . ? ('*p*' is wrong)
For example: If it rains we get wet; we are getting wet, therefore . . . ?
(No conclusion follows – we might have fallen in the river!)

Errors like these are common in children and adults. This is because binary (yes or no) thinking is so common and is often a source of unconscious error or manipulated truth. A common rhetorical ploy of politicians is that because two things are connected the absence of one necessitates the absence of the other – if *p*, then *q*; not *q*, therefore not *p*. Creative thinking, the ability to generate alternatives, to consider other factors, is a necessary complement to critical/deductive thinking. The truth often lies in factors not considered.

What makes such logical reasoning difficult is that attention must be focused entirely on what is said, not how it is said. In understanding a spoken sentence we process not only the words but also the background information and the speaker's intentions. In everyday reasoning we use language in context. Exercises in deductive logic do not easily transfer to ways in which we reason about the real world unless those exercises are being used in a process that links the two, such as the scientific method. Our everyday reasoning is embedded in the ways we understand the world, which include guessing, processing information, using common sense and the ways in which we use language to create meaning.

Logic and meaning

Deductive logic does not by itself guarantee clear thinking or good general reasoning. Those trained in formal logic are not necessarily any better at everyday thinking and reasoning than the rest of us. Reasoning depends on the meanings of words, the importance of definitions. Consider the following argument:

No cat has nine tails.
My cat has one tail more than no cat.
Therefore my cat has ten tails.

The argument is deductively true if the words have consistent meanings. The trouble is that 'no cat' changes meaning in the first and second statement. Many arguments in real life are not arguments about reasons but about definitions of words and concepts. They are not about the world but about the words we use to describe the world. The old debating ploy, 'It all depends what you mean by . . .' points to an insight into the nature of human discourse. Words can mean many things, both public and personal. They depend for their meaning not on dictionary definition but on context, shared assumptions and personal associations. You have only to ask a group of children or adults to brainstorm 'Love is . . .' or 'Happiness is . . .' to come up with many divergent definitions. Comparing dictionary definitions, personal associations and shared assumptions can help children to understand how people can use the same word to mean very different things.

Meaning also depends on tone of voice. Consider what the following utterance might mean if different words in the sentence were stressed: 'I like my mother's cooking.' Analyse different ways of saying the same sentence with children; discuss what the hidden meanings, messages or assumptions might be. We can intend the same words to convey different meanings in different contexts, explore how gestures, stress and tone can affect what words mean. Do people always mean what they say? Do they always say what they mean?

The Polish mathematician Korzybski[16] proposed three laws that he suggested might lead to fewer misunderstandings and conflicts. These were semantic rules to do with the nature of words.

- **The law of non-identity**: A is not A (the word we use to represent an object is not the object itself). Help children to realise that the word is not the same as the real thing by asking them what they can do with an ice cream, a piece of paper or a chair, that they cannot do with the words ice cream, paper and chair. What can they do with the words that they cannot do with the real things?
- **The law of non-allness**: A is not all A (the word does not represent all the object). Ask children to describe all about something. How long do they think it will take? What needs to be considered, for example shape, size, colour, weight, age, history, manufacture, efficiency? Children should become aware that there is no limit to the possible discussion about any one object. Can they specify the limits to their knowledge of a chosen object? The words we use do not (perhaps cannot) represent all of an object.
- **The law of self-reflexiveness**: A can be both A and not A (words can refer to things and to other words). We can use language to talk about language. We can say for example 'that's stupid' and refer to an action, or to words used in describing an action. Words can reflect or jump off in different ways. We need always to attend to and reflect on meaning. Explore with children ways of conveying meaning without words – communicate a message through mime or gesture. Does the message get through? How might it be interpreted? Would words be better? If so, which words? One teacher has on her classroom wall the reminder 'Use words with care'. It is a message we need reminding of from an early age.

The patterning of experience

Everyday reasoning depends on the meanings of words and also on the strength of evidence that supports a particular statement. The deductive logic of an argument does not guarantee its truth; assumptions must be supported by evidence. The question 'Do spiders have eight legs?' requires different forms of reasoning: defining the terms, seeking evidence (observing, collecting, classifying spiders) and fitting the elements of enquiry into a logical chain of reasoning. These forms of reasoning are ways in which we successfully pattern our experience. This ability to pattern experience into conceptual categories, classes or sets is a fundamental aspect of our intelligence. It is the basis of thought and communication, of reasoning and the scientific method. We pattern our experience through concepts or category names like *spiders, fire, fear, love*, which provide the building blocks of thought. A concept is an abstraction or generalisation from experience. It can be used to interpret fresh phenomena and data:

Is it an insect? A spider?

It enables us to perceive connections between items of knowledge:

spiders, octopus, octagon?

In teaching children to think we are aiming for children to make as many connections between concepts as possible, to perceive relationships, to build structures of understanding, and thereby to provide them with more opportunities to pattern future experience. We all have conceptual models of the world that have been built up, interconnected and elaborated over many years. What are the ways we can help children to learn these patterning processes?

Sequencing

Reasoning is concerned with the ability to perceive and understand relationships between ideas or concepts of things. One form of relationship is that of sequence, the way that one thing does or should follow another. Finding the right order is often essential for any activity or investigation. A key strategy for problem solving is sequencing a step-by-step approach to a solution.

Sequencing takes many forms. There is sequencing of time. Young children learn the sequence of days in the week and months in the year. Later they learn to sequence time with greater precision – hours, minutes, seconds and even (with the aid of watch or stopwatch) fractions of a second. They learn to apply the concepts of 'before', 'during' and 'after' with greater accuracy and sophistication. The learning of these relationships may be haphazard but it is not accidental: it is orchestrated by their experience of the world, by the help that others (adults, peers, parents, teachers) give them. Children can be helped in this process by thinking about their own lives. What happened this morning, today at school, yesterday, last week, this time last year? The questions 'What happened before?' and 'What happened after?' can be asked of any event. We are creatures of time and children need help in understanding this dimension in which we live – if only we had the time!

The sequencing of space and objects within space can be shown in the numbering, position and design of houses. Different types of sequence apply to the same object. For example, look where traffic lights are placed and at the temporal sequencing of lights. In observing and drawing patterns and objects in space one important question is 'Where should it be in relation to other things?' 'Is it in the right place?' 'Where might it go?' 'Where would you put it?' 'Why?'

From a young age children need to sequence activities, from putting on clothes to learning how to build or make something. All physical skills require the sequencing of activity. Children can be helped in this by verbalising what to do and by rehearsing in their minds what they intend to do. Getting up in the morning or making a drink are sequences that can be arranged by children, using pieces of card.

Figure 3.6 Making a drink.

The use of flow charts can assist children in the logical ordering of information. The aim is to break down activities into small steps, which are described in diagram form.

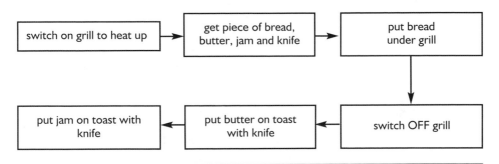

Figure 3.7 Making a piece of toast and jam.

Similar flow charts can be constructed for making a cup of tea, getting dressed in the morning or any other activity. Good organisation depends on the sequencing of operations because this helps to pinpoint gaps in information and weaknesses in planning. Flow charts encourage a systematic approach and more efficient use of time, material and resources. Children can gain a better overall view of the processes involved. The four basic components of-flow charts are:

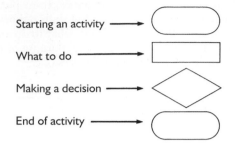

Starting an activity ⟶

What to do ⟶

Making a decision ⟶

End of activity ⟶

Figure 3.8

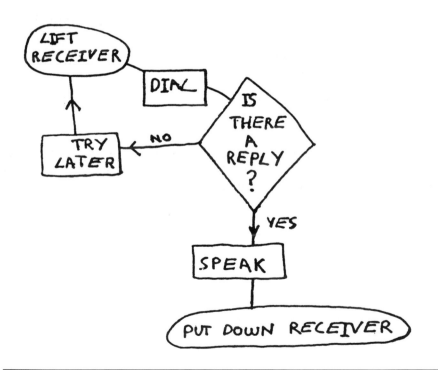

Figure 3.9 Children can make up their own flow diagrams involving as many yes/no branches as they like.

Figure 3.10 Crossing the road.

Another way of critically analysing information is by creating a decision tree diagram by asking questions that will help to sort and classify a collection of objects. Figure 3.11 shows a decision tree diagram classifying flowers.

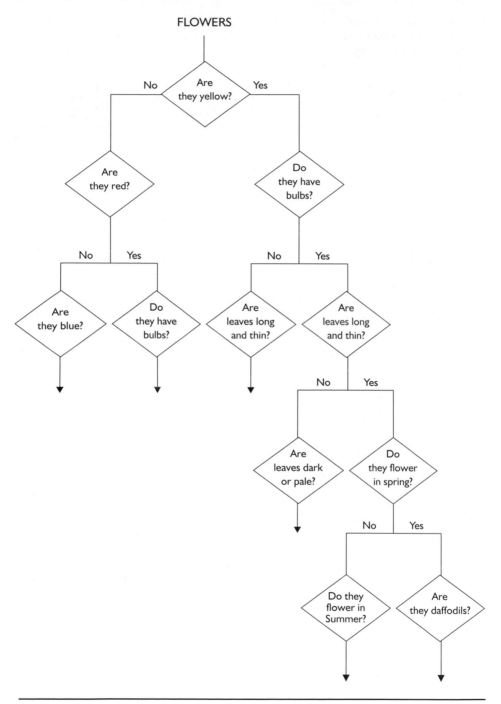

Figure 3.11

Information on any topic can be analysed by constructing a table. Computer programmes provide easy ways to construct and create tables. Children can be encouraged to think of their own key questions and categories for the table. For example a table on the topic of flowers could include:

Name of flower	Where grown	Height	Colour of flower	Size of flower	Number of petals

Figure 3.12

Traditionally, logicians used a form of tabulation called truth tables to assess the validity of statements. A simple form of this sorting process is the Carroll diagram, invented by Lewis Carroll who was not only the writer of the *Alice in Wonderland* books but also a skilled logician. Carroll diagrams can be used to represent the results of classifying using two different criteria. For example:

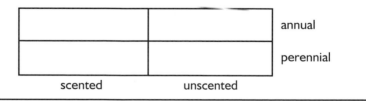

Figure 3.13

What underlies all higher order thinking is the sequencing of ideas. This is essential, for example, in the telling or retelling of stories. This is one reason why 'news time', the recounting of experience, is such a valuable exercise in infant classrooms. The sequencing of related ideas provides the impetus for many nursery rhymes, such as 'The House that Jack Built'. Important lessons can be learned through discussing the natural association or sequence of ideas running through popular traditional stories and poems such as:

> *For want of a nail the shoe was lost,*
> *For want of a shoe the horse was lost,*
> *For want of a horse the rider was lost,*
> *For want of a rider the battle was lost,*
> *And all for the want of a horse shoe nail.*

As children grow older they can appreciate the skill in the ordering and presenting of ideas by the great story tellers and learn the importance of sequencing ideas in their own stories and essay writing.

Classifying

Children need to be able to classify, to organise, differentiate and categorise their ideas. Their conceptual development relies on the ability to recognise similarities and differences. The process starts from birth with the classification of people (who is Mummy and not-Mummy) and continues (who are family and not-family) and extends outwards into the world. The child's ability to classify the world depends on the experience and support she receives. Young children learn to categorise their clothes and their possessions, which toys belong to the same set and why. Children of all ages enjoy spot-the-difference puzzles and can be encouraged to differentiate any group of near-identical pictures or objects. The 'what's the difference?' game can be extended to any two objects: in what ways are they similar/in what ways different (how many different ways)? For example, in what ways are any two foods like and unlike?

Children begin by learning to classify objects. Give them the opportunity of analysing the contents of a shelf drawer or cupboard in, for instance, the kitchen, garage or bedroom. The aim is to discover by experience how objects can be placed in different categories and how in organising them the child will need to choose between different attributes and criteria. As children get older they learn to abstract from experience, to play with, connect and relate their own concept of things. They are not limited to physical experience, they can manipulate ideas and images in the mind. Ask the child to name as many different living things as possible and then to work out how many different groups he can divide the list into. What are the distinguishing characteristics of each group? Other categories that might be chosen include foods, transport, clothes, homes, jobs, adverts, shops, plants, sports or games. Children can work on classifying the pros and cons of any idea (for example 'is it a good idea to move house?'), classifying the advantages and disadvantages (or, if you prefer, do a PMI, Plus Minus Interesting, analysis). Such a classification can be a useful exercise in developing judgement.

Judging

Children often find it hard to distinguish what they know from what they don't know. They often respond in ways they think are expected of them and are reticent about saying 'I don't know' when they are not sure of the truth of a claim. A common obstacle to critical thinking is the tendency to agree or disagree with statements immediately, without first reflecting on what we need to know to be certain in our judgement of the truth.

Teachers need to encourage the habit of saying 'I don't know' and of suspending judgement when there is insufficient evidence. For example, when a child is given a task of sorting objects into categories or discussing whether a concept does or does not apply, offer not only the clear-cut options like true or false but also categories where something may partially apply or where something is not proven. Children need practice in using true/false/unproven categories. Equally important is the encouragement children need to reflect on how they know. How do they find out? What facts are relevant? What do they need to know or understand before they decide? What standards or criteria are they using in forming their judgement? How would they judge it?

In buying a new toy or car, which factors are relevant – cost, colour, durability, availability, one like (or very different from) other people's? What is the best one available from a catalogue or the local shops? How would you quality-test the product? Whose opinion on the product would be relevant? Which one do you prefer? Why? Is it necessarily the best? How would you judge? How does this compare with the way other children judge things? 'Are you certain or are you withholding your judgement?'

One of the strongest tendencies of the uncritical mind is to see things in black and white, all right or all wrong. Beliefs that should be held with varying degrees of strength are held with certainty. Children should be encouraged to qualify their statements (and thus to extend their thinking) if they have insufficient evidence to be certain; they should be asked for the evidence on which their statements of belief are based and be encouraged to recognise the possibility that alternative claims might be true. Teachers themselves need to model the use of probability qualifiers such as 'I'm not sure', 'It's probably so', 'not very likely/highly unlikely', 'I doubt', 'I suspect', 'maybe', 'perhaps', 'often', 'seldom', 'in the majority of cases', 'rarely' and 'occasionally'.

Predicting

Concepts of probability can be explored through games of chance. If you toss a coin, is it going to be heads or tails? Are you sure? How sure are you? Older children can explore the odds, the strength of different probabilities. What are the odds (probabilities/chances) of a heads coming up if you toss two coins? What are the odds of throwing particular numbers with a dice, of picking a particular colour, suit or number from a pack of cards, of choosing a button of a particular colour from an assortment in a bag? Who is going to walk through the door next, a boy or girl? What are your reasons for thinking this is possibly/probably so? What will the weather be like tomorrow? Who will win the race? What will happen next?[17]

Theorising

An educated guess is a kind of theory, using evidence from the past to predict the future, reasoning from cause to effect. Children are not short of reasoning ability, they are short of experience. Many of their theories or hypotheses will be weak or faulty because they are still at a formative stage in their thinking. However, they can come up with thoughtful and plausible hypotheses from an early age, given sufficient stimulus from adults. Any number of 'why?' or 'what if ... ?' questions can be offered as challenges and children invited to suggest more. For example, why is the sea salty? When asked this question a group of 6 year olds suggested several theories: 'It's because of the seaweed', 'It helps the fish swim', 'There's salt at the bottom of the sea', 'Someone dropped a whole load of salt in it a long time ago'. Older children might be asked to brainstorm questions for which humans have yet to find answers. A list of unanswered questions might include:

- What causes cancer?
- Is there life on other planets?
- What is at the bottom of the deepest oceans?
- Is there a cure for the common cold?
- Are there such things as ghosts?

Questions to encourage children to theorise include:

- What do you think?
- How was it caused?
- What is your theory about it?

A theory can represent the first stage in critical enquiry. The child's theory can stimulate the search for evidence – and for investigating the good reasons that support the theory.

Understanding others

The term 'critical thinking' is sometimes defined as the ability to cultivate a balanced viewpoint, with being 'fair' and 'open minded'. Because children live in a social world of thinking and doing and ideas are a common currency, children need to be aware not only of their own thinking but also of the thinking of others. The critical thinker needs to have knowledge about himself as well as an understanding of others. Being open-minded may be the proper disposition of the human mind but it is not the natural disposition. Children need to be educated out of egocentricity. From their earliest days children begin developing their egocentric identity but they also come up against opposing points of view. There are various ways in which we can encourage children to see and experience another point of view:

- *Stories* – What would Red Riding Hood be feeling? What would the wolf be thinking? What is Grandma expecting to happen? What are the characters think-ing about at a particular point in the story? How do their views change? What do they intend to do? What should they be thinking, feeling and planning to happen?
- *Drama* – Act out the story, create situations and conversations between charac-ters. Mime the story and verbalise what the characters might be thinking. Invent a conflict situation, such as a dispute over the sharing of some sweets, friends falling out, a family dispute over which TV programme to see, a playground quarrel, standing up to the bully, being teased by others. What do the characters say? What do they think (are there differences between what they say and think)? Encourage children to take turns playing both sides of the argument. Explore what they think and feel about their acting experience, so that they become personalised individuals and not stereotypes. That children are capable of entering the lives and thoughts of others is demonstrated in their early play: 'You be doctor, I'll be nurse and my sister will be the person who's ill.'
- *Discussion* – How does it feel to be in another person's shoes? Which character would they like to be in the story? What kind of performer would they like to be in a circus? An understanding of other people does not come by simply being told about them but by making an imaginary leap and entering their lives.

The child can be asked to imagine being a certain person. Questions can help to focus on what life would be like for that person, such as:

- What would my family be like?
- Where would I live?

- What would I like to wear?
- Where would I like to go?
- What would I like to do?

A question-and-answer game could give a group of children the chance to guess or seek clues to the mystery person. The children could act, mime or write a description of themselves as this imaginary character, even an animal or mythical creature. What would it be like to be a lost dog, a cat that walks alone at night, a turkey just before Christmas? Probe the imaginary character with these questions:

- What kind of personality have you got?
- What kind of thoughts do you have?
- What are your worries and fears?
- What makes you angry?
- What do you most hope for?

Since children have been born into their own particular country and culture it is easy to be unaware of the values and ideas of those from other cultural groups. The experience and study of other cultures is an essential part of a child's education and a necessary part of the development of their critical thinking.

Understanding oneself

> *O wad some Pow'r the giftie gie us*
> *To see oursels as others see us.*
>   Robert Burns

Children can be invited from a young age to appraise their thoughts and actions. What are you thinking? What are you feeling? What are you learning? A key to critical thinking is self-questioning and there is no better way to encourage children to monitor their own thinking than for significant adults in a child's life to model an openness to self-criticism. This insight was formulated 150 years ago by John Stuart Mill:

> *In the case of any person whose judgement is really deserving of confidence, how has it become so? Because he has kept his mind open to criticism of his opinions and conduct. Because it has been his practice to listen to all that could be said against him: to profit by as much of it as was just, and expound to himself, and upon occasion to others, the fallacy of what was fallacious. Because he has felt that the only way in which a human being can make some approach to knowing the whole of a subject is by hearing what can be said about it by persons of every variety of opinion, and studying all modes in which it can be looked at by every character of mind. No wise man ever acquired wisdom in any mode but this: nor is it in the nature of human intellect to become wise in any other manner.[18]*

One way of helping to develop self-awareness is to focus the child's attention on himself. For example, draw a life-size silhouette of the child and glue as much information as possible on to the picture – photos, fingerprints, favourite foods, hobbies, pets, personal facts, height, weight, age. This project on Myself could be presented in book form as a scrapbook or simple autobiography. Other elements could include what I look like, how I behave, where I come from, my first memories, things I do best, my friends, things I think about when I am alone, my saddest moment, what makes me happy, what I am good at, any weaknesses, my favourite books, games and places, my ambitions for the future.

Self-analysis can help children to gain a deeper insight into their lives and take a more objective view of themselves. Questions can be posed for children to answer as honestly as possible, such as:

- Which of your possessions do you value most?
- What has been your greatest moment of success?
- Are there any changes you would like to make in your life?
- What do you like most in other people?
- What do you dislike most in other people?
- What do you most want to do that you have not done?
- In what ways are you like other people of your age?
- In what ways are you different from other people?
- Do/would you mind being different from other people?

Another question to stimulate critical and creative thinking about any situation is 'What are the problems?' The next question to think about will then be 'How can we solve our problem(s)?

Summary

Critical thinking means a readiness to reason, a willingness to challenge and a desire for truth. For Bloom 'evaluation' is the highest of the critical thinking skills, which include knowledge, comprehension, application, analysis and synthesis. Bloom's taxonomy can be used in planning teaching activities. A critical thinker aims to be reasonable and fair-minded. Skill in critical thinking can be developed through practice in questioning, giving reasons and the patterning of experience (sequencing, etc.). From an early age children should be expected to ask questions, give reasons, predict and theorise. To be 'open minded' and achieve a balanced viewpoint also requires knowledge of self and understanding of others.

4 Problem solving

And suppose we solve all the problems it presents? What happens? We end up with more problems than we started with. Because that's the way problems propagate their species. A problem left to itself dries up or goes rotten. But fertilise a problem with a solution – you'll hatch out dozens.

N.F. Simpson, *A Resounding Tinkle*, Act 1

Tom's father was worried. The school had reported that his son did not know his number bonds. When presented with the problem '6 add 4', Tom counted on his fingers '7, 8, 9, 10 … it's 10'. Tom got to the right answer but he could not seem to do it without counting on his fingers. 'Why can't you work it out in your head?' asked his father. Other sums produced more finger counting and more frustration – 'Why don't you remember the answer?' Then with '5 add 5' Tom smiled and said '10'. Heartened by this his father tried '5 add 6'. Tom counted on his fingers – 'It's 11'. 'Listen Tom, 5 add 5 is 10, 6 is one more than 5, so if 5 add 5 is 10, what is 6 add 5?' Tom looked troubled. He counted on his fingers from 6 to 11.

'Isn't it 11, Dad?'
'Tom, what is the connection between 5 add 5 and 5 add 6?'
'They both begin with 5.'

The session ended with Tom having an 'I-don't-get-it' feeling, and his father with the 'I-can't-help-him' feeling. What was going wrong? Perhaps it was to do with the type of problem, or the child's way of learning. How does a child come to know and to remember, and to gain the skills and attitudes that are necessary to solve problems? What are the ways of overcoming the 'I don't get it'/'I can't help him' feelings?

We all have problems of various kinds. Typical problems in our daily lives include finding a way to pay the bills, forgetting the name of someone you are about to introduce to a friend, finding time to fit in all the shopping, discovering a flat tyre and wondering what to do about it. We all know we have problems. The situation is complicated, however, by the fact that what is a problem for one person may not be a problem for another. It is not always easy to know when someone else, even one's own child, has a problem.

What underlies efforts to solve a problem is some form of cognitive processing; in other words thinking is essential to problem solving. Problem solving is applied thinking and can be contrasted with the two other kinds of thinking: creative (divergent) thinking and critical (analytical) thinking. These three kinds of thinking are closely inter-related. Creative and critical thinking are essentially forms of investigative thinking, which may entail forms of enquiry for their own sake or be applied for a purpose in problem solving.

Kinds of thinking: investigative and problem solving

Figure 4.1

The ability of the child to apply her thinking to the solving of problems will be the key to success in life. There are more immediate gains to be had from bringing children up as problem solvers. Problem-solving activities will stimulate and develop skills of thinking and reasoning. They utilise and make relevant the child's knowledge of facts and relationships. Getting results helps develop confidence and capability, the 'I-can-think-this-out-for-myself' attitude. It can also provide opportunities for children to share ideas and to learn to work effectively with others, the 'let's-work-this-out-together' approach.

Problem-solving activities not only promote knowledge, skills and attitudes; they also provide adults/teachers with opportunities to observe the way children approach problems, how they communicate and learn. There is no better way to check if a child understands a process or body of knowledge than to see if he can use that understanding in the solving of a problem. Feedback is gained on the way a child can apply skills and knowledge. Working on common problems can be a way to get the ferries moving between islands of experience, linking and extending the network of thinking.

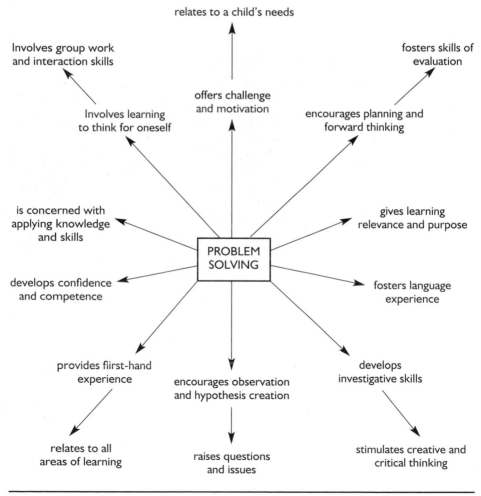

Figure 4.2

What is a problem?

It isn't that they can't see the solution. It is that they can't see the problem.
G.K. Chesterton

A problem is a task with a certain number of given conditions and items of information. It has a context, although the relevant factors that make up the given context may not be at all clear. The person confronting it wants or needs to find a solution. A useful question to ask in any situation is 'Who *owns* the problem?', 'Who wants to find the solution?' If there is no goal or desired end there is no problem. If a person has a problem she is blocked in some way from reaching a solution. The goal cannot be directly reached because there is an obstacle or series of obstacles in the way. It may not be immediately obvious what the obstacle is but there is something in the way and a conscious effort must be made if a solution is to be found and the goal reached. Problems can be defined as having these elements:

Givens → Obstacles → Goals
- *Givens* – initial conditions or context for the task.
- *Obstacles* – blocks such as not knowing the way, process or procedure for reaching the goal.
- *Goals* – objective, targets or desired ends.
- → *Efforts* – an attempt, activity or conscious effort is needed to find a solution.

We tend to use the word 'problem' loosely to cover a multitude of difficulties, as in the phrase 'what is your problem?' A problem can refer to a life-threatening situation or to a minor irritant. Such a wide difference in the scale of problem might suggest very different decision-making processes. However the minor irritant might turn out to be life threatening. The difference might be in the scale not the type of problem.

Real-life problems tend to be ill-defined and multifaceted. How to resolve a quarrel between two people, buying a new house, deciding a career. Such problems rarely have a single or final solution. They are open-search problems in which there is no one method that will guarantee the right answer, only a variety of possible approaches from which we choose a 'best fit' rather than an exact outcome. The solution becomes not right or wrong but the best in a given situation. The solution does not necessarily end the process: each resolution to a problem opens up another fertile field of problems. Life is a problem-solving process and to problems within the dimensions of space and time there is no end. Real-life problems or problems realistically modelled on life situations are open ended. They achieve practical purposes and are not perfect. They are typically not the problems children are presented with at school.

Most problems children are presented with at school are closed problems, which focus on one right answer. These tend to be artificial and well defined, disconnected from experience and unrelated to those aspects of life that children value most. They seek for single solutions, the 'right answer', which in classroom terms is directed towards getting ticks. Such problems or puzzles end with the satisfactory solution, reflecting the closed nature of the learning. They may be useful in checking what is known, in testing the memory or understanding of a single process, but they do not extend the enquiry.

Puzzle problems often rely on some sort of trick, lucky guess or creative way of looking at the problem. For example in the following nine-dot puzzle you must draw four straight lines to pass through all nine dots without taking the pencil off the paper or drawing any other lines.

```
•  •  •
•  •  •
•  •  •
```

The secret here is to continue the lines beyond the frame of the dots:

Puzzles like this can be enriched for children by extending them in more open-ended investigative ways, for example what is the fewest number of straight lines that will connect

16 dots
```
•  •  •  •
•  •  •  •
•  •  •  •
•  •  •  •
```

25 dots
```
•  •  •  •  •
•  •  •  •  •
•  •  •  •  •
•  •  •  •  •
•  •  •  •  •
```

Word puzzles also fall into the category of closed problems. What words are GANRE and TARIL anagrams of? Every five-letter anagram has 120 possible letter arrangements so there is much scope here for practising trial-and-error strategies. There may, of course, be more than one answer, for example GANRE = range and anger, TARIL = trail and trial. Extend the puzzle to more of an open-ended investigation by seeing what 3, 4, 5 letter anagrams children can invent. Can they find anagrams with more than one answer?

P	U	Z	Z
U	Z	Z	L
Z	Z	L	E
Z	L	E	S

Figure 4.3 Here is a puzzle problem invented by a primary child.

How many different ways can you find to make the word PUZZLE by following the letters in the word maze in Figure 4.3?

Some children love to work at puzzle problems and their appetite can be matched by choosing from the wide range of comics, paperbacks and newspapers that feature puzzles of all kinds. For example:

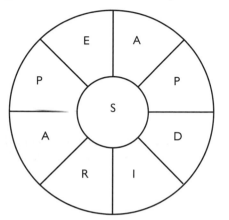

See how many words you can make with these letters, using the one in the centre in each word.

What target word(s) can you make using all letters?

Devise a target-word puzzle of your own

Figure 4.4 Target word.

Thirty-sixers

What you need: a pack of playing cards.
What to do: remove the aces and picture cards from the pack.
Arrange the 36 remaining cards in a 6 × 6 square so that:

1   the total of each row is 36
2   the total of each column is 36
3   no two cards of the same number are in the same row, column or diagonal
4   each row and column has three red and three black cards
5   one diagonal is made up of red cards only and the other of black cards only.

The Towers of Hanoi

The initial state is:

The goal state is:

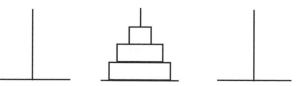

The problem can be modelled as follows.

Draw three circles marked A, B and C. Place three different-sized coins on A, largest on the bottom, smallest on the top. Move the coins one at a time, without ever placing a larger on top of a smaller coin, and transfer all the coins to B. What is the smallest possible number of moves?

How many moves did you take?*

large   medium   small

Vary the problem by trying with four coins/rings or five coins/rings or work backwards from the goal to the initial stage.

Some children (and adults) find such puzzles unbearably frustrating and don't like them at all. Puzzle problems can allow children to engage in enriching opportunities for recreational thinking. They point to the importance of flexibility, looking at problems from differing perspectives and trying a range of options.

One question that can be asked of any educational activity is 'what problem are we trying to solve?' Problems can be divided into five categories: real, realistic, tangible, contextual or abstract. Each type of problem can be represented in open-ended or closed forms and each can offer different kinds of intellectual stimulus.

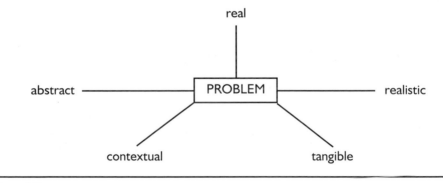

Figure 4.5

The following is an example of a problem that can be tackled in a variety of ways:

* The Towers of Hanoi answer. S = small coin, M = middle coin, L = large coin. Circles = A B C. 1. SA to B 2. MA to C 3. SB to C 4. LA to B 5. SC to A 6. MC to B 7. SA to B (seven moves)

- *Real problem* – if you had to deliver leaflets on your own to every house in the surrounding area, which would be the quickest route to take, starting from home or school?
- *Realistic* – look at a local map to trace and record possible routes.
- *Tangible* – create a model of the local road system and try travelling the possible routes with a model figure.
- *Contextual* – read a story to describe or explain why the leaflets are being delivered, where they are being delivered and what is the best way of delivering them.
- *Abstract* – record possible routes through a simplified grid of local roads. Devise codes of directions.

Much of our problem solving goes on at an unconscious level. Problem solving is not something we do on special occasions; we are doing it all the time. We tend to regard it as something special only because we don't normally pay attention to the way we do things, how we do them and why we do them. We don't examine or analyse our activities. We simply do things and take how we do them for granted (like the man in Molière's play who suddenly discovers he's been speaking prose all his life without knowing it). We all learn to walk, talk, think and solve problems somehow. We pick up these skills haphazardly. They are unstudied. We learn without paying attention, without noticing we are learning. As a result we develop hundreds of highly particular more or less useful habits for solving hundreds of particular problems. We make do. On the whole they are fairly poor and inefficient habits compared to what we could do with attention and study. We and our children can be helped by developing general principles that can transfer from one problem to another. What then are the skills and strategies of problem solving?

Skills and strategies: a case study

Gail was in the middle of reading Roald Dahl's *The BFG* when it had to be returned to the library. Unfortunately she could not renew the book because it was reserved for someone else. In her class the children were encouraged to share and discuss their problems. The children developed with their teacher certain problem-solving strategies to help in this process. The following questions were devised and used by the children to help solve their problems:

- *What is my problem?* – formulating the problem.
- *How can I explain it?* – interpreting the problem.
- *What can I do about it?* – constructing courses of action.
- *Which way is best?* – decision making.
- *How can I do it?* – implementing a solution.

In deciding whether they really have a problem the children use these questions: 'what do I want to do?' (objective) and 'what is stopping me from doing it?' (obstacle). When a child identifies a potential problem he is asked to discuss it and record it in writing.

Gail identified her problem in writing as follows:

- **What is my problem?** (Problem = objective + obstacle)
  Objective I wanted to finish the BFG
  Obstacle I couldn't renew the book
  Problem I cannot finish the story because someone else wants it.
- **How can I explain it?**
  1 I was in the middle of the story *The BFG* by Roald Dahl.
  2 Since we borrowed it from Oldham Library, WH has read it. He passed it on to me.
  3 It was a long book and I hadn't time to finish it before it was due back.
  4 I asked to renew the book but I couldn't because someone else had reserved it.

The children brainstorm and Gail lists the suggested solutions:

- **What can I do about it?**
  1 Ask WH how the story ended.
  2 Run away from the librarian with the book.
  3 Buy the book.
  4 Go to Chadderton library and ask if they have the book.
  5 Ask friends and relatives whether they have the book.
- **Which way is best?**
  She writes, 'We need to think very carefully when we come to this question. Look at each idea in turn and see if there are any snags – then CHOOSE.' Later she wrote, 'I chose to buy the paperback copy of *The BFG* as a solution to my problem.'
- **How can I do it?**
  Gail explains, 'We need to make a plan of action to carry out our choice so that we can decide which order to do things in. Next we must get together all the things we need to help us. Then CARRY OUT THE PLAN.' Plan of action:
  1 Ask Dad for permission to go to Oldham.
  2 Make sure I have enough money to buy the book.
  3 Ask Dad to take me to Oldham.
  4 Decide which shop to go in.
  5 Buy the book.

Gail completed her planning and action stage and she got the book. She had demonstrated her ability to generalise skills into a real-life situation when sufficient structure was given to acquire and practise those skills. She had obtained sound and meaningful results by using known strategies.[1]

Different problems require different kinds of skill and strategy. Children can, however, be helped to understand that certain broad strategies are common to the effective solution of most problems. The simplest set of strategies can be summed up as Plan–Do–Review, but before planning a course of action the child needs to understand the nature of the problem.

1 Understanding the problem

Children often fall at the first hurdle by not understanding the nature of the problem. Questions that can help here include:

- What is it that is known?
- What is it that is unknown?
- What kind of solution are you after?
- What is preventing you from reaching the solution?

Children need to be helped to express the meaning of the problem in their own terms. They are often not clear about the purpose of a problem, confusing means with ends. Children, particularly at school, tend to tackle problems in the spirit of the mountaineer who when asked why he wanted to climb Mount Everest replied 'Because it is there.' Children can get used to tackling problems in an unthinking way. We don't need to build better mousetraps for the sake of building better mousetraps but because we have a problem with mice.

2 Planning the action

Children need to think systematically to work out a plan, to consider strategies, not jump to hasty conclusions. Many take a 'one-shot' approach to problems, acting impulsively either by taking a wild guess or giving up. Good problem solvers don't usually come up with instant solutions; they withhold judgement. A key role of a management consultant in business or industry is often to slow the group down in its problem-solving activities. For successful artists the preparation or incubation stage is usually a long one. Scientists spend longer setting up their experiments than in doing them. Planning is a key to success.

Learning to plan can begin in the nursery.[2] Young children who plan for themselves see that they can make things happen, they have control over their lives and come to view themselves as competent decision makers. They learn to become autonomous and develop a 'can-do' approach to problems. But, for the young child, adult help is important. The adult can offer encouragement and ideas and help the child to build a mental picture or framework of her own ideas. If the child is stuck or not yet competent in planning, the adult can offer choices and suggest possibilities of what to do.

Children are often thrown by what seems to be the great complexity of the tasks before them. The following are strategies that might help:

- *Consider all factors*. Try to get the total picture. Re-read the question, think what it might mean, consider the alternatives, as, for example, in the well-known riddle 'As I was going to St. Ives, I met a man with seven wives. Every wife had seven sacks, and every sack had seven cats, every cat had seven kittens. Kittens, cats, sacks and wives, how many were there going to St Ives?'[3] Parents and teachers can help children to focus on important facts and processes. There is in business management a rule of thumb known as the '20–80' rule, which states that 20% of the facts account for 80% of what is going on. There are a vital few facts that need to be sorted out from the trivial many.
- *Think of a similar problem*. How did you solve that? How might that help us? A child may have a lot of experience to bring to the situation that he is not immediately aware of. There is a need not only to have a range of experience relevant to the

problem but also to be able to make connections. Adults can help the process of bringing experience to mind. Analyse a previous success, working backwards from the solution. How was the obstacle overcome? According to Polya, 'finding a related problem' is the most important step in seeking a solution.

- *Simplify the problem.* Try part of the problem first. Encourage a step-by-step approach. For example, in trying to describe a complicated route from A to B, don't leave the child struggling with all the possibilities; plan short distances at a time. Similar advice was given by the psychologist Karen Horney to patients overwhelmed by the problems and anxieties of life: 'live in day-tight compartments' – that is, tackle only a day at a time. Break the problem into parts. If these are not manageable, continue until you arrive at problems of a manageable size.
- *Model the problem.* How can we show the problem? To a child a problem often seems out there, remote, intangible, difficult to come to grips with. They should be encouraged to model the problem with objects, diagrams and pictures etc. Take the water jug problem:

You have three jugs

The 8 litre jug is filled with water

Can you find some way of pouring the water back and forth between the jugs so that you end up with:

You must end up with 4 litres in the 8 litre jug and 4 litres in the 5 litre jug.

There are no markings on any of the jugs.
Show how you would fill and empty jugs, using the 8 litres of water and the three jugs.
What is the minimum number of moves needed to solve this problem?

Figure 4.6

Obviously real jugs and water would provide the best models, or three containers and eight counters could represent the jugs and litres of water, or jug shapes could be drawn. Modelling a problem will often suggest starting points or ways of experimenting with ideas in search of a solution.

- *Record the plan*. What do you intend to do? One of the drawbacks of human problem solving is the limitation of our short-term memory. Research[4] suggests that people are generally able to plan three or four moves ahead and that, if they have made such a plan, then they can proceed through a cluster of moves or attempted solutions in rapid succession. Children need to be encouraged to discuss or record their plans and to think of logistics, the material they need, who will do what when and how and the sequence of moves. 'Is the action plan ready?'

3 Tackling the task

Strategies for supporting the problem-solving child include:

- *Describing with interest what the child is doing*. Talking through what the child is doing not only supports the learning process but also models ways the child can use to monitor and express their own activity. 'It looks to me as if you are ...'
- *Asking the child what she is doing*. It is important that the adult does not presume to know exactly what a child is doing or making. By inviting the child ('tell me about what you are doing'), the adult indicates that what the child is doing is worthy of interest and attention.
- *Supporting the process when needed*. It is not always easy to break problems down into easy steps or subproblems. Sometimes it is necessary to try unlikely avenues, to choose paths that seem to move away from the solution (for example, if you were on the third floor of an unfamiliar building and wanted the way out, knowing the entrance faces north would you refuse to go down a south-facing stairway?). Children sometimes need clues, to be pushed in divergent directions, to be led into new avenues of enquiry, to be shown new tools and ways to use them.

Another difficulty with problem solving is that a child will tend to repeat the wrong routes, sometimes for good reasons (for example, it worked once before so it might work again) but sometimes error will be repeated for bad reasons (for example, going down the same dead end in a maze because the child has failed to recognise or identify the path). Getting the child to think aloud can help her to evaluate progress on a problem. It can help the child to relate what she is doing to her planned course of action and encourage her to consider other possible moves or ideas. It does not always work; there is often a gap between what we say and what we do. When all avenues have been explored does the child know what to do when she is stuck?

One strategy is to break the problem into smaller problems. For example take the problem of the Hobbits and the Orcs.[5] Three Hobbits and three Orcs need to cross a river. There is only one boat, which they must share. The boat can only hold two creatures at a time. The Orcs must never be allowed to outnumber the Hobbits on either bank of the river (or they will overpower and eat them). How do the Hobbits and Orcs cross the river in safety? Various strategies can help here: trial and error, stage by stage, or working backwards from a solution. Try drawing, modelling or acting out the problem. If all else fails you can always leave the problem and try later, or share it with others. ('A problem shared is a problem halved' – or doubled!)

4 Reviewing the situation

Review completes the planning and doing process. In looking back, children can see the relation between the problem, the plan and the attempted solution. Recall helps children to learn from their experience and to remember it next time they are planning an activity. Recall in a group helps children to share experiences. Some teachers feel that recall time is best undertaken not immediately after the task but after a period when the experience has 'sunk in' and a more detached view can be taken.

If you want to help children to review what they have done, ask them to teach you how to do it. Focus on a key concept in a process and explore its implications. Check to see if the child can transfer his approach to a similar kind of problem. Make explicit the application of the problem-solving process in as wide a field as possible. The aim of the review is to enable children to reflect on and to learn from their experience.

Success in problem solving

> *I didn't know I could do it till I done it.*
>   Five-year-old girl

Three sets of interacting factors are involved in problem solving (Figure 4.7):

- *Attitude* – interest, motivation and confidence.
- *Cognitive ability* – knowledge, memory and thinking skills.
- *Experience* – familiarity with content, context and strategies.

I Attitude

Poor problem solvers tend to find problems unpleasant or threatening. They tend to shy away from problems and to avoid thinking about them. They do not see themselves as problem solvers. They may not recognise the fact that problems are a normal part of life. We all have obstacles to overcome and gaps to cross with no visible means of support.

A 7 year old once said, 'I want to be an inventor but I don't know what to invent.' His difficulty was in finding problems. One characteristic of a good problem solver is to be good at finding problems, even actively seeking them out. Trouble is bad, but finding the source of trouble is good. Finding a problem does not create it, it gives you a chance of doing something about it. Whatever the topic, ask 'What problems does this present?'

Problem posing involves the use of imagination. How do traffic lights work? Where do those pipes lead? Why don't dead birds drop from the sky? There is a need to keep a range of possible solutions in mind and not to take the easy way out. Another characteristic of a good problem solver is that she accepts uncertainty. John Dewey[6] argued that all conscious thought has its genesis in the uncertainty evoked by a problem situation. Uncertainty does not mean indecision; it means deciding (metacognitively) to withhold judgement, to leave the options open. 'Thinking man is necessarily uncertain' (Erich Fromm).

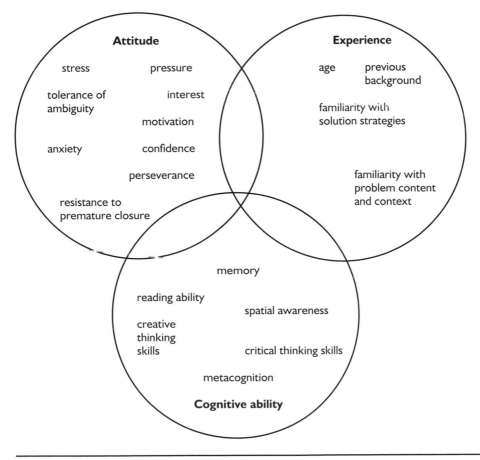

Figure 4.7 Some factors that influence the problem-solving process.[7]

Good problem solvers show confidence in their ability. Be confident in your child's ability, build on existing strengths. Take time to analyse what they are. Research shows that boosting confidence increases a child's ability to solve problems and keeps him from giving up too soon, before the right and bright ideas come up. Children need help to recognise intangible strengths such as memory, imagination and persistence. Start with easy tasks to build confidence and encourage the child to take time. The child needs challenge, the stimulus to think, investigate and attack problems. The child also needs the security provided by the most important external resource – you. The child needs security of SOS:

- *Structure* – in planning, personal help and resources.
- *Order* – a disciplined and anxiety-free environment.
- *Support* – in having someone to listen, praise and advise.

The teacher's attitudes that can help support the child include the following:

- learn with and alongside the child
- admit you don't know and can make mistakes
- trust the child to make his own decisions
- intervene only when appropriate
- encourage collaboration and discussion with others
- allow time for thinking things through
- reward the child when she shows courage in taking risks
- accept a range of results at different times and from different children
- praise and motivate the child's efforts
- praise and motivate your own effort!

2 Cognitive ability

What are the cognitive factors that contribute towards success in problem solving, and how can they be developed?

Cognitive ability includes knowledge, memory and metacognition.

There has been a widespread tendency to devalue the role of knowledge in education. Research[8] into the role of knowledge has blurred what was once regarded as a fundamental distinction in the process of problem solving: the distinction between knowledge and understanding. Phrases like 'merely applying a rule' or 'just remembering how to do it' express the low opinion generally held by educators of problem solving through applying remembered knowledge. 'Real problem solving' has often been described as that which involves skills and understanding. However it can be argued that all problem solving is based on knowledge, even if that knowledge is in the form of a known strategy such as trial-and-error. All problem solving requires 'know how'.

Research[9] shows that one key element distinguishes experts in problem solving from less successful novices – the expert knows more. A doctor, for example, needs to know about anatomy, a games player needs to know about his/her sport, a cook needs to know about food. It is estimated that it takes at least 10 years' exposure to the task environment of chess before even the most gifted of chess players can become a grand master. A master chess player, like a master chef, may have a knowledge base of about 50 000 facts, patterns and techniques at his/her command. The same may be said of experts in most fields. It is also true of the field in which we are all, or nearly all, natural experts: our native language.

Studies of the difference between good and poor problem solvers pointed to the importance of knowledge. But good problem solvers do not simply know more; they do more with what they know than poor problem solvers. The inactivity of poor problem solvers might be due to laziness but more probably it is because they do not know that there is anything for them to do because of 'you-either-know-it-or-you-don't' habits reinforced by dull schooling. They do not know how to generate their own knowledge. We need to encourage children to take an active role in their learning and show them how to use what they know to the best advantage.

Knowledge requires memory. The two are inextricably linked. Part of ensuring that our children have a sound and wide knowledge base from which to solve problems is to help them access that knowledge through memory. Memory is important in all thinking and is involved in every stage of problem solving. The essential difference between thinking and acting is that in thinking we are manipulating representations of things like words, numbers, symbols and images rather than the things themselves. In thinking we do not operate upon the world but on what we remember about the world. It is this that frees us and can free our children from the tyranny of time, space and objects. Unlike lower animals we are able to transcend the here and now and enter through memory and imagination into timeless realms of thought. Memory enables us to vastly extend the range of problems we can solve.

Memory is a source of power when it works and of weakness when it fails. Most of our problems are solved by the use of memory, often by recalling solutions to similar problems. Research[10] into how we remember has important implications for helping our children.

We remember best when what we need to remember:

- is important for us
- has some personal relevance
- is meaningful in itself
- can be connected to something we already know
- is of immediate use
- is of manageable size
- is repeated and strengthened through repetition.

Memory can be thought of as a kind of conveyor belt, which when in operation (awake) receives a constant stream of information, which it processes as follows:

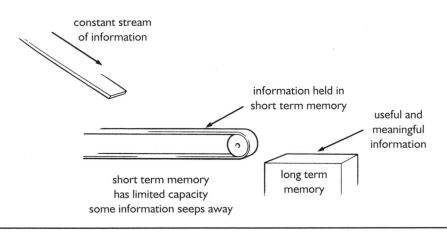

constant stream
of information

information held in
short term memory

useful and
meaningful
information

short term memory
has limited capacity
some information seeps away

long term
memory

Figure 4.8

Initially, information is received and passed into short-term memory, where it is rejected or passed into long-term memory. Unlike short-term memory, which can quickly become overloaded, long-term memory seems to be of unlimited capacity. It organises itself as a network of concepts (semantic memories) and images (episodic memories).[11] Semantic memories contain generalised information, abstractly coded into words and images that express our conceptual classification of things. Episodic or event-memory refers to images of observations or events stored and recalled like snapshots from the past. Visual and auditory memories are stored in this way. There is another kind of memory, which is stored almost unconsciously – kinaesthetic memory, which is the know-how we have based on touch and movement such as remembering how to swim.

We gain access to our memories through a production system involving various strategies and procedures. Some memories are better preserved than others. This may be due to the quality of the initial perception (how effectively the information was taken in) or how effectively it was connected into a network of related memories. Children process information in the same way as adults but adults have more efficient networks and processing systems. To help children remember we need to strengthen the production and networking systems in their memory. Children not only know less than adults; because of their lack of experience, they are weaker at knowing what to do with what they know.

To prevent overload, the brain filters out the irrelevant and tends to overlook things that it cannot relate to some internal or external pattern. Simply presenting structural material to a child, for example a rule out of context, is not sufficient to ensure effective thinking and learning. Simply leaving the child on her own without helping her to structure her thoughts and abstract connections and patterns will not help her thinking and learning. If there is to be a transfer of the learning into long-term memory the child must be taught to process the structured experience to her own understanding.

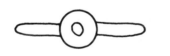

The brain is programmed to make connections, looking for linking features to make sense of an object. For example, what is shown in Figure 4.9?

Figure 4.9

Given a visual stimulus the brain seeks to connect it to remembered patterns of experience. Adults need to help children to look for significant patterns in the verbal or visual information given and to help them process the patterns through thinking, talking or writing. People talk of having poor memories, or a memory like a sieve, as if the problem was one of loss or inability to retain impressions. Memory failure is more often a failure of information processing. Recalling a memory is not just finding it in the right pigeon hole; it is a reconstructive process, tracing the fragments of memory in the network system and putting them together to make the concept or image you are after. This reconstructive process can be sensed in the 'tip of the tongue' experience, or when, for example, we say Jean instead of Jane. The processing of memory is not necessarily a conscious activity. Often things that we could not recall at a previous time occur to us later. Poor memory is not so much a psycho-physical dysfunction as poor habits of learning.

One of the poor habits of learning, or of teaching, that results in a failure of memory retention is caused by memory overload. Short-term memory is of limited capacity. Consider these questions: 'What is your telephone number?' 'What is your postcode?' 'What is your car number?' The answer may come tripping off the tongue because these have been encoded in manageable chunks. A famous research article[12] concluded that seven (plus or minus two) seemed to be the magical number of unconnected items – for example numbers, names, facts – that could be successfully stored and retrieved from short-term memory. It is perhaps no surprise that there are seven wonders of the world and seven days of the week. There are the Secret Seven and the Magnificent Seven but not the Great Eight. Try remembering the whole of a large set such as the names of the apostles; after seven (and sometimes before seven) remembering becomes difficult.

There are various activities through which we may seek to strengthen a child's memory, such as the following.

- **Kim's game** was named after the hero of Rudyard Kipling's novel, *Kim*. Part of Kim's training was to sit cross-legged on the floor in front of a low table covered with cloth while his teacher arranged semi-precious stones, beads and other objects of various colours, shapes and sizes on the cloth. After a short while he covered everything and asked the boy to tell him exactly what he had seen and the position of each item in relation to the others. A variation of this was to send the boy out of the room and change the arrangement of the objects, removing some, replacing others, and then to challenge the boy to tell him what had changed. This exercise could be reproduced, starting with a few items and working up to the recall of more complex combinations.

- **Memory** is a variation of Kim's game and fun with a large group of children/people. Make a list of 10 simple words, numbering them from one to 10. Read the list, including the numbers, out loud to the group. Now say any number from one to 10. The first player to tell you which word on the list corresponds with the number scores a point. Make a new list after a few rounds. Try reading it again in any order but the right order. The player who can recite/reconstruct/remember the list in the original order wins the game.

- **Suitcase**. The players are going on a long journey with a large suitcase. The first player packs the suitcase, verbally, with anything he fancies. For example, 'I packed my suitcase with a tennis racket.' The next player repeats the words and adds another item, for example, 'I packed my suitcase with a tennis racket and a bag of crisps.' Each player repeats the list in exactly the same order as it has been packed. When a player forgets an item he is out. A variation of this game is:

- **Alphabet suitcase**, when each item must begin with the next letter of the alphabet (allowing 'Ex' for 'x'). A harder version is to pack your alphabetical suitcase for a particular purpose, for example a picnic (items must be related to the purpose and packable or they can be challenged and disallowed).

- **Pelmanism** is a memory game played with a pack of cards, playing cards or picture cards. Lay them face up first for all to see, then face down. Players take turns to describe a card and turn it face up. If correct they keep it. The player who picks the most correctly identified cards wins the game.

- **Chinese whispers**. Whisper an interesting sentence or short story to one child, who must then whisper it to the next child and so on down the line. Check with the last child, or continue round in a circle, to see if/how the story has changed. A variation is to whisper a long story (or tell it where no one can hear) to a child who then goes out of the room. The next child goes out to hear the story from the first child. Then a third child goes out to hear it from the second child. Then a fourth from the third and so on. The last child retells story to the whole group. Discuss the way the story has changed and why. What might have helped them to remember it better?

A child constructs an individual understanding of the world through an interaction of experience (stored as memories) and mental processing.[13] To be able to retrieve more from the child's information system she must learn to store it better. The storing of information is not a passive process but an activity that needs to engage the mind. To store strong memories you have to attend to the information and you have to do things with it. Learning to spell is a case in point. A child does not learn to remember a new spelling by simply being told or shown it. She needs to look at it, to write it and to check it afterwards. A good memory is a matter of what we do rather than what we have. Some memories have such a profound effect on us, are so deeply etched into our experience, that we will remember them always, but most memories tend to fade from short-term memory unless reinforced by use. We need to continue to work on them if they are to be easily retrieved or reconstructed from long-term memory.

Repetition alone is an inefficient form of memorisation. Memory is best achieved by elaborate encoding, via *MORE* processing of the information.

- **Meaning**. A child will tend to remember things that are made meaningful by the context, relating things to what he already knows, and by understanding, ensuring that what is to be memorised is understood and can be explained by the child in different words.
- **Organisation**. A child will tend to remember information that has been structured into patterns, either visually, verbally or symbolically. Examples of this structuring occur in multiplication tables, mnemonics, rhymes (for example, '30 days hath September') and categories or sets such as the four suits in a pack of cards. Children will search actively for some relationship in what they have to remember. They can be helped to organise large amounts into small parts (the step-by-step approach) but not more than a few parts (three to five). Three is a powerful combination (for example, the Trinity), four also (for example, the compass points) and so are fives (for example, fingers). Children often learn the alphabet through the song:

ABCD,   EFG,
HIJK,   LMNOP,
QRS,   TUV,
WX,   Y and Z

The problem of remembering unconnected strings is demonstrated by trying to say the alphabet backwards (notice that the trouble-points in this tend to occur in the breaks in the above grouping). Memory links are also strengthened by rhyming, for example G and P.

- **Repetition**. 'What you don't use you lose!' The memory process is strengthened by repetition. Children should be encouraged to test themselves, seeing which bits cause trouble and need repeating. One strategy is overlearning, which is to repeat the information even if you think you know it. Another strategy is active recall, which involves trying to recall the original without looking at it, such as the learn-to-spell strategy of Look (at the word) Cover (it) Write and Check. A third strategy is intermittent practice, going over the material with periods of rest in between to allow for consolidation.

- **Elaboration** – using what has been learned in new contexts, locating it in a wider framework, connecting it to other knowledge or experience and expressing or experiencing it through another medium, for example visually. An example from the context of learning spellings would be to use the learned word in writing some meaningful sentence. The principle involved here is that the child should apply different forms of intelligence to what is being learned and thereby to extend the framework of connections so that it becomes more firmly embedded in the memory.

A most effective and often under-used aid to memory is imagery. The effectiveness of imagery was first noted, according to tradition, by the Greek poet Simonides. He discovered the technique when the roof fell in at a banquet he was attending. As the only person to survive the tragedy, Simonides was presented with the problem of identifying the crushed bodies. He found he could identify them by recalling who sat where round the banqueting table. He went on to generalise this technique by suggesting that one could remember items by forming images of them and mentally placing them in special locations. Greek and Roman orators used this technique to remember major points in their speeches, by generating images and mentally locating the images round a room.[14] A modern variation is called Galton's Walk, from James Galton's suggestion of taking an imaginary walk down a familiar path and locating items to be remembered along the walk.

Children can be encouraged to make mental images of what they wish to remember and perhaps to locate them in a familiar scene. Mnemonics are like verbal images that can aid memory. A mnemonic is a memory nudge.

memory   nudge

For example some people are helped to spell the word *necessary* by

one collar   two socks

remembering 'one collar and two socks', or beautiful by 'big elephants aren't ugly'. Encourage your child to develop his own personal tricks to remember the words that are needed. Exercise visual intelligence.

Another major aid to memory is the memo pad.

> *'The horror of that moment', the King went on, 'I shall never, never forget.' 'You will, though,' the Queen said, 'if you don't make a memorandum of it'.*
> Lewis Carroll, *Alice in Wonderland*

Encourage your child to memo, jot, note, scribble, scrawl, write or draw on notebook, memo pad, scrap of paper, jotter, rough book, log book, think book, exercise book, back of envelope or whatever is at hand to help relieve unnecessary demands on short-term memory. There are sound reasons for creating a visual memory store.

Memory seems to be stored in 'chunks' of knowledge such as patterns of sound, shape and symbol. Words are stored as chunks of knowledge, as are phrases, rhymes, quotations, sayings, titles, proverbs, riddles, jokes, slogans and addresses. What makes a person fluent in a language is not simply that he knows a lot of words but that he has a rich knowledge of different word patterns. It is the same with other problem-solving experts. The expert chess player does not simply know how to work out the best move in a given position, she has access to a vast store of 'chunks', of remembered positions, variations and configurations of pieces, which she can call upon. Memory, like learning, should not rely on haphazard accretions, it needs to be organised and put to use.

Knowing what we know, how we remember, our attitudes to a problem and what strategies to use is part of the metacognitive[15] understanding we develop through experience. What are the starting points for this experience?

Experience – starting points for problem solving

A problem-solving approach to teaching argues that thinking is essentially unfinished. It is an ongoing activity. Not about knowledge that once known becomes dead, what Whitehead[16] described as 'inert facts', but about knowledge for a purpose. We need to know x in order to know/do/solve y. Knowledge is an instrument of action, modifiable and open-ended.[17] By offering challenge we help children to move from dependence to independence, we help them to decode the world in which they live and to create their own authentic responses to it. Where do we help them to find starting points for investigation and problem solving? The ideas in Figure 4.10 take the child as the focus and explore ways in which the child's experience can become a catalyst for problem solving.

I In the home

- *Decoration* – design colour schemes, wallpaper, wallcovering – cost, plan, what tools, plan the jobs, do the decoration.
- *Furniture* – design a better chair/table/cupboard/bath/bed – new covers, decoration.
- *Clothes* – design a better hat/shoes/pair of glasses/watch/clock/badge/mirror/tool/penknife/comb/key ring.

- *Design* a favourite bedroom, secret den, hideout.
- *How to make washing up quicker and easier*, or bed-making, or cleaning windows, or keeping the house tidy.
- *Keeping warm in winter* – problem/solutions.
- *Help in the house* – a machine/invention/idea that would be helpful in the house, problems to solve, jobs to do.
- *Building* – how to build a better, cheaper, quicker house.
- *Design a home for a pet animal* – what problems does your design solve, different designs, make real or model home. Design something that would prevent your cat or dog fighting.
- *Design your own garden* – a place to play, eat or sit out in, a pond, shed, greenhouse, place to grow flowers or vegetables.
- *Garden furniture designs*, garden ornaments, bird bath, bird scarer, flower or fruit picker, garden tool, water fountain, plant pot, garden seat, sundial, wheelbarrow, water barrel, useful gnome.
- *A House of the Future* – design a dream house; what problems would you hope to solve?, outside/inside/location.
- *Design new games*, toys for home use, a machine to help practise your favourite hobby, game or sport.
- *Stop thief* – how to stop burglars entering your home; how to protect your belongings, what precautions to take.
- *Repairs* – what needs mending, how, why, when?

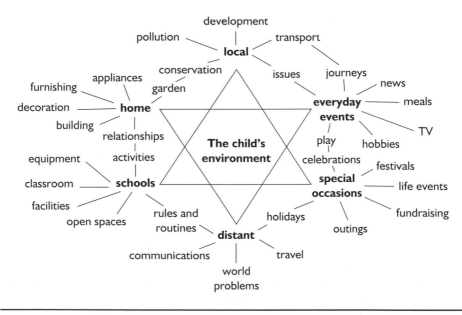

Figure 4.10

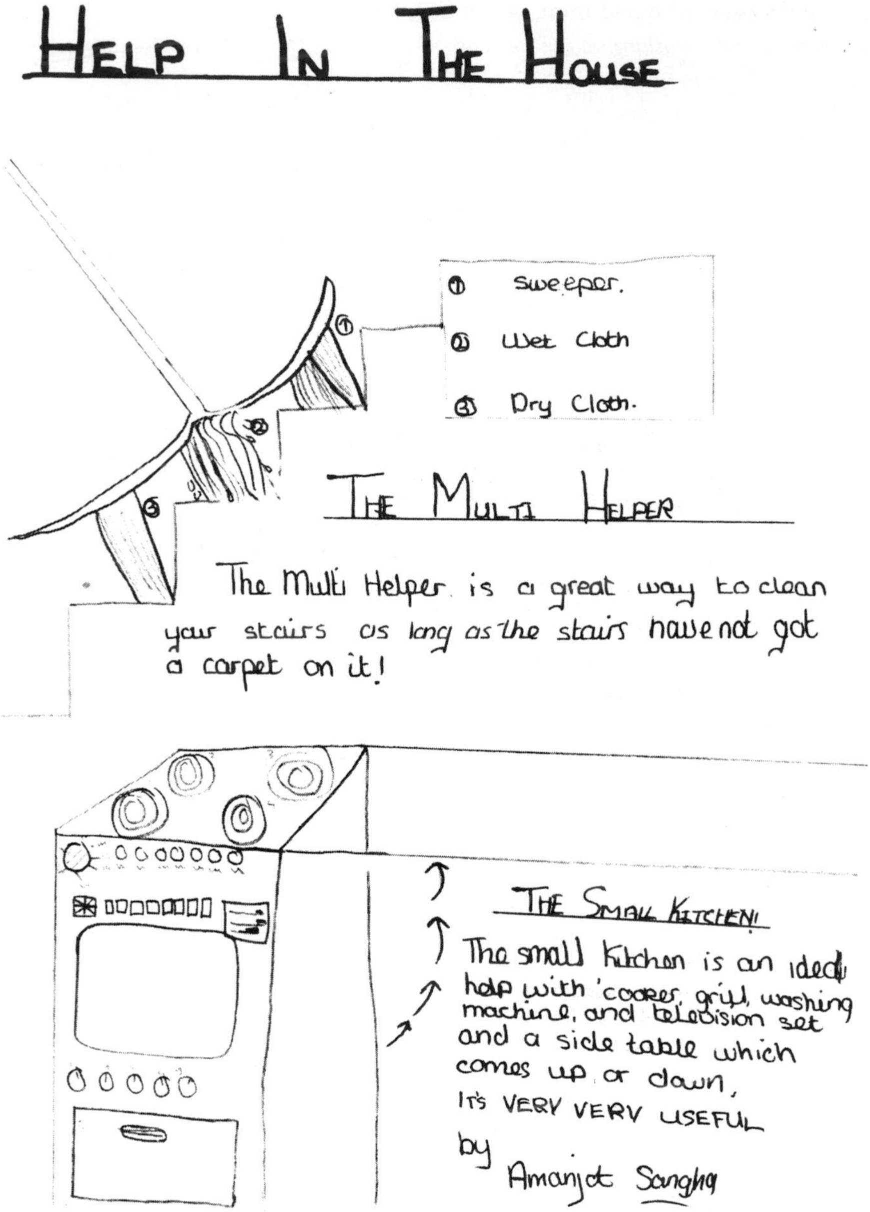

HELP IN THE HOUSE

①	sweeper.
②	Wet Cloth
③	Dry Cloth.

THE MULTI HELPER

The Multi Helper is a great way to clean your stairs as long as the stairs have not got a carpet on it!

THE SMALL KITCHEN!

The small kitchen is an ideal help with 'cooker, grill, washing machine, and television set and a side table which comes up or down.

It's VERY VERY USEFUL

by Amanjot Sangha

Figure 4.11 Help in the house.

2 At school

- *What school would I like?* Facilities, equipment, children, teachers, activities.
- *School rules* – invent rules for children/teachers. What problems would they solve, which are most important?
- *Punishments* – are they needed? Are they fair? Ways of preventing unfairness.
- *School-day problems*, timing, timetable needed?
- *Create an advert* for your school/class/teacher.
- *Routes round the school* – how many, which are best, shortest routes (in case of fire), covered routes (when raining), how to find way round (signposts, maps), design or make useful signs, directions.
- *Open spaces* – field, sports pitch, garden, new facilities, e.g. pond, wild area, trail, maps and plans.
- *Playground* – design/make play equipment, climbing frame, painted designs, teaching aids.
- *Play problems*, how to stop accidents, e.g. dangerous games, how to prevent upsets/quarrels/bullying – should there be divided areas, different play times, monitors? Should there be playtimes?
- *School uniform* – should there be one? Problems, designs?
- *School meals* – problems, menus (healthy eating) how best timed, served, cost?
- *Classroom organisation* – seating arrangements, storage, display. What the class lacks, how better organised.
- *Disabled facilities* – wheelchair access, problems, solutions.
- *Library* – types of book, shelf space, rota of visits, tidiness, problems?
- *Sports Day* – when, what races, refreshments, equipment, points or teams? What if it rains, what if there's an injury?
- *School play/production* – what type, who will take part, who will come, programme, charge, seating, invitations, adverts.

3 The local environment

- *Keep the neighbourhood tidy* – how to discourage litter/encourage tidiness, design litter bins, where best put?
- *Routes to places of interest*, quickest, safest, most interesting.
- *How could local transport be improved?* Transport of the future using road, rail, sea or air, consider speed, safety, payment and pollution factors.
- *Factories* – think of what you would like to make, design factory products, advertising, plan costing, promotion, packaging, set up production plans, then produce.
- *Local issues* – what is the main local problem, causes, possible cures, what can you do about it? Have you any local contacts?
- *Local park or green space*, how to improve it, design a play area for children.
- *Conservation* – what should be conserved, why, how, where, when?
- *Local routes* – to nearest places of interest.

- *OAPs* – how to help them, how they can help us, problems of old age.
- *Design a leisure complex* to include a wide range of activities that would appeal to local people.

4 Everyday events

Figure 4.12

- *Design something to solve a particular problem*, for example a cup that never spills
- *Timing* – how to be on time, best times for different activities, how to wake up in the morning.
- *Bedroom* – how to organise, keep tidy, when to go to bed.
- *Meals* – prepare your favourite meal, problems of different tastes, how to buy, prepare and store foods.
- *TV* – what makes the best programmes, problems of watching, e.g. violence, which channel, problems described in programmes.
- *How would you care for a baby?* Design/make a baby's bed, baby toys, baby feeder, baby buggy, baby carrier, indestructible baby book.
- *Design something to help you keep warm in winter*, how to overcome the cold, problems of the elderly.
- *Daily journeys* – routes, problems, different modes of transport, timing, timetables, how far?

- *News* – disputes, accidents, disasters, reporting accurately, bias, evidence, proof.
- *Lost!* – how to avoid losing things, how to retrieve a ball stuck high in a tree, a coin that has fallen down a drain.
- *Design a bicycle to solve a special problem* – a bicycle for a musician, a postman, new accessories, extra comfort.
- *Play* – who to play with, when, for how long, what to play, hobbies, sports.
- *Homework* – should it be done, how long, who by, what kind?
- *Disputes with friends/family/strangers* – causes, cures.
- *Redesign the human body* – how would you make it better, solve particular problems?

5 Special occasions

- *Buying presents* – who for? Best present, design/make a present. How much to spend, choice of present (e.g. from catalogue)?
- *Buying a new car* – what are the most important criteria for choosing, best design. Can you make a working model?
- *Parties* – what type, when, how long, which games, how to organise food, who can help – problems?
- *Outings* – where can we go, how can we get there, how much will it cost, who will come, how long will it take, what to do there?
- *Fundraising* – how to raise money for a good cause, who needs money, how much (set target), how to raise it (plan)?
- *Plan a travel holiday* – destinations, journeys, alternatives, problems – funding, when to go, who to go with, what to do.
- *Fete or fair* – what type of stall, how to collect money, how to organise, what the money will be used for?
- *Shopping trip* – where to shop, best buys, best routes, lists, savings, best design for supermarket/toyshop, packaging.
- *Life-changing events* – birth, marriage, death. Moving house/school. Divorce/separation of parents – how to face the problems.
- *Festivals* – why, how, where, when to celebrate.

6 Distant problems

- *Problems of survival in distant climes* – desert, icy regions, jungles, remote islands – problems? Survival kit? For example, you have gone fishing and your boat has drifted out to sea out of sight of land. You have a box of matches, oars, a torch (with batteries), binoculars, a penknife, a lifebelt, string, a bottle of water, a small sail and mast, a compass, fish-hooks and fishing rod, a book, a pencil, some chocolate, a bucket. Number them in order of necessity for your survival (1 is the most important, 15 the least important).

- *Travel* – getting to distant places, routes, alternative modes of transport?
- *Problems of war and peace, international disputes* – how should they be settled?
- *Problems of famine and the world's hungry* – how can they be helped?
- *Problems of disease* – what are the major problems, who (WHO) can help?
- *Problems of homelessness* – causes and cures, e.g. design an emergency shelter
- *Problems caused by natural disaster* – floods, fires, earthquakes, hurricanes.
- *Problems of inequality of wealth* – how is it created, should it be shared?
- *Problems of communications* – foreign languages, media, signs and symbols.

Extending the experience

Develop the problem. Explore problems that arise. Pose new questions and problems. 'Can you try a different way?' 'What could you change?' 'What have you found out?'

Does experience of a problem make it easier for children to solve new problems that are similar to the original problem? The evidence from research is mixed. It was once thought that young people could be taught to 'think logically' by instructing them in Latin, or in the rules of logic, but celebrated studies by Thorndike[18] in the 1920s punctured this idea. Simply telling children what the rules are is not sufficient to transfer that skill to new problems. Evidence[19] points to four important conditions for the transfer of skill from one context to another:

- Transfer of skills requires some of the processes or knowledge to be identical between the new problem and the problem that has been solved – *have you met this kind of problem before?*
- Learners need to be made aware of similarities in the skills involved – *how did you do it last time?*
- Learners need help to recognise the relationship between similar problems – *what other problem is this like?*
- Ideally the second problem should be simpler than the first, for problem-solving skills to be reinforced – *try/make up another problem like this one.*

As Dr Johnson said, 'It is not sufficiently considered that men more frequently require to be reminded than informed.'

Left to themselves, children are not very good at bringing their previous experience to bear on solving related problems.[20] Both structural factors (how clear the problem structure is) and psychological factors (how clearly the problem is expressed and understood) are important. How a problem is presented has a powerful effect on a child's ability to understand and relate it to previous experience. Clarity and simplicity of presentation are the keynotes, together with clues seeded into a child's previous experience. These help the child gain some metacognitive control over the process of problem finding and problem solving. The best answer that the child gives will be his own. As the young boy Tom said to his exasperated father, 'It's wrong when I do it your way, but it's right when I do it my way.' And he continued to work out number problems on his fingers, sometimes correctly, sometimes wrongly, until he was convinced of a better way, a way he only possessed when he had conquered it for himself.

Summary

Problem solving is applied thinking. Real problems are often ill defined and multi-faceted. They are open to a range of possible solutions, not closed like puzzles. Every problem has givens (initial conditions), an obstacle and an objective, and requires conscious effort. Any educational activity can involve a real, realistic, tangible, contextual or abstract problem. Children need to develop skills and strategies of problem solving. Problem-solving strategies involve formulating, defining, implementing and reviewing possible solutions. Success in problem solving requires positive attitudes, cognitive skills and knowledge, including the ability to remember. Problem-solving skills are developed through tackling a wide range of problems.

5 Instrumental enrichment

What the child does in cooperation with others he will learn to do alone
Lev Vygotsky

John's brow furrowed. The teacher had shown him the way the puzzle could be put together, how one piece linked with another and how there was a place for each piece in the pattern. It was not as if the puzzle was new to him. He had done it only the day before, with some help from Sarah. He had seen others doing it quickly and easily. But how did it go? Which piece should he start with? What was the secret? He picked up two pieces at random and tried forcing them together. That didn't seem to work. All of a sudden he crashed the pieces together. He looked at the ungainly heap, then slowly pushed them over the edge of the table on to the floor.

Children try to solve problems but not all children succeed. Many children fail at quite simple problem-solving tasks. Why is it that children of similar age and physical development can achieve very different degrees of success while attempting the same kinds of problem? To succeed in solving problems children require a store of experience to apply to new tasks. But why do some children, even when they have had relevant experience, still fail to learn from that experience? Why can some children master a skill after careful tuition yet within a short space of time apparently lose that skill? Faced with this frustrating phenomenon it is not surprising that many teachers fall back on that familiar appeal, 'must try harder'. It is true that application to a task, the willpower to think things through, can be a key to success. But for many children sheer effort is not sufficient: they don't know what kind of effort to make.

Why do children fail?

According to the Israeli psychologist Reuven Feuerstein,[1] children who find it difficult to learn from experience or to respond to teaching may be suffering from cognitive deficiencies. They may not have developed the information-processing capacity to store, organise and use the information that they are given. They are victims of information rather than controllers of information. Instead of using past experience to help them succeed with new problems and tasks, they react either impulsively or passively. They become haphazard in their responses or inert in the face of a challenge they cannot immediately solve or understand. If intelligence is the ability to adapt to new situations, they are unintelligent. They have not learnt how to structure their thinking to enable them to learn from mistakes and to act rationally in new situations. Usually, such a child will score badly in an IQ test.

Feuerstein asks, what is the point of just measuring the child's intelligence and labelling him with a tag of slowness or subnormality? The point is to change the child.[2] For Feuerstein one of the great weaknesses of the traditional approach to IQ testing is that it cannot distinguish performance from potential. Every child can achieve some mark or level of attainment in a test but this will not indicate the level of possible development. In assessing potential we need to seek reasons for past failure and look for ways of providing opportunities for learning that will help a child fulfil her potential.

One reason why children fail is that they lack culturally transmitted tools of learning. Much of Feuerstein's early work was to do with helping immigrant families settle into their new homeland of Israel. Some children of immigrant families such as Moroccan Jews were found to be so backward that it was suggested that they would never successfully integrate into Israeli society. Even on culturally unbiased tests these children were found to be exceptionally low functioning. They had become, in Feuerstein's words, 'victims of information' with a very poor grasp of reality and low levels of perception. They had not learned how to store and use information presented in the school and other life situations. They were either passive or highly impulsive and snatching at possible solutions out of a blind hope or a burning frustration. There seemed to be no structure or strategy to their thinking. But why was this so? Was it because, as some experts suggested, Moroccan Jews were in some way genetically impaired?

The Moroccan children improved dramatically with specialised help. Their learning functions had not been genetically impaired – perhaps their backwardness was due to their being from a primitive, pre-industrial community? Not so, for other Jewish immigrants from pre-industrial societies, such as the Falashas from Ethiopia, produced children who were well adapted to their new lives in Israel and who showed great capacities for learning. Feuerstein discovered that the communities from which the Moroccan Jews came had been uprooted, scattered and fragmented in Morocco. They had become the urbanised poor, losing or rejecting the traditional values of their parents. They had become culturally deprived, alienated both psychologically and socially from the roots of a culture that in turn had become impoverished through social upheaval. They had lost their cultural roots.

The Falashas, in contrast to the urbanised Moroccans, lived in rural isolation in the highlands of Ethiopia. There they had preserved an archaic but integrated culture in which children had a valued role and were introduced at an early age to the rituals and cultural traditions of the community. Like many children in developing countries they were given important tasks to perform, such as being in charge of flocks of animals, from an early age. They were also given cognitively demanding duties such as memorising passages from the Torah. Because of the great scarcity of books (traditionally handwritten) in the villages, those who learned to read by sitting in a group around one book learned to read from many angles, upside down, left to right and right to left! Falasha immigrants surprised their Israeli teachers and social workers with their adaptability to the new social situation. Many of their youngsters progressed into higher education.

For Feuerstein a potent factor in developing a child's cognitive abilities, and one that helps to explain the success of the Falashas, is the absorbing of a rich and coherent culture. Children who have learnt one culture, he argues, usually have the capacity to learn another. Those who have been deprived of a rich cultural inheritance do not have that advantage. Feuerstein found that children from culturally rich backgrounds, like the Falashas, were more receptive and better able to understand a new culture than either children from poor immigrant families from Britain or the USA or even deprived Israeli children.

Teaching children to think means, among other things, the ability to make use of new experiences. One way of decoding experience is through social values and shared habits of thought. Cultural experience provides a powerful means for human beings to interpret reality. The values, social rituals, traditions, customs, myths and stories that are handed down also provide the necessary raw materials that the child uses to develop his information-processing capacities. A culture provides connecting links between concepts, offering a scaffolding of understanding on which a child can build. Lack of such essential mediating experience is what Feuerstein means by cultural deprivation; it deprives the child of the vital structuring that is needed for full cognitive development. Without cultural enrichment the world becomes, in the words of William James, one great 'buzzing, blooming confusion'.

The role of mediation

Children need as much sensory stimulation as possible for their intellectual growth. Children's minds develop through processing their interactions with the world. These mental operations work in response to sensory stimuli, which in turn modify their intellectual structures so that they are able to assimilate new levels of information. Thus emphasis on direct 'hands-on' experience has become a cornerstone of child-centred education. Feuerstein argues, however, that this approach, which is largely the legacy of Piaget and his followers, lacks one crucial element: the role of the mediator.

A mediator is any knowledgeable person, usually an adult, who shapes the way the child perceives the world. Parents and significant others in a child's life, grandparents, siblings, caretakers and teachers, are not simply sources of stimulation for the child. They control the stimuli a child receives and in so doing help to structure the child's universe in patterns similar to their own. They transmit a culture that determines the child's attitudes, perceptions and behaviour. Parents and teachers mould a child's world by selective ordering, emphasising and explaining. For Feuerstein, culture is not simply absorbed as some sort of hidden curriculum in a child's life, it is something actively imposed on a child and it is necessary.

Basic thinking skills are built up by parents and teachers through what Feuerstein calls 'mediated learning experiences'. In a mediated learning experience the adult intervenes between the child and the environment. The mediator 'transforms, reorders, organises, groups and frames the stimuli in the direction of some specifically intended goal or purpose'.[3] When parents say, for example, that objects and actions are 'good/bad', 'right/wrong', 'important/unimportant', they are transmitting cultural values to the child. These meanings can be imbued with powerful emotional and moral significance. They can be deeply motivating. 'Give me a child until he is seven', said the Jesuit Fathers, 'and he is mine for life.'

Virtually any experience can be a mediated learning experience if someone intervenes to make the sensory experience 'transcend itself'. For example, a child may see the traffic lights change and learn something from the experience. However if an accompanying adult explains why the lights change, how they work or the need for safety rules, it becomes a mediated learning experience. Even a simple request like 'Please buy three bottles of milk' can be extended to show the reasoning behind the request. 'Please buy three bottles of milk so that we will have enough left over for tomorrow when the shops are closed.'[4] The content of the experience (whether the learning is about dinosaurs or the functions of the brain) is not what is important for Feuerstein. What matters is the extent to which the mediated experience offers insight into the thinking involved in the task. In the words of Feuerstein, 'You can take a child to a zoo and he might find it interesting, but it won't teach him logic.'[5] Feuerstein argues that if all child–adult interactions were learning experiences then it would narrow the huge gulf that divides the high-achieving from the low-achieving child. It is the mediators who provide the meaning in a child's world. If the beauty of a sunset is not pointed out to a child then the experience will be lacking in vitality and relevance. A child will not make the effort of directing attention to a stimulus that carries no significance. Parents and teachers are the child's makers of meaning. Only through a given framework of meaning can a child construct, adapt and develop his own meaningful responses to the world.

The culture that is passed on provides vitality and relevance to learning. Feuerstein argues: 'One of the greatest causes of failure at school is the attempt by many teachers to remain neutral towards the material they are conferring on the children.' A stimulus, to be learning experience, should carry significance and meaning that relates to the wider context of the child's culture. A given culture can be challenged or rejected at a later stage. What a child needs is a starting point of offered meanings to give him his first bearings in an unfamiliar world.

The way a parent offers meanings to a child is different from the way meanings are given in a dictionary. A human interaction conveys more than any teaching machine or artefact can do. There is a difference between a static toy and one moved along by a parent. What is common to these differences is the purposive nature of human interaction. When the parent pushes the toy or explains an event it is an intentional act and this alters the nature of the stimulus. An intentional act, says Feuerstein, intensifies its significance, it produces a state of vigilance and focuses attention. A bird in the hand (when being shown to a child by a loving parent) is worth two seen in a bush. A mediated learning experience conveys meaning and purpose, where both mediator and child become more attentive and responsive.

Another characteristic of effective mediation is that it transcends the immediate experience. Successful teaching lies in pointing to general values or principles over and above the individual task. For example, letting the child play with the keys of a typewriter can help teach the transcending principle of cause and effect. A family or class outing can provide opportunities for learning about planning, timing and problem solving. In responding to simple questions the parent or teacher can stimulate the child's thinking beyond the immediate facts to a general principle. Almost every situation provides opportunities for adults to give more than the child asks for. This potential is easily overlooked. Children can be told never to play with the typewriter, they can be 'seen and not heard' on outings, their toys can be left unexplained. Telling the child 'Don't touch that saucepan' cannot be a mediated learning experience but saying 'Don't touch that saucepan because it's hot and you might get burnt' conveys principles of cause and effect that transcend the immediate experience.

According to Feuerstein, poor thinking skills often result from having too few mediated learning experiences. These cognitive deficiencies[6] in turn reduce the individual child's ability to benefit from everyday opportunities for learning. What underlies these deficiencies is the child's passive approach to the environment. The retarded performer views himself as a passive receiver of information, not as someone who is a user and generator of information. Feuerstein quotes the case of a girl who, when asked how long it took her to go to school, did not know. However she did know when she caught the school bus and what time she arrived in school. She also knew the arithmetic to compute the difference. What she did not see was that she could produce new information merely by thinking about and processing what she knew. As a consequence the girl lacked a sense of competence and control about her life and learning.

A sense of incompetence is one of the most difficult deficiencies to reverse. It can be repeatedly confirmed by a child's low expectations and become a self-fulfilling prophecy. Feuerstein suggests that feelings of inadequacy and poor self-image are inevitable tendencies of childhood because of the child's growing awareness of inadequacy compared with adults and other peers. Children can often be seen compensating for this sense of incompetence through fantasy play. Positive strategies are needed that will mediate in the child a confidence in his own reasoning powers. This self-reliance can be built up only by a pattern of successful responses to challenge.

'I want to do it myself' is not the natural response of every child. It is the excitement of success that encourages the child to seek new goals and gives her the motivation to try to reach them. Children who have not been challenged ('go on you try to do it/work it out') and have not been rewarded by success ('I did it myself') often do not have the internal need to set their own goals. This need to look for goals can be encouraged by such questions as 'Where shall we go, and how shall we get there?' 'What do we need to take with us?' 'What shall we do now/then?' Planning by the child supported by the adult is as important as achieving a desired outcome.

Successful living needs planning; it also requires the self-regulation of behaviour. Children need to inhibit instinctive or impulsive behaviour, and not only when they are crossing the road. The impulsiveness of under-achieving children can be helped in two ways. First, by teachers and parents modelling controlled and considered responses to stimuli and second, by offering opportunities, what Feuerstein calls 'instruments', for reflective thinking. These are situations where children must assess for themselves the information they need, check for errors or missing data and evaluate an outcome. Feuerstein aims to encourage the idea that children can achieve things they once thought impossible. A failure of some teaching methods is that children are given little idea of the progress they are making; they are not taught how to review and evaluate their performance. Children need to be made aware of when they can do things alone that beforehand required the help of others.

All children have potential, what the Soviet psychologist Vygotsky called 'zone of proximal development' (ZPD). Vygotsky found that traditional measures of attainment and intelligence lacked one vital ingredient. They did not assess what a child might achieve given the right help and support. Vygotsky found that one 8-year-old child might, with some slight assistance such as being given a leading question or first step towards a solution, solve problems designed for 12 year olds. Another child might not go beyond problems intended for 9 year olds. The difference between a child's actual mental age and the level he reaches in solving problems with some help indicates his potential (ZPD). 'With assistance every child can do more than he can by himself – though only within the limits set by the state of his development.'[7]

Psychologists, following the lead of Piaget, have regarded the child as an active learner, interacting with the environment and forming increasingly complex structures of thought. This active learner, much studied under laboratory conditions, was conceived as a rather isolated being, working alone at her problems. We now see that given the appropriate social context the child can handle far more sophisticated problems than she can alone. Language plays a key role in this process. Vygotsky argued that concepts are first acquired 'externally' in dialogue, then gradually become internalised as ways of thought. The instruments of language and culture help promote the growth of mental structures. Peers, teachers and parents challenge a child's cognitive approach to a problem and support the child by providing a scaffolding of understanding and so extend her thinking. This development of a child's concepts depends on a social context and on the linguistic resources within the culture. We make sense of words and concepts by locating them in our known world. The meaning we derive from words, as the philosopher Frege argued, depends on both the sense (definition) and reference (context) of particular speech acts. It would be difficult, if not impossible, for a child to develop a concept that is not expressed in her own cultural or social context. As Vygotsky says: 'All the higher functions originate as actual relations between human individuals.'[8]

The social world of the child is given order by a system of rules and conventions. 'We get up at 7', 'Girls wear dresses, boys don't', 'You shouldn't hit other people' are the kind of messages that give order to a child's world, that make it predictable and provide a framework for living.[9] Initially the child obeys through compulsion and conditioning: if the rules are not followed then order and routines are disturbed, adults get upset, accidents happen and other unforeseen events can occur. Gradually the child comes to see that if social and cultural rules are broken things may not work well. The child also learns that rules are underpinned by reasons. If the rules are not followed the game cannot be played, the shared conventions so necessary for group interaction break down. Eventually the child sees beyond the conventional rules to the principles involved and can in turn generate further rules from those principles. The various dimensions of rule-governed activity include the rules of language (what Wittgenstein called the 'language game'), rules of play (in children's games), moral rules, social rules, rules categorising sexual roles, rules governing home and school. Would it be possible to live a life with others entirely by one's own rules? Do children need rules or guidelines to help them work effectively with others? Does working in a rule-governed way with others improve a child's ability to think and learn?

Research[10] shows that children working in pairs and groups produce more effective solutions to logical problems than children working alone. The social process of discussion and argument acts as a catalyst to thinking. The opportunity to suggest, reject and spark off new ideas helps to synthesise and consolidate a child's thinking. There are three interacting systems thathelp in this process:

- the individual intrapsychological context
- the social interpersonal context
- the cultural context.

Teachers, adults and others in the child's social context describe the boundaries and the vistas of the child's world. In particular their mediation creates the 'expectation of intelligence' which plays such an important role in the child's thinking and behaviour.

Helping the child

Feuerstein has identified certain crucial ways in which the adults in a child's life foster cognitive development. If any of these links are missing then the child's cognitive ability will be impaired.

1 Helping the child to 'see'

We now know that very young children can see much more clearly than was once thought possible. Their natural style of seeing, however, is to scan the environment around them. They need help in learning to focus perception and attention. Initially it is the mother who helps her child to focus on objects by persuading the child to follow her eyes and gestures. Such parent–child interactions Feuerstein calls 'mediated focusing'. An absence of this mediation in helping children to focus attention on single objects can have profound effects. It can mean the child growing up with poor perceptual skills, including 'blurred' or 'sweeping' perception. Perceptual skills are necessary for recognising shapes and patterns, and for comparing and differentiating objects in the environment. Children who lack effective mediation find it hard to attend to an object longer than it takes to register its existence. They lack the ability to discriminate and select. They find it hard to perform the necessary prerequisite of logical/critical thinking, putting objects into mental categories.

Does your child's attention roam aimlessly and superficially? In the words of D.H. Lawrence:

> Thought is gazing on the face of life, and reading what can be read,
> Thought is pondering over experience, and coming to a conclusion.
> Thought is not a trick or an exercise or a set of dodges,
> Thought is a man in his wholeness wholly attending.

The parent or teacher can help the child to look beyond the surface of things more precisely, more closely and more accurately. Feuerstein has developed his own 'instruments of enrichment' to help older children who lack these skills.

2 Helping the child to select

Children are bombarded with visual and other sensory stimuli. They cannot concentrate on every stimulus in the given world so they learn to shut off the world or to rely on random unthinking responses. They look but do not see. Their responses become haphazard and unfocused, unable to select, to attend or to concentrate. But skill in selection can be taught through the modelling behaviour of adults and through mediation. Gradually the child can be encouraged to think and concentrate for himself. To aid this process Feuerstein's instrumental enrichment exercises stress the need to consciously seek out information and also to transmit this information with care and precision.

3 Helping the child to plan

Research[11] on children with learning difficulties shows that their most common characteristic is a lack of planning behaviour. When such children are told to make a plan their performance often improves. But they rarely engage in planning spontaneously. Learning to plan begins as a mediated experience. From a young age parents instil in children the need to order their lives: bath before bed, wash hands before a meal and after the toilet. 'Do this first, then that.' Routines are reinforced, both consciously and unconsciously. The conventions instilled by parents become internalised. The child learns that he lives in a world of ordered events and develops the skill to plan ahead and to represent the future in abstract temporal terms. The child is able to keep in mind a goal and to plan and schedule events that lead to that end. Parents help reinforce this process of planning by encouraging children to plan holidays, shopping trips, the day or week ahead. Children can be helped to learn the value of positive anticipation: 'The rule is jam tomorrow and jam yesterday – but never jam today.'

4 Helping to develop self-control

Another prime reason for learning failure is impulsiveness. Children need to invest more time and energy in recognising and defining problems, to inhibit their first thoughts and impulses and to foster a more reflective and cautious approach. The slogan 'Take time to think' is one that could prove useful in home and school. Without the mediation of self-control children's lives can become ruled by impulse, grabbing whatever is wanted, erratic in temper, uncontrolled in behaviour, quick to enter into conflict with others. Taking turns, waiting for others to finish, not snatching, these are not simply the conventions of courtesy; they help children to gain control over their impulses and so control over their lives. One of the observed features of juvenile delinquents, according to Feuerstein, is their inability to conceive the consequences of their actions. They do not visualise the future, their acts are 'situational', they have limited control over themselves as agents and they only respond to the surface features of the situation.

The way self-control is mediated can help to enhance cognitive development. The simple negative, 'don't do that again or else,' teaches a primitive concept of cause and effect. But a logically rich response, 'don't do that because if you do x will happen' or 'x and/or y' or 'x and/or y followed by z'. These sequences will engage the child in a chain of reasoned argument. They encourage the child to stop and think.

5 Helping to develop care and precision

'Look/listen/think carefully' are the sorts of verbal cue adults use to help children take care and develop precision in their thinking and perceiving. Parents quite rightly insist on their children describing or saying exactly what they want rather than merely pointing, grunting or mumbling. Children can be quick to pick up this need for accuracy and be ready to challenge their verbally lazy parents or teachers.

One common problem with perception is the difficulty many children have in using more than one source of information at any one time. They tend to rely on the dominant feature, looking for the one crucial clue, the one obviously right answer. Once again, impulsiveness can inhibit precise processing. Questions to help children get a clearer conceptual grip on the elements of any given situation include:

What else can you see?
Is that all there is?
What other features/aspects/clues are there?

Another problem with perception is that thoughtful analysis tends to become governed by the field of perception. Children can be 'field dependent', lacking the capacity to impose a frame of reference in which they can place the objects that surround them, placing their perceptions in a wider context. Children may see the trees but do they see the wood? Can they relate the wood to other geographical features, to the nature of forests? They may know what certain terms mean, for example 'left/right' or 'forward/back' but not all will be able to use these terms as tools to categorise objects and events. They may know the compass directions of 'north, south, east and west' but not be able to give an accurate geographical direction or describe accurately the way to a nearby place well known to them.

Perception is a matter of seeing within and relating without. It involves looking into a field of perception with care and precision and connecting what is seen to a wider field or context. For example, in visiting a stately home children may not see much – probably only what is most obvious to them. Adults can turn the visit into a mediated learning experience by helping to focus the child on to specific objects of interest in the house, relating stories of the occupants and evidence of significant events, looking within, beneath the surface of things, with care and precision. The house can be related to a wider context socially, geographically or historically. What do the rooms tell you about the social life of the occupants? Why is the house situated where it is? What changes have taken place over the years? Why? Such investigations relate what is seen to wider contexts, developing frameworks of understanding, extending the range of a child's perception.

Children need help in placing events and objects in time and space and so creating their own cognitive models or maps. We can see an example of how children create their own cognitive maps, their frameworks of understanding, through the development of map-making skills.[12] These involve the interaction of two factors, the individual expression of the child's own codes of representation (encoded ideas) and the social conventions to which the child's map symbolisation and abstraction eventually conform. Children learn best by active personal involvement mediated through a rich cultural and social context.

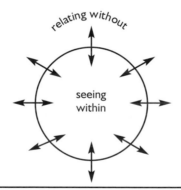

Figure 5.1 Extending perception.

The process of learning is, for Feuerstein, characterised by three phases or mental acts, input, elaboration and output:[13]

- **Input**: gathering information
  1 *Clear perception* – using all our senses to gather clear and complete information.
  2 *Systematic search* – using a plan so we do not miss something or repeat ourselves.
  3 *Labelling* – naming so we can remember/talk about it more clearly.

4 *Spatial orientation* – describing where things occur.

5 *Temporal orientation* – describing when things occur.

6 *Conservation of size and shape* – what characteristics of things always stay the same?

7 *Using two sources of information* – considering more than one thing at a time.

8 *Precision and accuracy* – when it matters.

- **Elaboration**: processing information

  1 *Defining* the problem or task.

  2 *Selecting relevant cues* that apply to the problem.

  3 *Interiorisation* – having a picture in mind of what we are looking for or doing.

  4 *Making a plan* – including steps to reach our goal.

  5 *Remembering various bits of information* – broadening our mental field.

  6 *Looking for relationships* – linking objects, events and experiences.

  7 *Comparing* – similarities and differences.

  8 *Categorising* – finding which category the object or experience fits into.

  9 *Hypothetical thinking* – considering different possibilities and their consequences.

  10 *Using logical evidence* to prove or defend our opinion.

- **Output**: expressing solutions

  1 *Overcoming egocentric communication* by clear and precise language.

  2 *Overcoming trial and error* by thinking things through.

  3 *Restraining impulsive behaviour*   self-monitoring, checking, restraining.

  4 *Overcoming blocking by using strategies* – leaving the problem, returning to it later.

  5 *Being clear and precise* in our response.

The input phase is the child's capacity to gather and organise information. Children often fail to solve problems because they have only partially collected (or have miscon-strued) the necessary data. To help the gathering and interpretation of information children need certain verbal tools with which they can extend their conceptual grasp of things, words-in-use such as 'detail', 'characteristic', 'identity', 'cause', 'theory', 'symbol'. These words are tools and not just labels, for they help the child to receive and differentiate data.

The elaboration phase is the 'thinking things through' phase, when we have to work our way through confusion and doubt, confronting the elements of a problem. In the elaboration phase children try to master and organise the stimuli presented to them. Children need to be shown how to project relationships between objects or events, to generate information from other information and to seek for reasons and relationships. They need to reflect on experience, to sum up the situation and to express their own opinions.

Part of the elaboration phase is the selection of relevant data, the picking out of pat-terns and structures of meaning. Ways of mediating this process of selectivity might include asking children to sum up a story and see if they have perceived the overall pattern, the key characters, events and 'ideas' behind the story. Can they differentiate between the characters? What was the author aiming to do in writing the story?

Children's grasp of information is often episodic; they need prompting to locate for themselves the links between the separated episodes of their experience, to link up and organise a structure of understanding. How does what they are doing now link with what they have done and are going to do?

The output phase is when children communicate their thinking, share their ideas, try out their solutions. The need is there but the expression or output may not meet that need. One cause of failure is lack of accuracy and precision – vagueness. What does the child mean? Another failing is egocentricity, the child not bothering to express himself clearly because he automatically assumes everyone else understands him. Will others understand? Another cause may be emotional blocking, the insecurity that expresses itself in impulsive behaviour and lack of cooperation. How does he feel about it? Lack of verbal skills will mean the child will not have the vocabulary necessary to express a full range of meanings. He will lack the labels to classify, the words to connect. What is he trying to say?

There are other causes of poor input, elaboration or output such as a child's fatigue, stress, lack of motivation, unfamiliarity with subject matter or problems presented in a confused manner. We should distinguish between the child's inability to carry out specific intellectual tasks and her level of intelligence. Some children may have specific cognitive deficiencies. What these children need, suggests Feuerstein, are activities or *instruments* thatwill provide the intellectual enrichment they have been lacking. It may be that all children would benefit from the kinds of enrichment that he and his followers suggest.

Instruments of enrichment

Instrumental enrichment (IE) consists of a series of intellectual games that require no background knowledge. Feuerstein calls them instruments because each is designed to be instrumental in helping children overcome specific cognitive deficiencies. The aim is to instil in children a need for intellectual activity that will help them in achieving a sense of control over their environment. A fundamental aim of IE is to change children's images of themselves from passive receivers of information to active creators of information. Teachers and other adults can mediate questions like 'How did I succeed?' or 'Why did I fail?' The encouragement of self-awareness and insight into why the child succeeded or failed is regarded as more important than the child's actual success or failure. IE is as much to do with attitudes as it is with skills, for they are interlinked.

The slogan of the IE programme, 'just a minute . . . let me think', stresses the need to allow children time for thinking. It helps to build a sense of security in the task. The child is in control, he can take time, he is not being tested. But if one basic need for the child is security the other is challenge. Feuerstein created 15 units or instruments that would offer intellectual challenge to children. These are meant to be mediated learning experiences with the teacher offering support and challenge through the process, asking for example such questions as:

What is the problem?
What strategy are you using?
Have you looked for different ways?
What plan have you got?
Which do you think is best?

The aim of mediation is to effect a transfer, what Feuerstein calls 'bridging', applying the skills and strategies learnt to other aspects of the children's lives. Instrumental enrichment is not intended to replace traditional subject areas but to act as a supplement that will make bridges to all subject areas, to help students become active, self-motivated and independent thinkers in all that they do.

The instruments are a series of paper-and-pencil exercises, introduced by teachers, followed by discussions to prompt insight and applications to other areas of learning. Instruments based on Professor Feuerstein's ideas include the following:

The organisation of dots

The child is presented with what seem like random arrays of dots. The task is to find relationships and patterns within the field of such dots such as squares, triangles, diamonds and stars, much like the way one picks out a constellation of stars in the night sky. The aim is to help train children to search systematically, to formulate hypotheses, to perceive clearly and create their own order and information, not simply to scan vaguely or impulsively. In this way they begin developing strategies for linking perceived events into a system from which they can create understanding, sense and meaning from the given environment.

Orientation in space

Poor spatial awareness (underdeveloped spatial intelligence) can impede a child's progress. We tend to assume that children can understand and follow certain directions such as front, back, left, right, up, down, above, below, north and south. Orientation in space is a series of instruments in which students are asked to identify relationships between objects. For example in one task they are asked to stick or draw a picture of a boy in the middle of a garden scene, then decide which of the objects in the picture, for example house, flowers, tree, bench, is right, left, in front of or behind the boy.

Games and puzzles such as draughts or chess can also help to develop spatial awareness, as well as the need to plan strategies and derive information from a given situation. In any game the child can be asked to describe the positions and relationships between the pieces or players. In chess the piece that causes children the most problems is the knight. The knight does not move in straight lines but makes spatial leaps according to a complex rule. Children can be helped by being given a vocabulary for spatial relationships such as direction (e.g. diagonal) position (e.g. adjacent) and distance (e.g. lengths). In drawing they can be introduced to ways of presenting different views (e.g. front, side, rear, top, elevation) proportion and perspective. They can also be challenged with that most perplexing of questions, 'What is space?'

Comparisons

How are a factory and a church alike and how are they different? How is milk like salt; how is it different? Which other letters of the alphabet resemble the letter h? (Choose five and rank them according to how closely they resemble h or another chosen letter.) Looking for similarities and differences between objects involves considering the dimensions of size, shape, number and colour. For example in comparing milk and salt:

- *common factors* – colour, nourishment, used in cooking, sold in shops
- *differences* – texture, taste, origin, use.

Whether the objects are fingerprints or snowflakes, no two have the same patterns. We can ask the child concerning any two objects 'How are they similar?' and 'How are they different?' We can also ask them to compare abstract concepts in terms of function, composition and power. For example, how would you compare ugly and wicked?

Analytic perception

Here the task is to break a whole into its component parts, for example finding a shape embedded in a complex pattern. A simple way of encouraging analytic perception with young children would be to take them on a shapes trail. This can be done in any street. Look at the buildings and tick any of these shapes you can see:

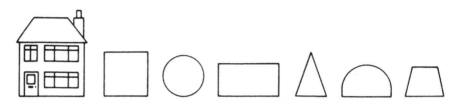

Figure 5.2 Look at the buildings and tick the shapes you can see.

Ask older children to identify shapes in intricate patterns. What shapes make up the pattern? What shapes are hidden in the pattern? Children need to know that any whole can be divided into parts, that every part is a whole and that new wholes can be created by recombining the parts. (For example, what patterns can the child make from a given selection of shapes?)

Categorisation

Anything can be fitted into a category, or into several categories, including you and me. Give the child a set of pictured objects (for example, cut out from magazines). Into what categories or sets could they be put (for example, forms of transport, tools, clothing, objects giving off light). How many different ways could they be categorised? What smaller classes or sets could be made from the larger categories?

Designing a zoo is an interesting task for older children, which involves categorisation. List or collect pictures of animals for your zoo. Put the animals into categories so that like animals can be housed together. Design a zoo to show the compounds, pens and houses in which the groups of animals could be accommodated. Which animals need trees, water or special heating? Which animals could be housed together? Which must be kept apart? Which would be safe to touch? Which are dangerous? Which feed on similar foods?

Family relations

The study of the family is a useful way for children to learn about various kinds of relationship. Feuerstein notes that some youngsters have little grasp of the abstract meaning of relational terms. When asked, for example, 'Why is he your cousin?' they may answer 'Because he helps me.'[14] Children need to develop an awareness of family relationships and how to define family terms. Some relationships are reciprocal, or symmetrical, for example brother/sister, husband/wife. Some are hierarchical, for example, son – father – grandfather – great-grandfather. An individual can fall into many categories, can be simultaneously daughter, wife, mother, grandmother, aunt, niece, sister-in-law. The union of two families through marriage alters relationships, as does the birth of new generations. Children can construct, with help, their own family trees. They can research the family relationships of the famous, for example the royal family. They can create family trees for characters in story books or fictitious families of their own creation. They may also enjoy the challenge of puzzling out obscure family relationships. For example, try the following puzzle for younger children:

> Two people are going for a swim.
> One person is the father of the other person's son.
> How are the two people related?

The problem of the family party is for older children:

> To my family party I invited two fathers, two mothers, one grandmother, three
> grandchildren, two sons, two daughters, one brother, two sisters, one father-in-law, one
> mother-in-law, one daughter-in-law and four children.
> What a big party. I make that 22 people.
> Don't be silly, there were only seven of us.
> How come?[15]

Temporal relations

It is impossible to define an object or event without referring either to its spatial (where) or temporal (when) attributes. Every thing has a time and place. Young children and deprived adolescents have a narrow temporal field, centred in the present, with a limited orientation towards the past or anticipation of the future. Mediated experiences are necessary to provide the concepts and systems of reference through which children come to understand the relativity and measurability of time.

Children need to be introduced to time both as a fixed interval and a dimension. What is the difference between the subjective perception of time and objective measurement? Can the child judge the passing of a minute? What happened this time last year? When do they think they learnt to ride a bike, got the measles, started school? Time is also a dimension understood through such mediated concepts as 'before' and 'after', 'early' and 'late' and in relation to distance and velocity, 'fast and slow'. Ways to help the child locate events in time are discussed further in Chapter 7.

Feuerstein suggests an understanding of the sequential nature of time and events can be developed through mathematical problems such as:

> A stork flew from Toronto to New York City. On the first day it flew a distance of 15 miles.
> On the second day it flew at the same speed yet covered a distance of 22 miles. Explain.[16]

Consider what temporal problems you could pose for your children to consider that derive from shared everyday experience.

Numerical progressions

Children may fail to identify relationships between seemingly unconnected events simply because they have not been taught to search systematically for underlying patterns and principles of organisation. To cite one of Feuerstein's examples, the pot that was once full of water is now empty. What might the cause/effect relationship be between these two states of affairs? Children should be encouraged to look for laws and relationships linking instances that at first sight may seem to have no connection.

By generating rules based on past observations the child learns that she is able to predict future outcomes, and so changes from a passive recipient to an active generator of information. In mathematical terms this can include identifying a pattern in a series of shapes, recognising the changes that occur from one item to the next or seeing principles manifest in patterns of numbers. For example, look at the following series, identify a pattern and predict what comes next: 1, 3, 6, 10, 15 —.

Instructions

Through following instructions children are encouraged to plan, to decode information and to translate it into action. Carrying out instructions can help in the reduction of egocentricity, by getting the child to consider the viewpoint of the instructor. Impulsiveness will need to be restrained and action deferred until the relevant information has been gathered and processed. Children will need to infer, to rely on partial cues, to clarify ambiguities and to take decisions. Games, model making kits and craftwork of many kinds give opportunities for children to decode and follow instructions. Sometimes these instructions will provide what Chomsky calls 'degraded information', poorly presented, unclear or inadequate instructions. Ask the child to analyse given sets of instructions: are they clear, well-ordered, complete? Get them to devise their own rules for games, recipes or craft instructions, then share and quality-test.

In Feuerstein's instrument the instructions often direct the student to draw various figures. For example:

> On a line draw a triangle, two squares and a circle, not according to size order. The squares are to be equal in size, the triangle is to be larger than the squares and smaller than the circle; and the largest figure is to be on the left side.[17]

Children can also be asked to give instructions to a partner, for example to draw the following diagrams (kept hidden from view).

Illustrations

As the child moves through life, he experiences, his eyes scan, illustrations of various kinds. Occasionally he may stop to ponder what the illustrated scene might mean, what the pictorial clues are conveying and what purposes the graphic artist might have had in mind. Feuerstein intersperses illustrations among the other exercises of IE. These items consist of cartoons and the child's task is to say what is going on in the scenes depicted and why the cartoons are funny (if they are funny). In one, a cleaner's broom handle tears a hole in a painting of an ocean scene, and a torrent of water pours forth.

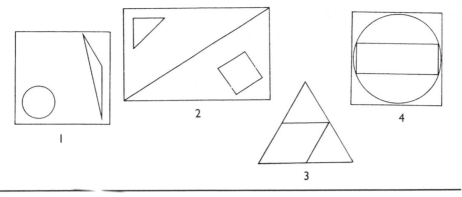

Figure 5.3

Children may go through life not drawing meaning from the graphic messages that surround them. To avoid information overload they may 'shut off', allowing themselves to take in only the superficial features of a given visual stimulus. Through mediation children can be helped to realise that to understand what one sees requires focusing attention, looking for clues, creating a meaning from the image. Illustrations are not random events, they serve purposes. What is the picture trying to say? What is its purpose? How would you express it?[18] Feuerstein has devised several other instruments that constitute a more advanced level of IE. These include:

- *Representational stencil design,* in which the student is asked to recreate a complex model design by choosing from a number of stencils, having to decide which to use and in what order to reproduce the design. The mediated use of visual puzzles such as jigsaws and tangrams (children can create their own) is of value for all ages.
- *Transitive relations* deals with inferences drawn from relationships that can be described as 'greater than', 'equal to' or 'less than'. For example, 'Adam likes maths more than history and history less than geography. Is it possible to know which Adam likes more, maths or geography?'[19] The question 'Is it possible to know?' is an important one when faced, as in most human problems, with incomplete information. The child faced with uncertainty should not feel helpless. Many matters can consciously be left undecided. The question then becomes 'What further information do we need?' 'What would help us decide?' '*Can* we know?' For example, Jane is taller than Ann. Mary is shorter than Jane. Is Mary taller or shorter than Ann?
- *Syllogisms* deal with formal propositional logic. One of the easier examples used by Feuerstein[20] is:
    No midgets are giants.
    Tom Thumb is a midget.
    Conclusion: _____ is not a _____.

Instrumental enrichment materials are relatively free from traditional school curriculum content. This is to help focus attention on the process of thinking rather than on the products. As intellectual puzzles many may seem to be of a trivial nature, similar to the traditional IQ test. The tasks themselves are relatively unimportant; their purpose is merely to provide a basis for mediated learning experiences through which the students develop their cognitive abilities. The teacher provides groundwork for the paper and pencil exercises through the introductory discussion. This usually lasts for no more than 10 minutes and includes a discussion of the thinking skills required for the exercise. The lesson concludes with a brief summary restating the points made in the introduction and evaluating the extent to which goals have been achieved. Over time the students take on the responsibility for summarising the lesson.

Instrumental enrichment lessons are generally intended for children who are 11 years old and over, functioning at below their average age level. Many lessons can be drawn from Feuerstein's approach that could usefully be adapted for younger children and more able children. Higher order thinking skills are based on a series of fundamental processes, which need developing in children of all abilities.

All children face stumbling blocks on the road to learning, which may hold up their ability to tackle a problem. Such stumbling blocks may be due to a number of factors:

- *Content* – the subject matter may be unfamiliar, they may not have the necessary knowledge. Mediated support may help them get over this 'hump'.
- *Mode* – the mode of presentation may 'throw' the child, whether it be verbal, pictorial, diagrammatic, symbolic. Offer the child a wide range of modes.
- *Procedures* – the child may be deficient in the specific cognitive skills or operations necessary for the information to be processed. The child may need to have practised, or the teacher may need to recall to the child's mind, the component processes involved in the task.
- *Phase of problem* – the child may ignore a crucial stage in the learning experience, for example through impulsiveness. He may have ignored the need for more input, for defining the problem, for working things through (elaboration) or for clearly expressing the results (output). The teacher may need to mediate a planful approach to the task.
- *Complexity* – sometimes the sheer detail of information overwhelms the child and help may be needed, to show how complex tasks can be handled successfully by breaking information down into small steps and manageable bits.
- *Abstraction* – as the child moves further away from concrete events she moves into more abstract realms of thinking. Children can often cope with quite complex tasks that are embedded in a familiar and objective world, but when removed from reality they find problems with encoding the task in symbolic form. They may well need to go back to concrete examples, or for the teacher to translate to and from natural and symbolic situations.
- *Efficiency* – many affective factors can influence the child's level of speed and accuracy in a task. Levels of anxiety and motivation play important roles in determining success. Reflective thinking in particular, needs time and children need to be encouraged to take time in selecting and adapting their strategies. 'Festina lente' (make haste slowly) should be a guiding principle for all teaching and learning.

Does the IE approach to cognitive development work? The evidence of research has shown 'that IE has a substantial effect, well justifying the time and expense of the programme, on pupils' metacognition: their ability to process fresh learning'.[21] An important part of the teacher's task is to encourage 'bridging', to apply the lessons previously learnt to new material.[22] However, 'the final step of showing that this effect can translate into school achievement' has not been conclusively demonstrated.[23]

There have been a number of attempts to extend the principles of Feuerstein's IE to a wider audience of teachers and pupils in mainstream schools. Two of the most successful of these programmes are the Somerset Thinking Skills Course[24] and the Oxfordshire Skills Programme.[25] Such programmes show that the principles of IE can be adapted and extended to a wider range of children than the retarded adolescent for whom they were originally intended. But do they provide a complete programme of development even for cognitively impaired children? Feuerstein's instruments provide well for basic geometrical, numerical and logical structures. Their literacy and linguistic content is not so high as in other thinking skills programmes. Much depends on the ways the exercises are mediated and on the bridging to other areas of learning. Long training periods for teachers are regarded by Feuerstein and his followers as necessary for effectively implementing the IE programme.

Feuerstein's instruments may be successful in developing logico-mathematical domains of intelligence but perhaps ignore other forms of intelligence. One of the reasons the IQ scores among Feuerstein's Moroccan immigrants were very low might have been the fact that they were faced with test problems of a logico-mathematical kind. They might have done better on tests that exercised other more practical forms of intelligence. In the 1930s the Russian psychologist Luria[26] found that the illiterate peasants of central Asia rejected formal tests of deductive reasoning but made intelligent judgements about facts of direct concern to them. Marcel Mauss, the French social anthropologist, observed Moroccan children carrying out skilful tasks, for example:

practising a trade at the age of 5 years – braiding and sewing with remarkable dexterity – delicate work which presupposes a very fine geometrical and arithmetical sense. The Moroccan child is a technician and starts work at an earlier age than do our children. On certain matters he reasons earlier and faster, although in a different way – i.e. manually – than do the children of our good bourgeois families.[27]

Feuerstein is surely right that, with suitable training we should be able to increase a child's powers of attention, judgement, reasoning and memory and thereby to improve her performance in all areas of the school curriculum. He is also right to stress the variability of human development. As an example he quotes the case of Rabbi Akiva, one of the most celebrated of Jewish wise men, who could not read until he was 40 years old. The progress of human beings, if it is not perfectible, is at any rate unpredictable. No one knows for sure what a child's potential might be. The processes that underlie an individual's performance are always capable of improved functioning. He is surely right to reject IQ scores as representing fixed levels of ability and to follow Vygotsky in focusing on the child's potential for achievement. Children especially are in a permanent state of becoming, and where that process will end, who can say? But if human beings are in a continual, if often imperceptible, state of change, then what of society? Is that not also in a state of development and change? Feuerstein lays great emphasis on the value of a cultural tradition. Following a tradition too rigidly can, however, lead to the stifling of a person's critical and creative abilities. A child may absorb all the skills of a closed society and not have the ability to judge or to question the values of that society. Individual cognitive skills may be enhanced and the power of logical thinking developed to a fine degree without necessarily affecting a child's judgement of moral, social or aesthetic questions. We may need other ways to open a child's mind to the deeper questions about society and human existence, not only to challenge the child but to get the child to challenge us and our culture. Perhaps there is something more important than the developing of cognitive skills, perhaps we can help even the youngest child to embark on a search for wisdom, the development of that child's own values and philosophy of life.

Summary

Children who fail to learn may be suffering from cognitive deficiencies or may lack the culturally transmitted tools of learning. Cognitive deficiencies can result in the child being a passive receiver of information, with poor self-image and prone to impulsivity. The mediation of others, usually adults, can help structure and give meaning to their experience. Such children need opportunities, what Feuerstein calls 'instruments' for reflective thinking. The instruments are a series of intellectual games that are content-free, such as drawing puzzles, that help children to be more observant, selective, planful, controlled, precise. Some children need specific enrichment activities to help overcome the blocks to learning.

6 Philosophy for children

The unexamined life is not worth living
    Socrates

A group of 6 year olds was discussing a story the teacher had told them about rabbits:

Teacher	Can animals think?
Child	Yes, they can talk.
Child	If they couldn't think they couldn't get away from their enemies.
Child	Like my guinea pigs hide under the sofa to get away from us.
Teacher	How do you know that they think?
Child	They've got brains, haven't they?
Child	If they didn't have brains they would die.
Child	They would just walk about without knowing what to do.
Child	They'd be up in heaven.
Child	They're not as clever as us, they've got littler brains.
Child	They talk to us in their animal language.
Child	Rabbits can't talk.
Child	They can in stories.
Child	Foxes can think. They catch rabbits and eat them.
Child	All animals can think but they're not as clever as we are.
Teacher	If all animals can think and rabbits are animals then all rabbits can think. Is that right?
Child	I know some rabbits who can't think.
Teacher	Which rabbits are they?
Child	Stuffed rabbits. I've got a stuffed rabbit at home. You can make it squeak.
Child	That's not a proper rabbit, it's been made.
Child	I've got a doll that can speak.
Teacher	Does it know what it is saying?
Child	Only when you turn it upside down. You can hear it.
Child	It doesn't know anything. It's not real like us.

Young children are born talkers. They chat, describe, question and argue for much of their time. Such talk may spur their thinking, getting them to reason, justify, seek causes, explain events, structure and make sense of their experience. Or their talking may involve minimal and repetitive responses, idle thoughtless chatter, the dull work of dull minds. How do we convert a child's low-level verbal responses into higher order thinking and talking? Do we need to?

A professor of philosophy at Columbia University, Matthew Lipman, became aware of the low level of thinking skills that students were bringing to the college. He decided that if the problem was to be dealt with effectively it would have to be tackled early, before thinking habits became entrenched. It was 1968, a time of student protest and unrest. As Lipman explained:

There was so much rigidity among both students and the university administration, so little communication, so little recourse to reason. I was beginning to have serious doubts about the value of teaching philosophy. It didn't seem to have any impact on what people did. I began to think that the problem I was seeing in the university couldn't be solved there, that thinking was something that had to be taught much earlier, so that by the time a student graduated from high school, skillful, independent thinking would have become a habit.[1]

If education is supposed to be about teaching young people to think, why does the educational system produce so many unthinking people? Lipman's answer is that we do not sufficiently encourage the child to think for himself, to form independent judgements, to be proud of his personal insights, to be proud of having a point of view he can call his own, to be pleased with his prowess in reasoning.[2]

We should begin early, says Lipman, as soon as the child enters school, and make improving thinking an aim that permeates every area of learning. Further than this, children should be offered a course of study in thinking itself.

How is thinking to be taught? Thinking about thinking for Lipman involves the study of the individual skills of which thinking is composed. Lipman lists over 30 separate skills that children should learn.[3] A key skill and the first in Lipman's list is 'Formulating concepts precisely'. The philosopher Leibniz once said that 'our clear concepts are like islands which rise above the ocean of obscure ones'. For some children these islands can be few and far between. The classic question 'What do you mean by ... ?' can help clarify the ideas behind the words used. In applying a concept to a set of cases, children should be encouraged to identify examples that are clearly within the boundaries of a concept and those that fall outside the boundaries. Many of Lipman's discussion plans concentrate on borderline cases. He suggests, for example, the following questions to explore the concept of friendship:

- Do people have to be the same age to be friends?
- Can two people be friends and still not like each other very much?
- Is it ever possible for friends to lie to one another?

(See below for more questions on the concept of friendship).

The aim is for children to become 'more thoughtful, more reflective, more considerate and more reasonable individuals'. Most of these skills and the dispositions to use them are learned best through language, by creating a 'community of enquiry', where children engage in dialogue as a cooperative venture.

Dialogue

Ever since the time of Socrates the search for wisdom has meant dialogue. Philosophy (Greek for 'to love wisdom') begins with wonder and seeks answers through dialogue to the most fundamental questions about life. Children, too, can engage in talk about deep and puzzling questions. As Vygotsky[4] and others have shown, children are able to function at an intellectually higher level when in collaborative or cooperative situations. Lipman aims to enlist the child's social impulses and to use dialogue as a means to the development of thinking. But how is one to get children to engage in philosophical discussion?

Lipman decided that the best way to teach children to think was through stories. He therefore wrote a short children's novel called *Harry Stottlemeier's Discovery* for this purpose⁵ (the title is a play on the name Aristotle). The story begins with Harry, a thoughtful boy, making a mistake in class one day. He hears his teacher explain that all planets revolve around the sun. Then, lost in a daydream, he misses the explanation about comets, which also revolve around the sun. The teacher asks him, 'What has a long tail, and revolves about the sun once every 77 years?' The correct answer is Halley's comet but since Harry has not been listening he doesn't know this. Remembering that all planets revolve round the sun, Harry concludes that this too must be a planet. The class laughs when he gives the wrong answer, for they have heard their teacher explain that comets travel round the sun but are not planets.

Harry is saved by the bell and when walking home tries to work out why his answer was wrong. He thinks to himself, 'All planets revolve about the sun, but not everything that revolves about the sun is a planet.' Suddenly Harry has an idea: a sentence can't be reversed. 'If you put the last part of a sentence first, it'll no longer be true'. He tries a few examples, 'All oaks are trees, but not all trees are oaks', 'All cucumbers are vegetables, but not all vegetables are cucumbers.' It's true that 'all planets revolve about the sun' but if you turn it round and say that 'all things that revolve about the sun are planets' then it's no longer true.

Harry is pleased with his discovery; then he meets his friend Lisa. As is the way with friends, she is quick to point out that Harry's rule does not always work. The sentence 'No eagles are lions', she says, can be reversed and still be true, 'No lions are eagles'. Logic is more complicated than Harry thinks. However he and Lisa soon discover a new rule, 'If a true sentence begins with the word no, then its reverse is also true. But if it begins with all, then its reverse is false.'

Later, Harry finds a practical use for his discovery. A neighbour, talking to his mother, suggests that Mrs Bates is a radical because radicals talk about how we should help the poor and Mrs Bates talks about helping the poor. This argument must be wrong, thinks Harry. It may be true that 'all radicals want to help the poor' but its reverse 'everyone who wants to help the poor is a radical' is not true.

Other characters in the story are introduced and more questions of logic are raised. Harry, Lisa and friends begin to think about thinking and to apply their discoveries to real-life situations, both outside and within the classroom. They come to realise the importance of defining their words in precise ways. Lisa is asked by her teacher to help think of a topic theme for the weekend homework. The teacher suggests writing about The Greatest Thing in the World. After reflecting for a moment Lisa replies 'Yiiich!'

> 'Yiiich?' repeated Mrs Halsey.
>
> 'I mean I wouldn't like to' said Lisa. 'Anyhow what do you mean greatest? Biggest or Most Important?'
>
> The teacher looks puzzled, then exclaims 'Oh, you're right! It could mean both things, couldn't it?'

What Lipman tries to demonstrate in story form is how children might behave in a genuine 'community of enquiry'. His characters discuss not only everyday problems to do with what words mean and how to use them but also such philosophical topics as the nature of thinking and the way minds work. Lisa says:

My mind . . . why it's like a world of its own. It's like my room. In my room I have my
Barbie dolls on a shelf, and sometimes I pick up one to play with and sometimes another.
And I do the same with my thoughts. I have my favourite thoughts. And I have others I
don't even want to think about.

'But thoughts aren't really real' Jill remarked, 'I mean they're not real like the things in
your room. My thought of Sandy isn't the real Sandy. The real Sandy is all full of fur. But
my thought of Sandy isn't furry at all!'[6]

The discussions between these characters and their discoveries may be unusual but
they are not unique. Ideas about the nature of thinking, mind, truth and the use of
words have been the subject of philosophical debate for centuries. But the famous
names of philosophy and their works are never mentioned in Lipman's books, nor do
standard philosophical terms appear. This is a deliberate policy, done 'so that children
can come to grips with ideas and not merely with labels'.[7] Lipman wants children to
think about the ideas that lie beneath the veil of words, to share and discuss issues of
common interest that arise.

If we want children to become reflective adults, Lipman argues, we must encourage
them to be reflective children. And how do you get children to be reflective? By
encouraging discussion, by getting them to talk things through. There is a common
misapprehension that it is thinking or reflection that generates the need to talk. More
often it is dialogue that generates reflection and a thoughtful response. An important
part of the Philosophy for Children approach is having thoughtful and often animated
discussions, often on subjects and in ways that were traditionally thought to be inap-
plicable to young children.

For reasons that go back to Plato the discussion of philosophical issues has been with-
held from the young. This reluctance to attempt philosophy with children is possibly
a product of an archaic view of education. Plato argued that children should be pro-
hibited from doing philosophy for their own protection. In Book 4 of *The Republic* he
argues that children should not be exposed to dialectical argument for 'it fills people
with indiscipline'. He gives an example of how philosophical dialogue might corrupt
young people:

What happens when he is confronted with the question, 'What do you mean by fair?' When
he gives the answer tradition has taught him, he is refuted in argument and when that has
happened many times and on many different grounds, he is driven to think that there's no
difference between fair and foul, and so on with all the other moral virtues, like right and
good, that he used to revere.[8]

One reason why Plato thinks children should be protected from philosophy is in
order to protect philosophy and adults from children.

You may have noticed how young men, after their first taste of argument, are always
contradicting people just for the fun of it ... like puppies who love to pull and tear at anyone
within reach ... so when they have proved a lot of people wrong, often themselves, they soon
slip into the belief that nothing they believed before was true; with the result that they
discredit themselves and the whole business of philosophy in the eyes of the world.[9]

It may be that what Plato was condemning was not the practice of philosophy with
children as such but the reduction of philosophy to logical inquisition and empty rheto-
ric. Certainly in earlier dialogues Socrates talks to young and old alike. Perhaps we

should remember Plato's admonition that 'you must be very careful how you introduce them to such discussions'.[10] Lipman's Philosophy for Children programme introduces children to philosophical issues through the discussion of a chosen passage of a book, such as *Harry Stottlemeier's Discovery*, which the children have read. The teacher generates discussion by asking the children what they wish to discuss about the passage and by prompting them in a Socratic manner with open-ended questions. What emerges may be discussion about the use and meaning of words (children can be fascinated by logical rules) but it is more likely to revolve around the perennial questions that interest people of any age. Is it true? Is it real? Is it right? Is it fair? Who are friends? Why are things like they are?

When children talk about questions such as these, they begin to learn that it is not enough just to have an opinion. You need to have reasons to justify your views. You must be clear to convey meaning in what you say. You must make distinctions, come up with examples, be prepared for counter-arguments and develop thoughts to their logical conclusion. Children learn through this process to listen to their peers and to respect other points of view. A tolerance of the opinions of others grows alongside the realisation that there are no definitive answers, no absolute rights and wrongs, to many philosophical questions. They learn to question dogmatism, to challenge assumptions, to examine arguments. Plato is right to argue that, if any belief is as defensible as any other or if argumentative victory determines what is right, then we should want none of it. But it should be possible to introduce philosophy to children in another way through cooperative discussions. Dialogue is not a battle with winners and losers but is a way of enquiry into what is right, true and of value, in partnership with others.

A group of 9 year olds was discussing what is real and what isn't real. Is time real? What about dreams? The discussion was animated, moving quickly from child to child. 'When you're asleep you're out of it, you're not aware of anything at all, so nothing is real to you,' said Tina, 'not even yourself.' 'Yes,' added Gillian, 'something is only real while you see or think of it.' Jena, however, thought otherwise. 'If someone walks into your room and watches you sleeping, you're real to that person, so you must still be real.' 'Besides,' said Marc, 'while you sleep your mind is always working, even when you're not aware of it, and you dream while you're sleeping too.' Someone else remarked that dreams aren't real. Marc replied, 'Even if dreams aren't real, the fact that you dream them is.'[11]

In a class of 10 year olds, discussion of what is real and not real was equally fast moving, orchestrated where necessary by the teacher.

Teacher	What about a reflection in the mirror. Is that real?
Andrew	Only when you are looking in the mirror.
Robert	Yes, something is only real if you know it's there.
Louise	But a reflection is still there even if I am not looking into it.
Rupert	Not if it is a totally black room or room that is all one colour, like all yellows.
Louise	Yes, I can still imagine a reflection even if I am not looking in a mirror, so it must be real. A reflection is something that doesn't seem to be real but is real.[12]

As discussion continued, the ideas bounced back and forth from mirrors to artificial flowers, to photographs, coming to no definite conclusion but involving all who wished to contribute in a cooperative search for understanding.

A class of 7 year olds was involved in discussing whether Superman was real or not. For half an hour the conversation flowed. Superman couldn't be real because no real person could see through things the way Superman can. Different viewpoints produced fresh arguments. Superman was real in people's minds and people's minds are real. What are real things like? How could you tell if something was not real? Where would Superman fit between these two categories? Finally the children decided that Superman 'fell somewhere between the two categories'.[13] What children often find difficult at first is to understand that the right or wrong answer is not going to be given to them but is something they must decide on for themselves. Once they catch on, however, the concept can be liberating. They are free to think on their own.

Productive discussion does not, of course, just happen. There are practical problems to face. Children often find it difficult to take turns in debate. It is not always easy to persuade them to follow a line of argument through or, once they have developed their own idea, to listen to the ideas of others. The success of a discussion depends on the teacher's skill in facilitating dialogue. How do we foster effective discussion?

Running a discussion

First establish a suitable physical environment. Discussion can flourish in many different settings. If it is to take place in a classroom during the school day we face a built-in paradox. Discussion is most worthwhile when each of the participants has a desire to pursue it. But class activities are usually mapped out in advance by the teacher. Children will be involved whether they want to or not. If it is left as an option, many children, not knowing what the discussion was or could be, would tend to choose not to be involved. What the teacher can do is to try to make the session as interesting and fruitful as possible and to be aware of factors that can influence the success or failure of the discussion.[14]

Physical environment is important in several ways. A minimal requirement is that everyone should be able to hear each other's voices without the need for shouting or straining. On a surprising number of occasions teachers try to battle through bumps, crashes, machine noise, obtrusive music and the sounds of uproar coming from adjacent places. Even with the door shut, sounds of talking and moving desks can travel from room to room, diverting the concentration of all. Be prepared to put off your discussion to a quieter time.

Dialogue is best achieved in a stress-free setting. Noise can be one cause of stress and so can interruption. A knock on the door, a ringing bell or a stranger entering the room can all sabotage the flow of discussion. If it happens at a crucial or absorbing moment the thread can be broken and continuity destroyed. One way to avoid this is to pin a notice on the door saying, for example 'Discussion in progress. Please don't interrupt' and to make sure that others understand and respect the meaning of the message.

Another cause of unintended interruption may be the activities of children in the room not engaged in the discussion. The disadvantages are obvious: if other children are talking or making a noise it distracts those involved in discussion; if the other children are working silently they in turn may be distracted by the group talking. If the class is regarded as a community of enquiry, there is a strong argument for involving all the children in the discussion, either as a class activity or in groups.

One way to avoid disturbance indoors is to take the group outside, if the weather is suitable. In ancient Greece they created 'philosophers' gardens' for just such purposes. Any open space may do – corner of the playground, quiet area in a public park, the school garden or a rooftop. Once a suitable environment has been found, how should the group be arranged?

In a philosophical discussion the views of all participants, including the teacher or leader, are equally valuable and worthy of consideration. This equality should be reflected in the setting or seating arrangements of the group. A circle would seem the best option but a rigidly defined circle has one disadvantage: it leaves a large empty space in the middle (prompting perhaps an expectation of performance – bring on the clowns!). A formal circle imparts a serious atmosphere but it may seem rather regimented (each in their preordained place) and inhibit the free flow of ideas. Every class varies in its character and reactions to situations. The ideal is to achieve a sense of purpose in comfortable surroundings and there is no one seating arrangement that will suit all circumstances.

Fruitful discussion can take place in formal seating arrangements, for example, children in rows facing the front, or informally, for example all sitting in a group on the floor. Teachers need to decide what seating arrangement is best for their own class and be prepared to experiment with different methods. Whatever method is adopted it should facilitate and be productive of dialogue between children as well as between teacher and child.

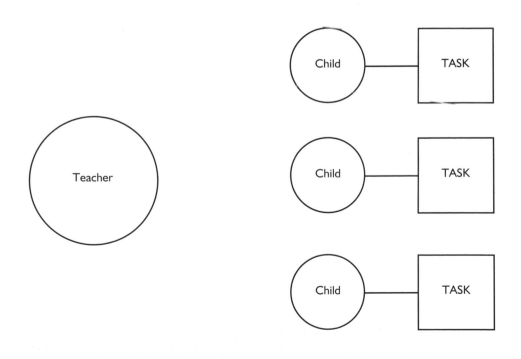

Figure 6.1 Individual task structure, where each child is engaged in a task, monitored by the teacher, who might move from child to child discussing, diagnosing and assisting.

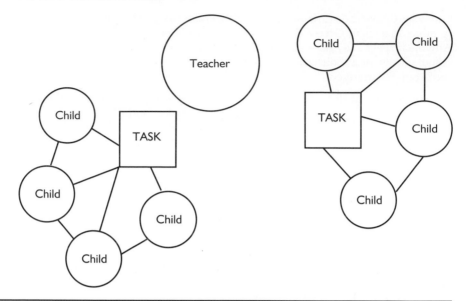

Figure 6.2 Group task structure, where small groups are set up, possibly to provide feedback to the larger group later.

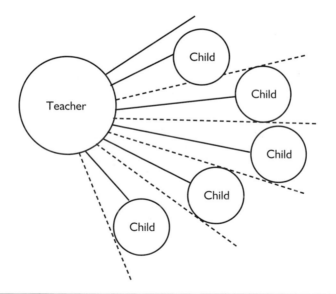

Figure 6.3 Tutorial structure is designed for the teacher to provide individual help to individual group members.

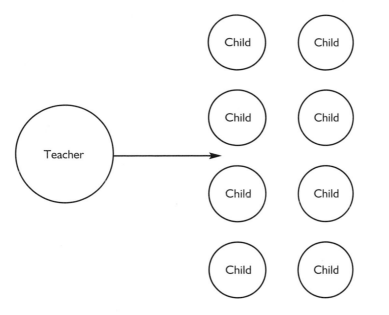

Figure 6.4 Didactic structure, typically organised for class teaching and used generally to inform, direct, instruct, report, explain, present or review.

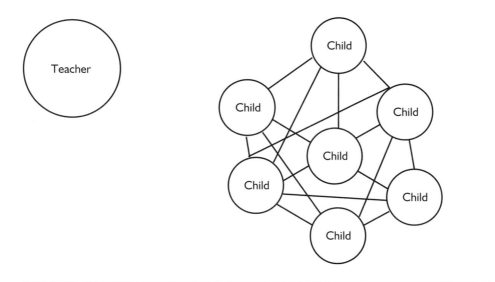

Figure 6.5 Conference structure allows free discussion or conferencing between children, an opportunity for them to discuss something of interest.

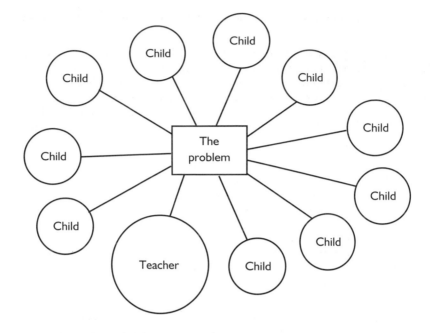

Figure 6.6 Class meeting structure to discuss or brainstorm a problem or topic, gathering and sharing ideas, with the teacher as participant rather than leader.

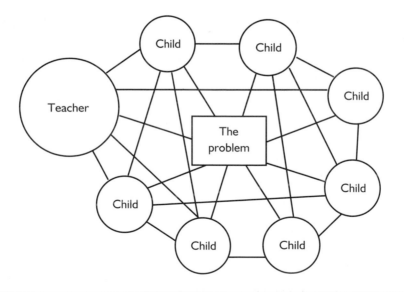

Figure 6.7 Socratic structure, a process approach where the teacher becomes the facilitator of investigation, aimed at encouraging children to discuss, listen, clarify and justify their thinking.

Within the physical setting certain rules may need to be agreed before discussion takes place.

Why are rules necessary for discussion? This may be a question to ask the children. If children are given freedom to talk, why have rules that will restrict that freedom? The golden rule is, of course, that one's own freedom should not interfere with the freedom of others. Individuals within a democratic community have equal rights. A child who talks all the time denies the rights of others to be heard. Each person should be allowed an equal chance to speak and to put forward their own point of view and if we wish to be listened to then we should listen to others.

There is no point in giving a point of view unless someone is listening. Few of us are capable of listening to more than one person at a time so another basic rule should be, only one person to speak at a time. Listening implies not only hearing the words but paying attention to the meaning of what is being said. This is not a natural thing for children to do. School is typically a place where children learn to listen to the teacher but not to each other. The skills of listening need to be practised. The ideal discussion, in which everyone listens to the person speaking then each by mutual consent is allowed to reply, is rare among adults, let alone children. It works best when certain ground-rules for discussion are followed. Which rules are best and who should set them?

To prevent problems and ensure fair chances for all, it is usually the teacher (or leader) who selects the person to speak. The pattern is often as follows:

- teacher asks a question
- several hands go up
- teacher selects a child to answer
- while child is speaking several hands remain raised, ready to answer the original question.

The result of this can be that those with their hands up are not listening to the child who is speaking. Even if they are following what is being said their chief concern remains with the point they have in mind. What occurs then may be a series of disconnected answers, with little chance of real dialogue. The general admonition 'Everyone must listen' is not as effective as a particular rule, such as 'no hand up while someone is speaking'.

Listening is hard work: it requires self-discipline. Children are naturally impatient. They want to be heard and dislike having to wait for their turn to speak. Point out to them that they do not have to wait to listen, that listening is an important part of discussing, that if they listen to others then they will be listened to. Other rules of the discussion game could include provision for everyone who wants to contribute being able to have a turn, that remarks should be relevant to the question being discussed, or that no one should interrupt a speaker. It may also be necessary to agree a rule about general discipline matters. What do you do if a child continually sabotages the discussion by disruptive behaviour? This is clearly unfair on the others. One strategy might be to ask the child to sit outside the group to listen, or to undertake some other work for a short period of time. Offer the child the opportunity to re-enter the group after a period of 'time out', if the child so wishes.

Whatever rules are adopted the chances of them being followed will be much greater if the children themselves have been involved in their formulation. It may be better to begin with no formal rules at all and then, when the need becomes apparent, to allow time for them to be discussed. Another approach would be to transfer the rules children employ in small-group discussion to the larger group.

In one class of 7–8 year olds[15] the teacher found that getting the children to contribute to whole-class discussions was no problem but being an active listener was much harder. The children had not developed the art of critical listening. They found it difficult to listen to each other, to understand what was meant, to recognise the implications, to discriminate between what they agreed with and what they didn't and finally to offer constructive and critical comment in a way thatthe recipient would find easy to consider. The teacher, together with the children, decided to establish a 'code of conduct' to put in use when they were discussing the stories they were writing. The rules that emerged were as follows:

- listen carefully and follow the story
- think of two good things to say
- ask if something wasn't very clear to you
- suggest something which you think might make it better.

Having established successful strategies for 'critical listening' for use in the children's writing groups, the teacher sought to extend the approach to discussions in general. The class was asked to suggest the criteria for a good discussion. The children decided to write them in the order they thought would happen during a discussion. Their final list was as follows:

- explain well
- listen to other people
- take turns to talk
- wait until the other person finishes
- say things that help other people
- keep to the subject
- share ideas with the rest of the group
- give suggestions and ideas
- be careful how you say things so that other people won't get upset
- ask each other questions so as to make things clear
- sort out and test ideas
- choose one idea together
- try not to be bossy in the group.

Having decided the aims of what they ought to do in a discussion, the children moved on to thinking how best to achieve those aims in practice. How could they get better at discussing things? In pairs the children tried to brainstorm some tips that would help others. Each idea was written on to card and all tips relating to a particular criterion were collected into a zip-bag. These then became the focus for further class discussion. Many useful strategies were suggested, for example:

To explain well

- wait till everybody is listening
- make things clear
- ask a friend for advice
- make notes to help you to remember
- put your ideas in order
- speak well so other people can hear
- choose your words carefully so others can understand.

To listen to others

- ask someone to talk to you
- try to understand what they say
- remember what they say
- look at the person who is speaking
- make sure everyone is quiet.

Developing discussion skills in children is a slow and gradual process. Identifying the skills needed is an important first step both for teacher and child. If the search for rules and strategies is shared it is likely that individuals involved will be more aware of their own needs and the needs of others. This awareness may extend to activities outside the classroom. For example, just after playtime a child from the class mentioned above was heard to remark, 'I know why we didn't have a good game together . . . I didn't listen to what the others wanted.'

Children need to learn to listen to each other. Equally important is for teachers to become sympathetic listeners. The traditional teacher–pupil role tends to reinforce the idea that it is the teacher who talks and the pupils who pay attention. The thoughtful teacher needs to pay close attention to what the children say. This means responding to what children are saying rather than what you think they mean. Achieving this will bring certain benefits such as a clearer idea of what children are actually thinking (and if they are thinking). You will be placed in a better position to ask a follow-up question or to make a relevant response. You will be demonstrating the value placed on what the child has to communicate. And you will be modelling what you hope the child will become, an active listener. But how do we improve the quality of our listening?

The following SOLVER[16] checklist offers some ways to check out your 'attending behaviour' and possible starting points for self-appraisal:

S *Seating* – do the seating arrangements create blocks to effective communication, for example do I sit behind a desk, do I turn away from children or sit at an awkward angle? My aim should be to face directly towards the children with no barriers between us.

O *Openness* – do I create 'body barriers', for example by folding my arms, crossing my legs or tensing my body, or is my posture open, relaxed and welcoming?

L *Listening* – am I learning as I listen? Do I lean forward a little, concentrate on

what is being said and show I am alert and listening? Or do I create blocks by
letting my attention wander, by being unresponsive and showing boredom?

V *Verbal cues* – do I encourage and support the child talking by offering verbal cues
that say I want to hear more, such as grunts of approval, words of interest
('really?') and 'door openers' such as 'what happened next?'

E *Eye contact* – do I give full eye contact to children who talk to me or when I talk
to them? does my eye contact encourage the child to 'open up' in discussion or
do I look past them or through them?

R *Response* – do I respond when a child speaks to me? What messages do I convey?
Am I a relaxed and friendly person to whom children will talk openly or do I
seem distant, rigid, forbidding?

Carl Rogers[17] refers to the quality of presence that is so vital for sympathetic listening. Am
I present, fully attending, or has my mind moved on to something else? Am I engaged in
the process, or do I rush on unheedingly to the next question? Dialogue that involves
organising one's thoughts, communicating and responding takes time. How much time
do I spend listening to the children and how much talking? Do I dominate the talk, or do
I allow time for the children to fully explore the elements that interest them?

My attending behaviour may be exemplary but is it evenly shared? Do all children get an
equal share of my time or do I allow some children to dominate? Am I listening only for
what I want to hear or do I take an active interest in a variety of responses? Am I looking
for the 'right answer' or for evidence of good thinking? What kind of feedback do I give
that shows I have been really listening and thus encouraging the continuation of talk?

There are certain discussion-leading techniques[18] thatwill help provide the positive
feedback to sustain children's talk:

- ask what other children think
- encourage difference of opinion
- be ready to allow the group to continue discussion without your intervention.

Above all, what materials and activities can provide good starting points for discussion?[19]

Starting points for discussion

Professor Matthew Lipman has produced a comprehensive programme of materials,
published by the Institute for the Advancement of Philosophy for Children (IAPC)[20] at
Montclair College, intended to aid the development of philosophical discussion in the
classroom. Each session takes the form of an enquiry into one or more issues that arise
from reading a given text. The IAPC curriculum comprises the following published
materials (see Table 6.1).

Normally each Philosophy for Children session starts by reading or re-reading part of
the story. The section should be long enough to allow the group some choice between
possible topics (usually between half a page and three pages). The group can take turns
in reading the passage (with children who do not want to read simply saying 'pass') or
the teacher can read while the rest follow. Having read through the passage the teacher
finds out what interested the class by asking a general question like 'What did you find
interesting/puzzling (etc.)?' Children choose their own points of interest from the

passage. If their response is slow, invite them to look over what was read again to see if something curious may have escaped their notice. The children's questions can be written on a display board as a visual record of the group's response to the particular passage. Writing up the child's name next to her contribution shows that every individual suggestion is valued. If a child finds difficulty in formulating her question, ask others in the group what issue they think she is trying to raise. Encourage the child to formulate a question using her own words rather than relying on the teacher's or using abbreviated quotations from the text.

Table 6.1 Philosophy for Children Programme (IAPC)

Age (years)	Grade	Children's novel	Instructional manual	Philosophical area	Educational area
5–7	K–2	Elfie	Getting our thoughts together	Reasoning and thinking	Exploring experience
7/8	2–3	Kio and Gus	Wondering at the world	Philosophy of nature	Environmental education
8/9	3–4	Pixie	Looking for meaning	Philosophy of language	Language and arts
10/11	5–6	Harry	Philosophical inquiry	Epistemology and logic	Thinking skills
12/13	7–8	Lisa	Ethical inquiry	Philosophy of value	Moral education
14/15	9–10	Suki	Writing: how and why	Philosophy of art	Writing and literature
16+	11–12	Mark	Social inquiry	Social philosophy	Social studies

Choose from the list an agreed topic to form the basis for discussion. The teacher aims to be the neutral chair of discussion,[21] a facilitator and manager of the process. However the teacher is required, 'albeit in a subtle manner relentlessly to "feed" rationality into the discussion'.[22] Within a framework of neutrality the teacher should:

- encourage children to build on one another's ideas
- try to get children to see the implications of what they say
- try to make children aware of their own assumptions
- encourage them to find reasons to justify their beliefs.

Texts for discussion can come from many sources. Here a teacher has chosen a passage from *Through the Looking Glass* (Chapter 5) to stimulate philosophical discussion with a class of 9–10-year-olds. A copy of the following excerpt (with line numbers) was given to each child:

'I wish I could manage to be glad!' the Queen said. 'Only I never can remember the rule. You must be very happy, living in this wood, and being glad whenever you like!'

'Only it is so very lonely here!' Alice said in a melancholy voice; and, at the
5   thought of her loneliness, two large tears came rolling down her cheeks.

'Oh don't go on like that!' cried the poor Queen, wringing her hands in despair. 'Consider what a great girl you are. Consider what a long way you've come to-day. Consider what o'clock it is. Consider anything, only don't cry!'

10   Alice could not help laughing at this, even in the midst of her tears. 'Can you keep from crying by considering things?' she asked.
        'That's the way it's done', the Queen said with great decision: 'nobody can do two things at once, you know. Let's consider your age to begin with – how old are you?'
        'I'm seven and a half, exactly.'
15   'You needn't say "exactually"', the Queen remarked. 'I can believe it without that. Now I'll give you something to believe. I'm just one hundred and one, five months and a day.'
        'I can't believe that!' said Alice.
        'Can't you?' the Queen said in a pitying tone. 'Try again: draw a long
20   breath, and shut your eyes.'
        Alice laughed. 'There's no use trying,' she said: 'one can't believe impossible things.'
        'I dare say you haven't had much practice', said the Queen. 'When I was your age I always did it for half-an-hour a day. Why, sometimes I've believed as
25   many as six impossible things before breakfast....'

The children were asked to choose something in the passage that puzzled or inter-ested them. After some initial hesitation one child suggested the phrase 'nobody can do two things at once'. 'Can you think of a good question about that?' asked the teacher, 'Can you do two things at once?' The question was written on the board with the name of the child. Several other suggestions came, each turned into a ques-tion, including:

Is it possible to live to be one hundred and one?
Can you believe impossible things?
What does 'wringing her hands' mean?
How can you be glad whenever you like?
Why do people cry?

The children were then asked to choose one of the questions to start the discussion. If necessary they would have voted on this but there was general agreement to try the question suggested first and to continue in the given order. During the discus-sions that followed the teacher was ready with key questions when needed, to extend the discussion, such as 'Is it possible to live to 200?' 'Have you a reason?' 'What do you mean by *possible*?' The discussion about wringing her hands was extended by the teacher to other forms of non-verbal communication: 'Why do we sometimes say things without using language?' The question about 'being glad whenever you like' led on to 'Can you choose to be glad, angry, sad?' 'Are there some things you can't choose to do?' After discussing the nature of crying, 'Can you decide not to cry?' 'Can you cry when you are happy?' 'Is crying wrong for boys?' The children were keen for the teacher to choose a topic. Prepared for this possibility the teacher chose 'I dare say you haven't had much practice', framing the question 'what things can be improved by practice?' and asking during the following discussion, 'can thinking be improved by practice?' By the end of this session the children's verdict was a resounding 'yes'.

Some matters of perennial concern include the following topics.

I Fairness

A young child was overheard remarking in the playground, 'In this game cheating is allowed.' The concept of fairness is not restricted to games. From the moment children start to play with brothers and sisters or friends they are aware of what is 'fair' or 'unfair'. Is it fair that Paul should stay up later than Sue just because he is older? Should Amy have more because she is bigger? How do we decide what is fair?

Piaget[23] pioneered the study of children's moral reasoning by telling children a story involving moral conflict and asking them what the characters should do and why. Examples of his stories are as follows:

A A little boy called John was in his room when he was called to dinner. He went into the dining room. But behind the door there was a chair and on the chair there was a tray with 15 cups on it. John couldn't have known that it was behind the door. He went in, the door knocked against the tray, and the 15 cups all got broken.

B Once there was a little boy whose name was Henry. One day when his mother was out he tried to get some jam out of the cupboard. He climbed up on to the chair and stretched out his arm. But the jam was too high up and he couldn't reach it. While he was trying to get it he knocked over a cup. The cup fell down and broke.

About each of these pairs of stories we ask two questions:

Are these children equally guilty?
Which of the two is the naughtlest and why?

It goes without saying that each of these questions is the occasion for a conversation more or less elaborate according to the child's reaction.

The link between morality and reasoning was further developed by Kohlberg,[24] who suggested that there are six stages of moral judgement. As with Piaget, children were told stories involving a moral dilemma and invited to comment on what should happen. This is his best known story problem.

> In Europe a woman was near death from a kind of cancer. There was one drug that the doctors thought might save her. It was a form of radium that a druggist in the same town had recently discovered. The drug was expensive to make but the druggist was charging 100 times as much as the drug cost him to make. He paid $20 for the radium and charged $2000 for a small dose of the drug. The sick woman's husband, Heinz, went to everyone he knew to borrow the money, but he could get together only about $1000, half what he needed. He told the druggist that his wife was dying and asked him to sell it cheaper or let him pay later. But the druggist said 'No, I've discovered the drug and I'm going to make money from it'. So Heinz gets desperate and considers breaking into the man's store to steal the drug for his wife.
>
> Should he? What should he do?

The belief that morality and reasoning are linked has its roots in Western philosophy, as does the linking of fairness with justice. John Rawls in his *A Theory of Justice*[25] follows the work of Piaget and Kohlberg in claiming that there are three stages of moral development through which we all pass:

1 the morality of authority
2 the morality of association
3 the morality of principles.

According to Rawls the only rational stage is the third one. He assumes that children are incapable of this stage and therefore should not be considered moral agents or held responsible for what they do.

There are serious problems with the theory of 'stages', ignoring as they do the educational process. They ignore the distinction between ethical rules and ethical acts (the possession of a moral rule does not necessarily mean that the rule will be acted on in particular cases). Rules tend to elevate 'justice' as the primary moral principle, when other principles such as caring for others might be equally important. Children tend to give different rationales for different kinds of rule, such as moral (for example, you should not kill), conventional (for example, you should wear clothes at school) and practical rules (for example, you should clean your teeth every day). Becoming a moral agent is a process of developing for oneself criteria for distinguishing the better from the worse and expressing that judgement in action. What would *you* do in a particular situation? It was St Augustine[26] who said that human insecurity and unhappiness derive from a lack of criteria by which to judge the good from the bad, the genuine from the fake, the beautiful from the ugly. And he suggested that 'there is no better way of seeing the truth than by the method of question and answer'.

Questions of fairness arise in real life and also in story books. And they can be tackled at a young age. For example, in the story of Goldilocks and the Three Bears, Baby Bear had the smallest bowl because he was the smallest bear. Was that fair?

- Did Baby Bear need as much as the other bears. Why?
- Could he eat as much as the big Bears. Why?
- Did he deserve as much as the big bears. Why?
- Do you think it was fair for Baby Bear to have the smallest bowl? Why?
- What problems have you seen like the one in the story?

2 Freedom

Children learn from a young age that their freedom is circumscribed by rules and prohibitions. They soon find that some of these rules do not seem to be binding on adults, for example always telling the truth. There may be some ways in which they have more freedom than adults. What is it to be free? How free do your children feel themselves to be? What would happen if children were completely free to do what they like? Ask the children what school would be like without teachers. How would they organise themselves and their day? Would they need to make any rules?

Wherever children go they see evidence of the rules that structure our social lives. Some of these rules appear on signs and notices, No smoking, This way, Keep left, Stop, Don't walk on the grass, Exit, Do not feed the animals, Private, Keep clear, No entry. Other unwritten rules provide coherence and order, the rituals of mealtime, of greeting people, of waiting in queues. The rules of games, the rules of living a good life, the rules of safety, the rule of law. Help facilitate discussion of social conventions with questions such as:

- *What is a rule?* Clarifying the idea.
- *Do you ever make rules?* Seeking examples.
- *Why do you make them?* Analysing underlying purposes.
- *Are there good rules and bad rules?* Classify: establish criteria. What are the differences between good rules and bad rules? Ask the children for examples of each and compare them.
- *Is it all right sometimes to ignore rules?* Recognise reasons.
- *Why do people sometimes break rules?* Develop insight into egocentricity.
- *Have the children broken rules sometimes?* Why? What were the consequences?
- *What kinds of rules are there?* Distinguish ideas. What are their purposes, their advantages and disadvantages?[27]

A group of 9 year olds were discussing whether it was ever right to break rules. The children decided that some rules, like Do not walk on the grass, might be broken, others, like rules of games, should not. The teacher took the discussion a stage further by asking about rules that should not be broken:

> *'Do you need a rule that says you must not break the rules?' 'Yes.' 'Which comes first, the rules or the You must not break the rules rule?' 'You have to know the rules, otherwise you would not know which rules you shouldn't break.' 'But do you need a rule that says You must not break the rule that you must not break the rules?' 'Yes.' 'What do you need then?' 'You need a rule which says you must not break the rule of the You must not break the rule of the You must not break the rule rules.' 'And do these ever end?' 'No ... they go on for ever.'*

3 Friendship

Who are my real friends? Whom should I trust? Who are not my friends? These are some of the important questions facing children as they try to mould and make sense of social relationships. Despite the fact that these and other concepts are of vital importance to the emotional well-being of the child there may be no opportunity in a crowded school curriculum for children to be helped to think for themselves about such issues.[28]

The following are questions that can stimulate discussion on the topic of friends.[29]

- Can people talk together a lot and still not be friends?
- Can people hardly ever talk together and still be friends?
- Are there some people who always fight with their friends?
- Are there some people who never fight with their friends?
- Are there some people who have no friends?
- Are there people who have friends, even though they have hardly anything else?
- Do you trust your friends more than anything else?
- Are there some people whom you trust more than your friends?
- Is it possible to be afraid of a friend?
- What is the difference between friends and family?
- Are there animals you could be friends with and other animals you could never be a friend with?

The following is part of a discussion with 8 to 9 year olds in Brisbane, Australia, reported by Ann Margaret Sharp.[30]

> 'Have you ever had a friend you didn't like all the time?' I asked.
> 'Yes' the class answered in chorus. 'I have a friend,' Karen said, 'whom I fight with a lot. We fight and fight and then we make up.'
> 'What makes him your best friend?' I asked.
> 'It's a her not a him' Judy said.
> 'Oh, what makes her your best friend?'
> 'She's a lot like me' Judy said.
> 'Oh' said Carol 'my best friend is nothing like me. That's why I like her.'
> 'Why is that?' I asked.
> 'Because she does and is the way I would like to be. Not the way I am. And I feel good when I'm around her.'

The discussion finished with the class recording eight criteria of friendship on the board, with at least one counter-example for each criterion. The children had moved towards clarifying an important concept in a systematic (critical) and imaginative (creative) way.

4 Truth

Children are taught from an early age to be truthful. They soon become aware, however, that others, notably adults, do not follow the same precept. In their everyday lives children are frequently faced with the dilemma of whether to tell the truth or not. They may have been told what they should do but they have not considered or worked out for themselves the 'whys' and 'wherefores' of truth telling. For example:

- What is good about telling the truth?
- Why is it wrong to tell lies?
- Is lying always wrong?
- What is a white lie?
- Are some lies worse than others?
- Have you ever told a lie? Can you remember why?
- Has anyone lied to you? How did you feel about it?

Often the best way to introduce discussion is through consideration of a story. The following is an excerpt from *The Adventures of Tom Sawyer* by Mark Twain and part of a discussion with 7 to 8 year olds that was prompted by it:

(The teacher's book has been torn. Tom knows that his friend Becky Thatcher was responsible. The teacher is determined to discover the culprit and punish him or her severely.)

> 'Who tore this book?'
> There was not a sound. One could have heard a pin drop. The stillness continued; the master searched face after face for signs of guilt. 'Benjamin Rodgers, did you tear this book?'
> A denial. Another pause.
> 'Joseph Harper, did you?'
> Another denial. Tom's uneasiness grew more and more intense under the slow torture of these proceedings. The master scanned the ranks of boys, considered a while, then turned to the girls:

'Amy Lawrence?'
A shake of the head.
'Gracie Miller?'
The same sign.
'Susan Harper, did you do this?'
Another negative. The next girl was Becky Thatcher. Tom was trembling from head to foot
with excitement, and a sense of the hopelessness of the situation.
'Rebecca Thatcher' – Tom glanced at her face; it was white with terror – 'did you tear – no
look me in the face' – (her hands rose in appeal) – 'did you tear this book?'
A thought shot like lightning through Tom's brain. He sprang to his feet and shouted:
'I done it!'

Teacher	Was Tom right to tell a lie? What do you think?
Child 1	Maybe.... I think he should have if he loved her that much.
Child 2	If he didn't love her he shouldn't ... or wouldn't.
Child 1	I'm not sure if it was right or wrong. I wouldn't have done it ... except for my wife.
Child 2	Lying's not wrong when it's being kind ....
Teacher	Does being kind make it right?
Child 2	When it's being loyal.
Child 1	I meant that.
Child 3	You do things for your friends and family that you wouldn't do for other people.
Teacher	You mean because they're special you should behave differently towards them?
Child 3	Yes ... in a way. They'd do the same for you.
Teacher	Do you think Becky Thatcher would do the same for Tom?
Child	She would if she loved him.
Child 2	I bet she wouldn't ... she might not love him.
Child 1	It's a kind of test.

5 Knowledge

How do you know when something is true?

A nursery class had just planted lettuce seeds when Eddie asked '... how do we know it's
really lettuce?' The teacher replied, 'The label says Lettuce'. 'What,' asked Eddie, 'if it's
really tomatoes?'

Gareth Matthews[31] took this as a starting point with a class of 8 to 11 year olds. He
bought two packets of seeds, one lettuce, one carrot, and passed them round the class
in clear plastic envelopes. What would be a sufficient condition to say, 'I know that
these are lettuce seeds?' The discussion that followed revealed a difference between
being certain (real knowledge) and having a strong belief (more-or-less knowing). The
children's discussion reflected the centuries old dispute in the field of philosophy
known as epistemology (the theory of knowledge) about what are the necessary and
sufficient conditions of knowledge. Can there be real knowledge where there is even
the possibility of being mistaken?

Another problematical area of much fascination to children is the world of dreams. It
fascinated the ancient Chinese philosopher Chuang Tzu, who one day dreamed he was

a butterfly and wondered if perhaps he was a butterfly dreaming he was a man. Centuries later St Augustine described a dream in which he tried to convince a man that the man was merely a figment of the dream. In Lewis Carroll's *Through the Looking Glass* Tweedledum suggests that Alice, because she is in a dream, doesn't cry real tears. Tim, aged six, posed the question 'Daddy how can we be sure that everything is not a dream?' Tim's father, temporarily stumped, gave the ideal open-ended reply, he asked Tim how he thought he would tell. After a pause Tim answered, 'Well I don't think everything is a dream, because in a dream people wouldn't go round asking if it was a dream.'[32] A piece of philosophical reasoning in a young child that the ancient philosophers would have been proud of.

Children also love to discuss marginal cases. Is Frankenstein a robot or a human? If a single drop of rain falls is it raining? Is a dog with a wet nose a wet dog? There are differences in degree that can be brought out in discussion (for example, we are all of different heights) and differences of kind (people of the same height may be different weights). Is it the same soup if it's sold in different cans? One of the values of philosophic enquiry of this kind is that it is a challenge to rigid thinking, the hardening of the mental categories, remaining stuck in the same narrow groove of thought.

Are you the same person you were when you were born? If you lost an arm would you be the same person? If you could change pieces of your body, how much could you change and still be you? In the Wizard of Oz the Tin Woodman had all his parts changed and the Scarecrow had no brain. If you and your friend swopped brains, who would you be? Children can be introduced to issues that get to the very stuff of the human mind and of the human identity. They are receptive to new ideas, new talking points, new puzzles; they do not lack the ability to discuss fundamental matters, only the opportunity.

6 Judgement

There is a whole range of moral issues on which children can exercise their judgement. Should you take what is not yours? Would you agree with the principle 'finders keepers'? Is it ever right to kill other human beings? Can you both love animals and eat them? Children, like adults, often hold moral viewpoints for unexamined reasons. Discussion involves exposing one's viewpoints to the scrutiny and judgement of others. Sometimes it involves holding a view that is independent from the group as in this excerpt from a discussion between Patrick Costello (PC) and some 8 to 11 year old children.

PC	What do you think about that question of shooting pheasants? Is that something that we should all be doing, do you think?
Russell	No.
PC	Who say Yes?
	(No one raises a hand)
PC	Who thinks it's something we shouldn't do?
	(Fifteen children raise their hands. Richard does not put his hand up.)
PC	Does this mean, Richard, that you think shooting pheasants is a good thing?
Richard	. . . if you like chicken you could shoot one and then you might like it so you carry on.

PC   So you think it's quite a good thing to do?
Richard   Yes and no.
PC   Why 'no' then?
Richard   Because it's out of season, you're shooting them ... you're not allowed to.
PC   So does that mean when it's out of season it's a bad thing to do?
Richard   Yes because you can go and farmers ...
PC   What about farmers?
Richard   They sometimes shoot them
            (*Comment: Richard equates what is morally right/wrong with what is lawful/unlawful*)
PC   What do you think about shooting pheasants Melanie?
Melanie   I think whoever shoots pheasants are cruel.
PC   Why is it cruel?
Melanie   Because, well how would Richard, or whoever shoots pheasants, like a pheasant or somebody to come up and shoot him?[33]

Melanie is here arguing not from the lawfulness of actions but from a universal aspect of ethics, the Golden Rule that we should treat others as we would have them treat us. She is in fact extending this rule from human to non-human animals to justify her argument about not shooting pheasants. The issue of animal rights is one that can often engage children in spirited discussion.

Children live in a real world of work, communication, mass media, mobility, economic needs and politics. They take a lively and positive interest in it, for it is also their world. As much as they respond to stories and enjoy 'pretend' games they are not the prisoners of fairyland. They are interested in what the latest computer can do, in what the day's news is about and what it is for a person to have a right to something. The media's daily coverage of politics and current events can provide a constant stimulus for talk and discussion. Children acquire information largely from TV but also from newspapers, images and vocabulary that can act as models for description, argument and analysis. A child may not be able to answer the question 'What is politics?' but can discuss information and ideas related to political activity – what it is to be free, to vote, to have rights, to form parties, to treat people fairly and to have different policies. Coming to know about politics is an act of conceptual construction that depends on the active role of the learner. Children's understanding grows gradually and they need help in developing their ideas and in building on hazy concepts.

In her research into children's thinking about politics, Olive Stevens[34] shows that 7 year olds find no difficulty in joining in a political discussion and are able to show awareness of highly complex issues. At this stage children tend to be egocentric in their concerns. When asked what a bad Prime Minister might do, one girl answered 'Making things so that no one can play on them.' Eight year olds tend to be less egocentric. Asked what a bad Prime Minister might do, Vince replied 'Put up signs saying "Keep Britain messy!"' Nine and 10 year olds are capable of more sustained discussion and of developing social constructions. When interpretations are illogical it is often because of lack of basic factual information. Eleven year olds become stronger in debate, elaborating freely on what interests them, though still needing help in sustaining a line of thinking.

Much of the political language of adults has been acquired by the age of nine. Also an awareness of world problems like hunger, disease and poverty, trading rights and international rivalries. Some children begin to show a strong commitment to social ideals. Children begin to grapple with sophisticated concepts. As one 11 year old remarked, 'I'd like to make the world ... more civil in its rights.' An interesting point of discussion for 11 year olds is whether children should vote, or perhaps whether there should be a family vote. Here are the views of two 11 year olds.[35]

Jamie	We've got to vote, I mean us children. We're not allowed to vote until we're 18, the government said that. But I think we should have more say – in the Common Market and things. We might make wrong suggestions but at least we've tried to be more mature in our ways.
Janet	We should really learn about the government in one great subject about the world. All the things that happen and the culture and social life, and all things like that – the whole.

Children have a great desire to learn about 'the whole' and to fit disparate elements of their experience – facts, images and opinions – together. In so doing they can begin the quest that we are all on.

As with politics so with religion. Children have an urge to question and to wonder at the strangeness of things. Philosophy begins in puzzlement. As in the question asked by a 7 year old, 'What was God doing before he made the world?', Wittgenstein said, 'A thinker is very much like a draughtsman whose aim it is to represent all the inter-relations between things.' Children are attempting to make these connections and relationships all the time. Piaget quotes his little girl asking, 'Daddy, is there really God?' Father answered that he was not certain. Daughter replied 'There must be, because he has a name.' Because it has a name must it in some sense exist? Life is something that we do not fully understand. Much of what we tell children, or try to explain for them, is highly questionable and deserves challenging. Skilled reasoning is learned through the social interaction of argument. Children eventually learn to use argument privately, though initially it is learned through interaction with others. Difference of opinion openly expressed is a point of growth. It makes for discussion and debate, the clarifying of ideas through talk. As Mark Twain said, 'It is not that we should all think alike, it is difference of opinion which makes horse races.'

A group of 10 year olds were discussing the roles of boys and girls in story books. One boy asserted that boys are always better than girls.

> 'You mean in the classroom as well as in the playground?' asked the teacher.
> 'Well certainly boys are better in sports than girls are,' replied the boy.
> 'In all sports?' asked the teacher.
> 'No, there are sports in which girls are better than boys,' argues a girl.
> 'No,' says another boy, 'even in girls' sports there are some boys who are better than girls.'
> A second girl objects, 'But there are some girls who are better than most boys, even in boys' sports.'[36]

After the initial sweeping statements the children gradually acknowledge that they have to speak more carefully and objectively. There is a need to offer and to weigh evidence. A need to share and to examine opinions. When Socrates said that the unexamined life is not worth living he meant that there is something disastrous about allowing our everyday ideas to remain in a state of unresolved conflict. Part of the point of education is to make us aware of current problems and conflicts of ideas and to show us alternative ways of dealing with them. Through discussion children can learn to become more logical, more critical, more reflective, more philosophical. Dialogue can help us to self-correct our thinking and to define more sharply those thoughts that are obscure and blurred. It offers a powerful means of problem solving. As Lipman says: 'the child who has gained proficiency in thinking skills is not merely a child who has grown but a child whose very capacity for growth has increased.'[37]

Summary

Philosophy for children aims to help children become more thoughtful, considerate and reasonable individuals through cooperative dialogue in a community of enquiry. Children are introduced to philosophical issues through discussion of stories. Children generate the questions for discussion. The discussion has a Socratic structure and is guided by agreed rules. Stories from a variety of sources can act as starting points, raising issues of universal concern such as fairness, freedom, friendship, truth and knowledge. Discussion of moral issues, conflicts of opinion and ideas from the real world develop concepts, skills and attitudes and offer children powerful means of problem solving.

7 Teaching for thinking: language and maths

A place where people ... learn to reason, learn to understand and above all learn to think for themselves.
    Judith (13 years) from Edward Blishen (ed.) *The School That I'd Like* (1969)

The traditional approach to learning, particularly in secondary schools, has been to assume that the right ideas are in the teacher's head and that children need to be exposed to these to gain understanding. In this transmission model of teaching the child's own ideas are unimportant. Some primary teachers take a different approach and use the discovery model. Here the right ideas are regarded as being somewhere out in the world and if children look in the right way they will find them. Once found or discovered these ideas will be the ones that become fixed in the child's questioning mind. The teacher's role is to provide the materials and expertise to make this possible and then to await results. But this approach can also neglect the value of the ideas that the child brings to the learning situation.

Teaching for thinking begins in valuing the child's own ideas. It embodies the recognition that children do not come to the learning process as 'vessels to be filled' (the transmission model) nor simply as 'fires to be lit' (the discovery model). This does not mean that the transmission or discovery modes have no place in learning. They have different functions in the process. The transmission model – 'Let me show you, or tell you, how to do it' – is ideally suited for low-level or preparatory tasks such as the conveying of information, instructions or orders. Being told what to do or how to do it can be of vital importance in learning such things as safety procedures, mechanical skills or the rules of the game. The child may need to be given the knowledge that can act as a catalyst for new understanding. The response demanded is low-level in the sense that what is being required is for the child to absorb and retain information. It is a reproductive mode.

The discovery model involves the child being actively engaged in a structured learning situation, in a productive mode of learning. The child becomes involved in processing information, in investigating, in making connections and solving problems. The discovery method does not necessarily utilise the ideas the child brings to the learning situation and whether, at the end of the activity after the problems have been solved and the discoveries made, there is any qualitative difference in the child's thinking cannot be guaranteed. At the heart of the educational process lies the problem of transfer. Have the ideas implicit in the activity been transferred into the child's thinking? What has the child brought to, contributed to and taken away from the experience? Does the teacher know? Does the child know? Is there a model of teaching that will better facilitate these ends?

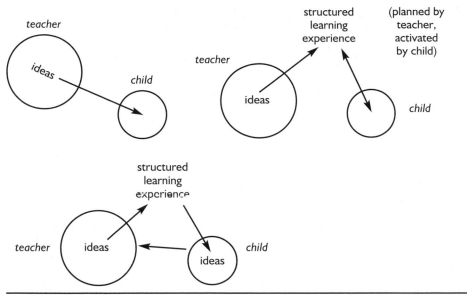

Figure 7.1 Modes of teaching.

The teaching for thinking model has at its heart a 'what-do-you-think?' approach to the child. It approaches learning through higher order levels of thinking. Its focus is not on a telling or doing approach but on a thinking approach. It aims for a transformational mode of learning. Taking the raw material of the child's ideas and processes (both cognitive and metacognitive) it aims to accelerate the learning process by allying knowing and doing with thinking. Teaching for thinking tries to combine reflection with practice. It starts from the ideas that children have and asks 'How can we help the children to develop their own ideas and their own thinking?'

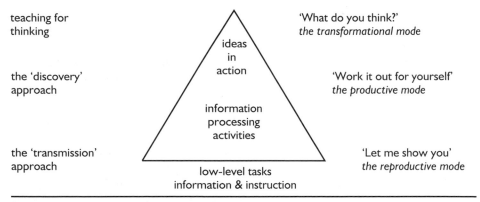

Figure 7.2 A hierarchy of teaching approaches.

This chapter will aim to show how teaching for thinking can be applied to all areas of a child's experience. These 'areas of experience' may be related to the subjects of the school curriculum and to the various forms of human intelligence. In the long debate that led to the National Curriculum it was widely agreed that the school curriculum should offer children different areas of experience. These include language and literature, mathematical, scientific and technological, the aesthetic area (music, art, craft, design), the physical area (physical education, dance and games), the moral area (personal and social education) and the spiritual area (religious education). Table 7.1 shows how these areas of experience are related to forms of intelligence and curriculum subjects.

Table 7.1 Areas of experience related to forms of intelligence and school subjects

Areas of experience	Forms of intelligence	School subjects
Language and literature	Linguistic	English and literacy
Mathematical	Logico-mathematical	Maths and numeracy
Scientific	Scientific/naturalist	Science and technology
Aesthetic: art and design	Visual/spatial	Art, craft, design
Aesthetic: music	Musical	Music
Physical	Bodily/kinaesthetic	PE, dance, games
Social, moral and spiritual	Interpersonal/emotional/ metacognitive	Social, cultural, citizenship PSE, moral education, RE

Much of the work that goes on in primary schools is of an integrated nature. The approach is often through themes, topics or projects. This reflects the world of the child, for whom knowledge is a seamless web. A study of trees, for example, can take in various forms of experience and be related to a wide range of different school subjects. The more skills, faculties and forms of intelligence that can be brought to bear on the task in hand, the richer and more varied the connections that can be formed in the child's mind. We need to show children different ways of looking at the world, different ways of patterning their experience, how to use in a thoughtful way different aspects of their intelligence.

Traditionally the curriculum has been divided into the arts and sciences, the arts being seen as creative and humanistic, the sciences as logico-technical and abstract. Teaching styles and timetabling arrangements have reinforced subject and departmental boundaries. What has been lacking, particularly at secondary level, is a curriculum and method of pursuing it that will equip children with transferable skills and expertise. The boundaries between arts and sciences need to be broken down and replaced with a model that presents thinking and problem solving as the heart of the learning enterprise. There is a science that infuses art and an art that infuses science, while maths and language infuse all subjects. A scientist can use thinking that is every bit as creative, divergent and original as the artist, for example in hypothesis formulation. The artist can work in a theoretical context as abstract and rule governed as the scientist, for example the musician composing variations on a theme. Technology most clearly unites art with science. The attempted colonisation of technology by science has been particularly damaging, divorcing the theoretical from the practical and reinforcing the sense of two cultures. Science has every bit as much to do with human concerns as the humanities and they in turn need the principles and resources of technology to achieve their highest purposes.

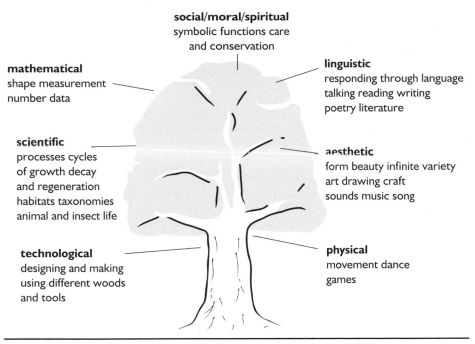

social/moral/spiritual
symbolic functions care
and conservation

mathematical
shape measurement
number data

linguistic
responding through language
talking reading writing
poetry literature

scientific
processes cycles
of growth decay
and regeneration
habitats taxonomies
animal and insect life

aesthetic
form beauty infinite variety
art drawing craft
sounds music song

technological
designing and making
using different woods
and tools

physical
movement dance
games

Figure 7.3 Here are some ways of looking at a tree involving different areas of experience and different forms of response.

A more useful distinction than arts versus sciences is that between the theoretical and the practical. In the German language there is a distinction between:

- *Wissenschaft* – theoretical knowledge, which may cover all subjects
- *Technik* – the practical ability to make and use things.

The theoretical aspects of a subject should be used to encourage free imaginative thought, speculation and conceptual connections between subjects or areas of study. The more cross-curricular connections and the more applications of knowledge that can be found, the greater will be the transferability of skills. Theoretical knowledge needs to be linked with the practical. The practical will include abilities to make things like working models and stage scenery and other forms of know-how such as the use of language. What is needed is a combination of 'knowing that' and 'knowing how', which together form the elements of 'knowing why'. All subjects should be seen as being involved in a common enterprise, uniting theory with practice, to help children become practising thinkers and thinking practitioners.

In schools teaching children to think is achieved through the curriculum. A school curriculum is not just the teaching provided but also what the child takes away from the learning experience. If there has been no gain in terms of knowledge and skills, and no change in thinking, no connections made, no transformation of any kind, then there has been no learning, no matter what activities the child has been engaged in. How can theory and practice be linked and transferable thinking skills be taught through the traditional subjects?

Language

... and so I learned not from those who taught, but from those who talked with me.
   St Augustine, *Confessions*

Language, what Moffett[1] calls 'the universe of discourse', is often said to involve the four modes of listening, talking, reading and writing. These are all aspects of the linguistic intelligence that is the powerhouse of a child's intellectual ability. Children will think more effectively the more skilled they become as listeners, speakers, readers and writers.

Growth in linguistic skills entails much practice. Children are embarked on a long apprenticeship[2] in developing thinking skills in the four modes of language. A fifth mode of language which is often overlooked, can play a vital role in developing language skills. This fifth mode is inner speech, which can help as much as outer speech when a child needs to decentre[3] and elaborate[4] his thinking.

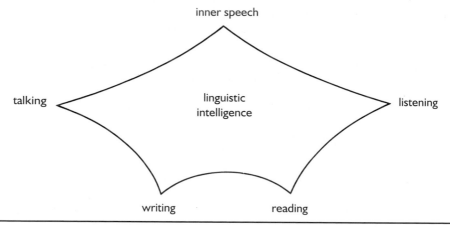

Figure 7.4 *Modes of language.*

The following are ways of developing the structures of thinking through the five modes of language.

1 Inner speech

When I'm stuck I can tell myself what to do, and it helps.
   Peter, age 8

Inner speech is the 'talking to ourselves' that we do sometimes when confronted with a problem. It is a human capacity that develops slowly and at variable rates in children. This inner talking is not simply the idle chatter of the mind. Inner speech plays a vital role in controlling and influencing our behaviour. What we say to ourselves affects our attitudes and actions. It also affects our understanding of the world. To describe something differently to oneself is to understand it differently. Psychotherapists have used the inner speech of patients to help modify ways of understanding and responding to the world.[5] Religious leaders have used inner speech in the form of prayer and meditation to heighten spiritual awareness. Psychologists have used it to maximise human performance in a wide range of sporting activities.[6]

Impulsive children often lack the patterns of inner speech that would help them to focus on matters in hand. Working on ways of 'talking through' what they are doing can help them to achieve a more careful, deliberate and thoughtful approach. We have all had experience of 'talking ourselves out of, or into, doing something'. Children too can talk themselves out of being creative or of being confident in tackling problems. They can also talk themselves into and through the challenges they face, monitoring and marshalling their knowledge and skills to tackle a task in hand.

Inner speech is of course no substitute for particular knowledge and skills but it can help to mobilise what the child knows and link it to what the child can do. An important way in which adults can help, as in all apprenticeship situations, is to model the thinking aloud process. In modelling thinking out loud with children we should aim not at the effortless manner of the expert smoothly showing how to deal with the situation but at the inner speech that it reflects. Struggling for direction, going back to beginnings, reviewing strategies, recognising new problems that arise, facing frustrations, overcoming setbacks, starting along false trails, hesitating over choices and expressing that swirl of hope and doubt are the characteristic responses of the true learner.

Some children gain by working in pairs or groups and thinking aloud while trying to solve shared problems.[7] There are two reasons why this can be valuable:

- by listening to classmates solving problems the child may learn about other people's approach to problem solving
- by expressing their thoughts to themselves and to others, the child's own approach to the problem can be checked and analysed.

The teacher can divide the class into pairs and have one member think aloud while the other is the response partner playing the role of listener/enquirer. In practice, children may find it difficult to keep to these rules and are likely to prefer to discuss problems on an equal footing. However, it can be useful to show how thinking aloud can be a shared activity and 'eavesdropping' on the process will provide a teacher with valuable and perhaps surprising insights into a child's thinking. It also shows the importance of audience, the need to listen, how to ask questions and the benefits of working together. Evidence suggests that getting children to talk about what they are doing, before, during and after working on a task, enhances their ability to think about it.[8] Talking about thinking, using inner or outer speech, encourages more thinking.

2 Talking and listening

We often think that if children are having trouble in learning they need more time at it. Research studies seem to back up this view.[9] They show that there is a relationship between the time the teacher devotes to having children engaged in learning activities and achievement in tests on the content of that learning. 'Time on task' seems the most influential factor linking class activities to success in achievement tests. But it is not simply the time spent that is crucial but the engagement of children's minds in the learning that enhances achievement. As Piaget said, all knowledge arises from interaction between learners and the learning environment. The message for teachers is that classrooms should be organised in ways that encourage active involvement in learning rather than passive response. Such organisation would include the stimulus of teacher-led class discussion as well as small-group investigations and individual work activities. Some children learn best individually, some in groups. But they only learn well when their minds are engaged and their thinking is supported and stimulated.

One way to encourage children's efforts in constructing understanding is to question their thinking. The child will often try to make sense of a question no matter how bizarre it seems. Asking children to respond to bizarre questions can produce interesting results.[10] To the question, 'One day there were two flies crawling up a wall, which got to the top first?' Five-year-old Jenny replied, 'The one on the left.' When asked why, she explained, 'Because he's the biggest.' To the same question, Andrew (aged 4 years 11 months) replied 'The first one.' When asked why that fly got to the top first, he responded 'Because he started first, silly.' When asked other questions that were intended to be unanswerable, such as 'Is milk bigger than water?' and 'Is red heavier than yellow?' children almost invariably provided answers. Children are ingenious in trying to make sense of situations presented to them and in creating their own frameworks of understanding. They take the fragments of meanings they find in the questions and transform them into something identifiable and coherent. When it was explained that the questions he had been answering were really unanswerable, 6-year-old Tom replied, 'They're not! I've just answered them!'

In Finland they have a proverb, 'When a fool talks to a wise man, who benefits the most?' Similarly, it is difficult to know who benefits most from the interaction between child and adult. Through talking and listening the adult learns much about what and how the child thinks and is given the fresh perspective of the child's-eye view of the world. The child also learns how to shape thoughts in words and how to communicate his understanding of the world. Ways to encourage the child to extend his thinking through talking include:

- *Pausing* – allow the child 'think time' during question-and-answer or discussion. Waiting for an answer demonstrates a trust in the child's ability to answer, an expectation of thoughtfulness even if the silence sometimes seems to be interminably long![11]
- *Accepting* – do not 'rush to judgement' on a child's response; give the child time and give yourself time to reply in a thoughtful way. Ways of accepting a child's idea are to restate it, to apply it, to recognise it, compare it to another idea or simply to acknowledge her view. Passive acceptance can be the non-verbal nod of the head, active acceptance will show understanding, or perhaps elaboration of the idea.
- *Clarifying* indicates that the teacher does not understand fully what the child is trying to say. Instead of 'rushing in' to explain to the child what he is trying to say, the adult requests more information and invites the child to elaborate on his idea. 'Can you explain what you mean by . . . ?' 'Tell me again, I couldn't quite understand . . . '

- *Facilitating* means sustaining talking and thinking through feedback and response. The teacher needs to provide opportunities for the child to check her ideas to see if they are correct. 'Are you sure?' 'Let's check it and see.'
- *Challenging* – to be understood by others is part of the stimulus a child needs but children also need challenge and should be encouraged to challenge each other and adults. 'Do you agree with what I/another child says?' 'Can you see any problems?' 'What do you think?'

3 Reading to think, thinking to read

Surveys[12] show that very few children aged between 11 and 15 are illiterate, in the sense that they are unable to decipher words that they are familiar with in their spoken language. But success at school and in social life requires far more than this. Many children who can understand what they read at a literal level find it difficult to understand a writer's underlying meaning or intentions. There is a tendency for them to interpret only what the words say, not what they mean. Children understand what is said, but they are often unable to infer why it is said.

The two general components of reading are decoding the words and comprehending the meaning. We want children not only to read the lines but also to read between the lines. A text provides only part of the information that readers need to make sense of the situations described. The reader supplies the rest, not merely by recording the message but by constructing a meaningful representation of the text.

what the child brings to the text – thinking skills, linguistic experience and previous knowledge

what the child takes from the text – meaning, purpose and understanding

Figure 7.5 The two-way process of reading.

Reading is a thinking activity. It involves critical thinking (the decoding of words, word parts, phrases and sentences) and creative thinking (the use of imagination, empathy, divergent outcomes and problem solving).

Fluent readers not only know more words and more about words; they are able to reason from language. They are able to use the semantic and syntactic clues to predict the meanings of unknown words. Such children progress far more quickly than those who rely on others for definitions of words. Research[13] has identified some of the metacognitive control processes necessary for fluent reading. When Vernon[14] reviewed the research on why children become backward in reading he concluded that 'cognitive confusion' was the chief characteristic of those who found it difficult to read. What is the nature of this cognitive confusion? One cause is that poor readers come to regard reading simply as a process of decoding isolated words and that success in reading means pronouncing words properly. They may consider a passage of random words as easier to read than a coherent story. Poor readers are slow to apply thinking to reading and are unwilling to make the cognitive effort needed to make sense of difficult texts. Good readers (and writers) are actively engaged in a problem-solving activity, striving for 'cognitive clarity'[15] by seeking meaning from words. Becoming a fluent reader does not consist in simply matching or associating words and letters with spoken forms; it consists in a number of discoveries that engage the processes of thinking.

Vygotsky,[16] in trying to account for why young children on entering school usually have fluent skills in speaking yet lack them in reading and writing, suggested that there were two reasons for this.

- **the abstract quality of written language – the fact that its meanings are not self-evident**
- **the vagueness children have about the usefulness of reading and writing, so that they have little motivation to apply themselves to the tasks of learning.**

Studies[17] of 5-year-old children show that they often do not know what people do when they read; they find it difficult to understand the purpose of written language and have problems with abstract concepts like 'word' and 'sound'. For example, one 5 year old reported that she had 'done reading' because she had finished her pre-reading book. Fast developers show more cognitive clarity about the activities of reading and writing. They know about the matching of sound and symbol, that words are units of meaning, that reading and writing have practical uses. Research[18] with 6 and 7 year olds confirms that children with slow progress show continuing conceptual confusion about reading and writing. They have little idea of what a sentence is and even the best readers can show uncertainty as to the value and function of reading and writing. To the question 'What do you do when you read?' many 6 and 7 year olds made no response.

In supporting children's learning we need to enhance children's knowledge of reading by giving them a rich and varied experience of words and books. We need to enhance their 'know-how' in reading by encouraging them to interact with and gain meanings from the text, through sharing and discussing books.[19] We also need to help children gain a knowledge of why reading and writing matter and to share with them our own reading experiences. Learning about reading is not just a child-centred experience, it is a process of development that lasts throughout life. The feeling that we have understood something simply because we have read it is not always to be trusted. Woody Allen reports a case in point:

> I took a course in speed reading, learning to read straight down the middle of the page, and was able to read War and Peace in 20 minutes. It's about Russia.

We need to give children cues on how to seek meaning from texts. The following are some ways to assess a child's reading comprehension thatembody active strategies typical of good readers that we might wish to encourage.

- *Monitoring for meaning*: checking what the child understands, skimming and selecting the main ideas, and signalling understanding e.g. by paraphrasing or summarising – 'What is it about?'
- *Questioning the text*: clarifying the meanings, monitoring doubts, checking on what is not understood or only partially understood – 'Why does it say that?'
- *Analysing text features*: looking at the textual context for clues to meaning, such as illustrations, captions, aspects of style, type of book – 'What clues have we got?'
- *Elaborating the text*: adding one's own thoughts and feelings, predicting what will come next, referring forwards and backwards, suggesting imagery, character responses, e.g. what the child would have done in the same situation – 'What will happen next?'
- *Judging the text*: evaluating the ideas, features and main points of the text – 'Does it make sense?'
- *Reasoning*: asking why things happened or might happen, analysing motivation of characters, seeking causes and effects, making inferences, developing hypotheses, theories and ideas – 'What is the reason for …?' 'What would happen if …?'
- *Reviewing*: looking back at the end of the reading experience to check on comprehension and coherence, responding to the text as a whole, evaluating the purposes of the writer, how and whether these were achieved – 'What did you think of the book? Why?'

If reviewing comes at the end of the reading process, then overviewing should come at the beginning. Preview the book by reading and thinking about the title, the cover design, the contents, illustrations, special pages such as maps, index, introduction. Fluent readers tend to try to decide what the book is about before they begin and they employ strategies to achieve this. The aim should be for the child to take charge of her own reading, to self-monitor and self-correct problems as they arise. Certain questions can be asked to focus the young child on her own individual approach to reading.[20] Such questions might include:

What made you choose this book?
Is it a difficult book?
What makes the book difficult?   Child's view of reading difficulties
Show me a difficult word – what makes it hard?
If you come to a word you don't know, when
    you are reading by yourself, what do you do?
Do you think children should learn to read?
Why?/Why not?   The purpose of reading
Why do you think grown-ups need to be able
    to read?
Do you think you are a good reader?
Why do you think that?   Child's view of own reading

Thinking through reading or writing can be hard work. This may be a reason why many people are disinclined to make the effort. Thinking through reading or writing can be pleasurable and rewarding, the enjoyment of solving the problem, meeting the challenge, being enriched by the experience. Not all books or writings achieve this. As Thurstone (1923) said 'A stimulus that does not serve as a tool for the child's satisfaction, as seen by the child, is simply not a stimulus.' If the material is not intrinsically interesting it is up to the teacher to let the child know why he should apply himself to a task.

Motivation may be achieved in any of three ways.

- *the child's natural interest* – intrinsic satisfaction
- *the teacher's motivation* – extrinsic rewards
- *success in the task* – combining satisfaction and reward.

Research[21] shows that intrinsic motivation is more easily undermined than created. This is one reason why many teachers prefer to teach reading through 'real books' rather than artificially restricted 'reading schemes'. They aim to provide children with a wide range of attractively produced books on a variety of themes so that children will learn to exercise choice between books of quality that will appeal. Attitudes are caught rather than taught. If children are to be 'hooked on books' they need not only mediated support (strategies for thinking) and opportunity (a wide range of motivating materials), they also need to share the enthusiasm of others. Enthusiasm inspires enthusiasm, while lack of enthusiasm tends to produce lack of interest and effort. No wonder that enthusiasm is the quality most called for in advertisements for teachers. 'A good reader' says Frank Smith, 'is a child who is willing to make mistakes' and it is a teacher's enthusiasm that can help sustain him in the creative act of making meaning from words both in reading and writing.

4 Writing – putting thoughts on paper

'Reading is a sort of rewriting', according to the French writer Jean-Paul Sartre. The link between reading and writing is a close one. Both require knowledge of spoken language and the ways ideas can be expressed in it. Both involve efforts to make meaning with and out of words, to actively process a text. Studies show a close correlation between achievement in reading and quality in writing. Writing activities can improve reading skills. Writing can also stimulate and develop thinking skills. As E.M. Forster said, 'How can I know what I think till I see what I say?'

Speaking and writing are two distinct modes of language, each with its own syntactic and textual characteristics. Speech is phonetic, whereas writing is graphic. Written language is both more explicit and more complex in its structures than spoken language. Because they are different modes of communication there is no necessary link between competence in speaking and in writing. Typically a 6 year old will produce written texts that match the spoken commentary of a 3 year old. That talk and writing are different activities can be seen in the very different ways that children will talk and write about the same experience. The child will tell the story once, whereas frequent versions of a written account may need to be made if he is to 'get it right'.

One of the primary contributions of writing to thinking is that it relieves the memory from the need to keep everything in the head at any one moment. Writers can develop lines of thought, patterns of description and reasoning that speakers would find too difficult to keep track of. Writing, unlike speaking, allows for revision, extension, interpolation and review. It can play a key role in cognitive development, particularly in the development of abstract thinking. However it is a complex process, probably the most complex set of challenges the child has to face at school; the child needs to stop to consider not only what to say but how to say it. For the different thinking elements that are involved in writing, see Figure 7.6.

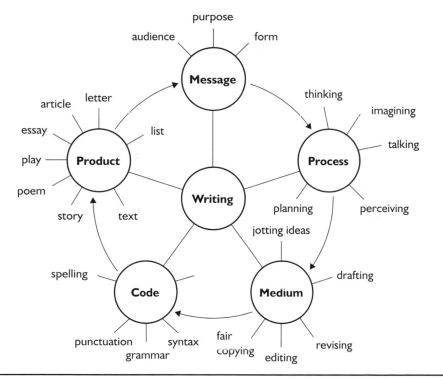

Figure 7.6 The elements of writing.

As adults we use writing to explore the perennial problems of the human condition, problems of freedom and conflict, expressing personal experiences and public concerns. Children's writing, too, can be a means of expressing and exploring the fundamental concerns of their own world, such as the reasons for things, the relationships between people and the results of actions. A valuable feature of the written word is that it casts communication in a form that can be made permanent, can be shared across time and space and can be made subject to critical appraisal. To see children writing (as opposed to copying) is to see intelligence at work and to see the creation of a focus for further thinking.

Writing is thought in action but it is not one unified process. The act of writing can be divided into two parts:

- *composition* – the creation of a text
- *transcription* – writing down the text.

Frank Smith[22] analyses these two jobs under the following headings.

Table 7.2

Composition	Transcription
(author)	(secretary)
Getting ideas	Physical effort of writing
Selecting words	Spelling
Grammar	Capitalisation, punctuation, paragraphs, legibility

Young children learn to compose long before they can accurately transcribe. Most problems associated with learning to write are problems to do with transcription. Most time spent teaching writing involves ways of improving the skills of transcription. Infusing thinking into the process will aid a child's skills in both composition and transcription. How does one infuse thinking into the tasks of writing for oneself and writing for others?

Writing for oneself – the use of journals and think books

Asking children what writing is for can produce revealing answers:

'You write down what's on the board.'

'Teacher tells you what to write.'

'You have to copy things.'

'It helps you spell better.'

'It's got to look neat.'

'So you can get a job when you grow up.'

Children are usually quite willing to let teachers, or other children, do their thinking for them. It is easier that way. They are more likely to get it 'right', or at least to get it 'done' and out of the way. Writing need not be like this. It need not be viewed by children as a secretarial skill alone, reproducing the right words (usually other people's words) in the right way at the right time. Writing can also be a tool for learning. Thinking is already occurring in the child's head. Ideas, plans, imaginings, daydreams, narrative experiences, questions, hopes, fears, struggles for meaning and understanding are part of the kaleidoscope of a child's daily thoughts. These are often unexamined and unexpressed but they form a rich resource for learning. As Ausubel says, 'The most important single factor influencing learning is what the learner already knows. Ascertain this and teach him accordingly.'[23]

When Theresa, aged 10, was asked to think about the way her own thinking worked she said:

> When I get my ideas I relax and they just pop into my head and then I write them down. Other people get their ideas in different ways but I don't see how they just pop into my head. I also wonder why and how one minute you have an idea and the next minute you forget it.

Bonnie wrote, 'I think if I stopped writing down my new ideas I would stop thinking them.'[24]

Children are often surprised to find that new ideas are just ordinary thinking carried a little bit further. One way into 'think writing' is to give the child a 'think book' or journal.

A think book is a notebook. It might also be called a learning log, a journal, a diary, a memo book. The audience for the think book is primarily the writer himself. 'Let the children show us what they need to know,' says Donald Graves.[25] In a think book the child can reflect back over recent learning experiences. The child is free to puzzle over any confusions, to catch any thoughts and to explore ideas that might otherwise get lost in the turmoil of everyday life. Think books can be used for writing about anything in a child's life that is of interest or concern.

Some teachers prepare a large think book for the whole class in which all the children can share what they think about the things they do in school. For example:

Are there things you like or dislike?

Are there things you find enjoyable, interesting, difficult?

Do you feel pleased with yourself or unhappy about something you have done?

Do you have any problems?

Do you have any suggestions about how to improve things for yourself or other people at school?

The book is made available at all times for children to write, or stick in, their comments. They may write their names beside their entries if they wish and the teacher will respond in writing when she feels it appropriate. The teacher can also act as scribe for younger children. In one infant class a young child wrote 'Why can't I make a Winnie the Pooh book?' The teacher wrote in reply 'I think making a Winnie the Pooh book is a lovely idea. We have very little time before the end of the term, so should we make one big class book for people to put things in or would you like to make books of your own? What does everyone else think of this?' The following morning it was read then discussed by the class before deciding what to do. Such a book can provide a focus for positive self-expression, like the child who said to his teacher 'I've had such a good morning, brilliant in fact, I really enjoyed it. I want to write it in the think book' or for deeply felt negative emotions like 'Why, oh why, do we have to go out to play? I hate it so!'[26]

Other teachers prefer to choose a focus for their think books, for example a 'reading' think book in which children's thoughts and feelings about books, stories and the reading process can be recorded. This also provides the teacher with an opportunity to stimulate thinking and canvass opinion: 'Who is not happy with the book they are reading? Why?' Think books can also be focused on other areas of the curriculum and they can include drawings, comments of visitors, questions to remember for future discussion, shared jokes, riddles, predictions or suggestions for future activities.

Many teachers are encouraging children to write for themselves in their own individual journals or think books. The book should be special, either home made or of the child's choice. A journal expresses an individual personality so should reflect the identity of the owner in its cover decoration and freedom to use illustration. Children who are daunted by the size of a book may stick pieces of paper into the journal, scrapbook fashion. Children who find it strange or difficult to write for themselves may find it easier to write for an imaginary audience, for example one in 50 years' time. It can be pointed out to them that their reactions to the unimportant details of daily life would be of great interest to future generations. Therefore everyone has something of value to say.

Most children enjoy writing their journals when they have something to say, at home or school, rather than at a fixed time in lessons. The 'think writing' produced in such journals reflects the current preoccupations of the individual child. Five year olds choose subjects as diverse as news items seen on television, how their scabs fell off and how the gears of a car work.[27] Thirteen-year-olds tend to explore adolescent fears and uncertainties as well as current affairs and relationships with adults. The *Diary of Adrian Mole* can often be an influence but the writing can extend to many types, for example poems, stories, dialogue, strange happenings, new ideas/concepts, news, doodles, thought experiments, worries and complaints. Because think books do not demand a special writing style the learner-writer is free to think on paper just as the words come. The personal voice comes through. The teacher's response can help draw the children into a written dialogue to explore the meaning of the child's message. The child's journal can be an expression of emotional needs as well as a tool for thinking. As one child reported, 'If I did not have a think book I would probably go nuts trying to keep the things I have written to myself.'

Sometimes children prefer to keep their journals to themselves, feeling free only then to reveal their inmost thoughts. Such privacy should of course be respected. The French writer and thinker Jean-Paul Sartre recounts in his autobiography the sense of fulfilment that came from writing in his notebooks at the age of nine.

> By writing I was existing . . . . My pen raced away so fast that often my wrist ached. I would throw the filled notebooks on the floor, I would eventually forget about them, they would disappear . . . . I wrote in order to write. I don't regret it. Had I been read I would have tried to please . . . . Being clandestine I was true.[28]

Writing for others

Many approaches to writing traditionally taught in schools do not reflect the mental and behavioural processes of good writers. These include telling the child:

- you start writing straight away
- you must get it right first time
- you must do it on your own
- crossing out is wrong.

Such advice is misleading, if not harmful, to the development of thoughtful writing. The processes that experienced writers use are the processes that will help even young children develop their writing/thinking skills. Among these processes are:

- pre-writing activities such as thinking, talking, brainstorming, note making, list making and planning
- writing activities such as drafting, expanding on ideas, revising and transcribing
- post-writing activities such as editing, conferencing, sharing and publishing.

The desire to write is the key of successful writing. Children have a need to communicate and writing is a powerful means of satisfying that need. The writing process begins with thinking about the nature of the message and for whom it is intended, as this will often determine the form the writing should take. At this initial stage such things as audience, purpose and form should be considered. There are various questions for the writer to think about.

• Who will receive the message?

The audiences might include families, friends, visitors, an older or younger child, teachers, people in another school or the wider community or simply the writer herself.

• Why are we writing?

Writing activities should have a purpose. Such purposes for writing might include: to amuse, to argue, to discuss, to describe, to recount, to remind, to report, to persuade or to touch the emotions.

• How should the message be presented?

Writing can take many forms and the forms should fit the function. The forms might include stories, poems, plays, essays, letters, journals, diaries, articles, posters, cartoons, tapes, lists and memos.

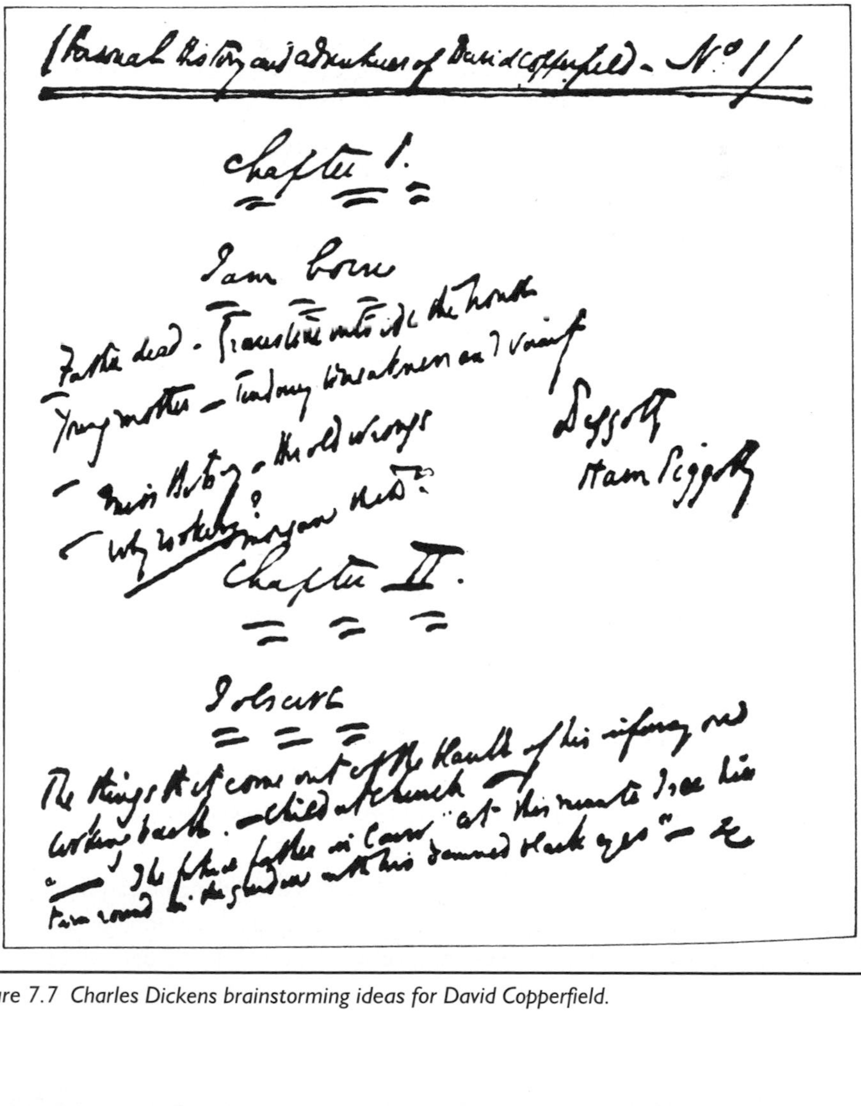

Figure 7.7 Charles Dickens brainstorming ideas for David Copperfield.

• What ideas have we got?

Once the purpose and audience have been decided then the writer needs to note down some preliminary ideas. Some ways of doing it include brainstorms, which can be individual ('I had a thinking time and wrote down all the ideas that came into my head' – 6 year old girl), group or class. A child or the teacher writes down all the ideas or keywords, however divergent or odd. Some of these words or ideas may be just what the child wants to use and develop at a later stage.

A flow diagram (see pp. 71–73), network, web or spidergram takes one idea as a starting point and others are placed around it. This approach is useful for getting lots of angles and aspects on one central topic. Ideas can branch off almost indefinitely but thought-links can be seen to relate back to the main point. Listing ideas (see p. 44) under sub-headings is useful for a logical presentation of ideas, showing different categories.

A mind map is a visual means of showing the two approaches that the child can take to any topic. What does he know about it? What does he feel about it? This division can be related to the left/right hemispheres of the brain as follows:

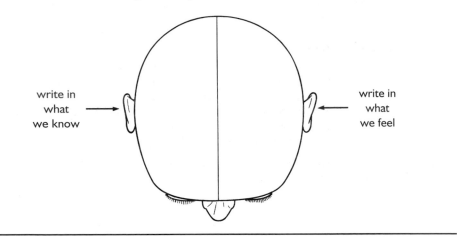

write in
what
we know

write in
what
we feel

Figure 7.8 A mind-map diagram.

• How should we write it?

Pre-writing activities encourage the view that planning is important and that writers discover much of what they want to say as they write. Writing researcher Donald Murray[29] found that professional writers spend on average 84% of their time pre-writing, 2% composing a rough draft and 14% revising. Inexperienced writers spent most of their time composing a single draft, with results that were often vague or skimpy.

Once the pre-writing, thinking and planning stage is complete the drafting stage can take a variety of forms:

- *Freewriting or speedwriting*, where the child writes everything he can think of for, say, 10 minutes as fast as possible. The aim is not to think too long or edit but to write ideas at speed ('from the brain, through the arm, via the pen, on to the paper').

- *Using a scribe* – when children dictate their writings to teachers or other adults they can compose and think at greater length than they would otherwise be able to do. It frees the child's mind to concentrate on the matter in hand. The child just thinks and talks. At first the scribe works mainly as a secretary. Later it will be useful to work together on the editing.
- *Using a tape recorder* can take the place of a scribe. Composing on a computer can minimise some of the problems of transcription, such as handwriting. Word-processing allows texts to be easily corrected so that an attractive final draft can be produced. The computer also offers good opportunities for collaborative writing, or conferencing.

First ideas are sometimes, but not always, the best. It helps to share these with other children and adults. Children can work with a particular response partner in twos or in a larger writers' group. Partners can help each other by making positive suggestions and criticisms and asking questions for clarification. Such discussion could take place before or after the first draft stage. This 'talking through' with a special person can help the child to work out what to do next.

• What should we do with the writing?

Once children have worked on their ideas and have produced a final draft, help may be needed with proof-reading for spelling and accuracy in punctuation. Care should be taken that the work is presented to its audience in a legible and attractive way. Quality in writing is rarely achieved by a one-off think/write process. Thought needs to be given to the end product so that the child has a sense of a task well done and the satisfaction of having an audience with whom to share the experience.

A key point in all cognitive research is that no one writer proceeds precisely as another would. Various stages are characteristic of successful writers but the degree to which these stages are followed varies according to the unique response of the individual writer and the kinds of tasks involved. The same writer may follow different processes when writing for different purposes. Each writing task is a unique journey.[30]

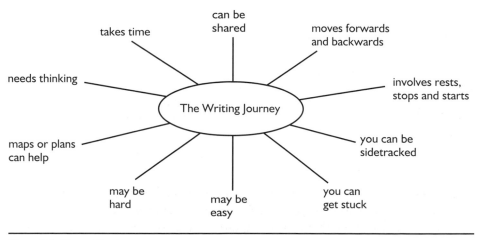

Figure 7.9 The writing journey.

Writing is a thinking journey and if we are encouraging children to find their own way then it is inevitable that sometimes they will make mistakes and get lost. It is important in our assessment of children's writing and other thinking activities, to distinguish between mistakes and misconceptions. Mistakes may be trivial errors, due to guessing or not thinking, or because the child has not understood the task. Misconceptions can impede learning, for they reveal that the child has not understood the matter and so will continue to make the same errors in the future. Misconceptions can advance learning in two ways. Firstly they may be evidence of bold chance-taking on the part of the child, for example an invented spelling, a theory that is wrong, a prediction that is not realised, a short cut that ends in a blind alley, an imaginative leap in the dark. Or they may be rational, intelligent guesswork that has arrived at the wrong solution. An error may have its own consistency, coherence and logic and it may simply point to an alternative set of conventions. Such signs of intelligence can often be misconstrued because of our own blindness. Errors can often be the evidence of intelligent, active, creative minds at work.[31]

From an early age children are corrected in all aspects of their lives. 'Don't do this!' 'Don't do that!' 'That's wrong!' That's not the way to do it!' There are often good reasons why we should stop and correct a child but these reasons should be articulated. We need to make clear whether what we are correcting refers to the writing code (syntax), the medium (handwriting), the process (thinking, imagining) or the product (finished piece of work). For a child, all correction marks error and from the child's point of view can devalue his whole effort. Discussion of errors should aim at being developmental and suggest strategies to support the child's future thinking. We learn in different ways; there is no one right way (even conventions such as letter writing can admit divergent forms). We need to discuss the different ways children may self-correct, self-monitor and self-create their own developmental strategies. As Piaget said, to understand is to invent. With writing it is the meaning that is of primary importance, more important than syntax or style. It is the heart of the writing process: 'What is the child trying to express?' As C. Day-Lewis said, 'We do not write in order to be understood. We write in order to understand.'

Maths

Child's riddle: *If numbers make you numb what do more numbers make you?*
Answer: *Number*

For centuries mathematicians could make no sense of numbers less than zero. To almost everyone in the Western world numbers started at 1 and continued in one direction, upwards. All numbers counted things: no things, no numbers. It was not until relatively recently that mathematicians accepted that there could be negative and imaginary numbers. However, at the age of four the mathematical genius Pol Erdos remarked to his mother, 'If you subtract 250 from 100, you get 150 below zero.'

Many children who have not the mathematical talent of Erdos can respond with creativity to thought-provoking questions such as, 'You know 10, 9, 8, 7, 6, 5, 4, 3, 2, 1, 0? What number comes next?' Here is a discussion of this question with 9-year-old Jake, who began by suggesting, after a pause:

Jake	1?
RF	You mean it goes … 3, 2, 1, nought, 1, 2?
Jake	Yes.
RF	So what follows 1… nought or 2?
Jake	It isn't 1 … I don't know.
RF	Well, what is 1 take away 2?
Jake	(*thinking, wrote* $1^2 - 2^1 = 1$). The answer is 1.
RF	How did you do it?
Jake	You take 1 from one number and add it to the other (*After several attempts at trying this, Jake suddenly wrote* $1 - 2 = -1$) It's take-away 1.
RF	What is 1 take away 3?
Jake	It's take-away 2. You go take-away 1, take-away 2, take-away 3 and so on ….

Other 8 to 9-year-old children have suggested, 'minus 1, minus 2', 'you owe 1, owe 2', or '1 less than nothing, 2 less than nothing'. They have extended the number system themselves, given:

- a questioning approach
- time to think and to try out ideas
- a mediating teacher to support thinking, test ideas and offer clues.

This kind of questioning technique is as old as Socrates, who on one famous occasion got a boy to prove a theorem of Pythagoras simply by stimulating him with questions.[32] To encourage children to think mathematically we need to become the 'midwives' to their ideas.

What characteristic features of logico-mathematical intelligence enable us to think mathematically? A key element in mathematical thinking is the ability to recognise patterns and to see relationships. Mathematics is a highly structured network of ideas. To think mathematically is to form connections in this network. Mathematics is not made up of isolated skills and bits of knowledge, it is an interrelated framework of concepts and procedures. What we need to do is to help children to see the structure inherent in mathematics, not just rules and facts learned in isolation.

Research into the psychology of learning mathematics suggests that there is an important distinction between instrumental and relational understanding.[33] Instrumental understanding is gained from learning rules (algorithms) and being able to apply those rules to particular circumstances. The trouble with rules is that they are easily forgotten. Relational understanding implies knowing the reasoning behind rules and this understanding can be gained if the child has thought through and can reconstruct the rules for himself. This learning tends to be deeper, more lasting and more easily recalled to memory. How are children to gain a deep rather than a shallow understanding of the structures of mathematical relationships?

In encouraging children to think mathematically we need to engage all aspects of a child's intelligence. Many traditional textbooks and teaching techniques have emphasised the symbolic at the expense of the other areas of thinking. Maths was seen as something 'out there' that must be learnt by way of symbols, rules and formulae rather than as something you need, with help, to process for yourself. The different ways of processing maths can be represented as follows:

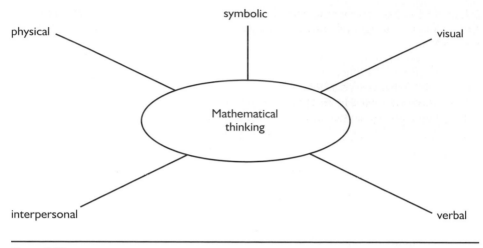

Figure 7.10

Mathematics is a way of solving problems in the mind, on paper and in real situations. Such problems can be modelled or represented in a variety of ways:

- *Verbally* – through inner speech and talking things through, using linguistic intelligence, putting planning procedures and processes into words, making sense and meaning for oneself.
- *Interpersonally* – learning through collaboration, observing others, working together to achieve a shared goal, exchanging and comparing ideas, asking questions, discussing problems.
- *Physically* – using physical objects in performing mathematical tasks, working with practical apparatus, equipment and mathematical tools, modelling a problem or process, having hands-on experience, using bodily–kinaesthetic skills, practical applications into the physical world.
- *Visually* – putting processes into pictorial form, making drawings or diagrams to make visible the problem, visualising patterns and shapes in the mind's eye, thinking in spatial terms, graphical communication, geometric designs, manipulating mental images.
- *Symbolically* – using written words and abstract symbols to interpret, record and work on mathematical problems, using different recording systems, logically exact languages, translating into mathematical codes.

One form of intelligence not represented here is the musical. There is a close link between music and mathematics. Musical rhythms can be seen as algorithms of sound. The composer Claude Debussy once said, 'Music is the arithmetic of sounds.' Like maths, musical notation is a symbolic code that depends on patterns of shape and number.

Recent mathematical research has focused on the ways in which children create their own solutions to mathematical problems.[34] One of the most important things teachers can do to assist creative mathematical thinking is to nurture these natural tendencies and encourage their development. Questions that promote mathematical discussion include:

Why do you think that?
Can you show me what you mean?
Are there other ways to do that?
Can you explain that in another way?
How would you explain it to someone else?
Where could you use that idea?
Can you make up another example?

Consider the problem, 20 is to 30 as 10 is to —?

a) 5 b) 10 c) 15 d) 20 e) 25

Most older mathematically able children will choose c) (20 is two-thirds of 30, 10 is two-thirds of 15). The answer given by a 13 year old was 10. Instead of yielding to the impulse to correct her answer, her father asked her why she thought 10 was the right answer. She explained '20 is to 30 as 10 is to 10. If you add 10 to 30 you get 40; and 20 is half of 40. If you add 10 to 10, you get 20; and 10 is half of 20. Am I right or what, eh?'[35]

It is very tempting to correct the mistakes and misconceptions of children. Many problems can, however, have more than one answer and almost all problems can be tackled by more than one approach. As one teacher said about the above problem, 'Isn't 20 as right as 15? 30 is 10 greater than 20; and 20 is 10 greater than 10 ' Even if they have made what seem obvious mistakes, children should be given the opportunity to explain them. Providing the answers may not enhance the thinking process; indeed, giving the right answer often puts a stop to the child's thinking. Our aim is not to make them dependent on the answer book or on others, but to grant them the maximum independence and to give them a sense of control over the process.

The different areas of mathematical thinking can be categorised as number, algebra, shape, measurement, data handling and problem solving.

Number

In getting children to think mathematically we are interested in their ideas about number rather than in particular methods of calculation. Indeed, if you ask children how they calculate (or even observe yourself at work) you will find a fascinating variety of individual methods. Peter, aged 7, was once asked if he knew what 'seven lots of eight' were. Peter answered, 'No.' He was then asked, 'Could you work it out?' There was a long pause, then Peter said, '56.' 'How did you know that?' 'Well' answered Peter, 'I knew 10 eights so I took away 8, that's 72, and another, and another – 56'. Peter had devised a method or algorithm all his own, idiosyncratic but mathematically sound.[36]

The variety of methods children may actually use in their heads contrasts with the standard pencil-and-paper methods they are usually taught in schools. Some of these methods were the invention of the Arab mathematician Al-Khowarismi, who was the keeper of the treasures of Haroun-el-Raschid, the Caliph of Baghdad, about 800AD. The word algorithm is derived from the name Al-Khowarism. An algorithm for subtraction is as follows:

²3̸ ¹1	Jane, aged 8, did the sum as follows:	31
− 1 6		16
1 5		25

When asked how she did it, Jane replied, '1 take away 6 is 5, 3 take away 1 is 2.' When asked if the answer was right, Jane said she didn't really know. However, given the problem '31 take away 16' to do in any way she wanted, Jane soon came up with the correct answer, 15, and she was able to check it both by her own paper-and-pencil method (involving groups of 10) and with a calculator.

John could not do the division sum $45 \div 3$ but found little difficulty in sharing 45 sweets between three people. Children who have problems with conventional methods can often develop their own mathematical strategies, given encouragement.

Mathematical thinking can be stimulated by challenging children to make up their own problems. 'The answer is "25p". Make up some questions that have this answer.' 'Think up a question for which "15 lorries" is the answer.' 'Write a problem that has the answer "360 sausages".' Encourage playing with numbers, for example 'Write down your telephone number. Using all the digits and plus, minus, multiply and divide symbols, how many different numbers can you make?' The calculator is an ideal aid for playing with and exploring numbers, for example, 'Choose a number, say 999, find the least number of moves to make 0 using the numbers 1 to 9 and only the plus, minus, divide and equals symbols.'

An important part of mathematical thinking is 'if ... then' thinking. It links to real-life thinking. You think, for example, 'If it rains tomorrow then we won't be able to have a picnic.' You would not say, 'If it rains tomorrow then it will be Sue's birthday.' In this case the last part of the sentence is not related to the first, even if tomorrow *is* Sue's birthday! Similarly 'if then' thinking can be done with numbers. If $2 \times 16 = 32$, then ... $16 \times 2 = 32$ or $32 \div 2 = 16$ would be correct. Later, children can be introduced to letters instead of numbers in 'if then' thinking, for example, if $2 \times n = 12$, then $4 \times n = ?$ In looking for number patterns and devising their own algorithms, children are being introduced to the foundations of algebra. As Bruner says, if you wish children to do algebraic equations in the eighth grade you need to introduce them to algebra, at their own level, in the second grade.

Algebra

Algebra develops out of the search for patterns in numbers. This search for patterns is a basic response of the human mind to all forms of experience. The search for pattern and order, what the psychologists call 'Gestalt', begins with the recognition of separate components and then working on them or playing with them to see if they fit into some overall configuration or order. The quality of a musical melody does not lie in its separate notes, nor a painting in individual brushstrokes, nor a shape in its conjoint lines, but in the conceptual ordering (what the Greeks called harmony) of its separate parts. Mathematical thinking, like other forms of thinking, is a search for patterns.

The traditional maths curriculum, as well as the 'new math' curriculum of the 1960s, was based on the logical structure of mathematics as perceived by mathematicians. One orthodoxy, the need to instruct children in a linear sequence of pencil-and-paper algorithms, was replaced by another, the need to introduce children from a young age to set theory. As Tom Lehrer said, 'New Maths – it's so simple, only a child can do it.' Neither approach achieved success in terms of children's understanding of concepts or in test results. Maths remained for many a source of fear and failure, if not of outright panic.[37] Neither the 'back-to-the-basics' fundamentalists nor the 'play way' progressives were able through their methods alone to generate the sorts of mathematical thinking in children that would offer confidence and understanding. Research now suggests that to be effective the teacher should utilise the ways children themselves impose pattern and structure on the mathematics they learn.

Children need a lot of experience in patterning numbers and these experiences should call on all forms of intelligence. From an early age children can be introduced to number rhymes and games, the sorting of objects into number sets, the progression of house numbers along a road, the colouring in of number patterns on number grids, numbering off groups of children and missing-number puzzles such as 1, 3, 6, 10, 15 –.

Questions to ask of any series of numbers might be:

What comes next?
What is missing?
What patterns can you see?

Sums are simply the logical patterning of numbers in particular ways. Older children can create their own number patterns with invented symbols. For example, $\odot$ is a symbol. It tells you what to do with numbers on both sides of it. If $3 \odot 4 = 6$ is a true statement, what might $\odot$ mean? (It can mean multiply the two numbers and then divide by 2.) You can use any symbol you like, as long as you can explain what it means. Make up some symbols, invent algorithms to go with them, let your children see you doing it, share your problems.[38]

Shape

Geometry is to do with the patterning of lines, surfaces and space. Here, too, what is important is not so much the marks that go on to the paper as the ideas that are formed in children's heads. Asked to explain what a circle was, a young child replied 'It's a round straight line with a hole in the middle.' Children need to be introduced to the skills of drawing and shape recognition. One child looked derisively at a circle I had drawn freehand and said, 'That's not a circle, that's a wobbly!' They also need to know the vocabulary of shape and the conventions of mathematical discourse. An older child puzzled for a long time about how to refer to the circumference of a circle before saying, 'It's the skin!' Investigating shapes provides many opportunities for experiment on how shapes can be fitted, dissected and tessellated.

As with all learning there are two questions that can be asked about a lesson involving geometric shape:

What knowledge/ideas does the child bring to the experience?
What knowledge/ideas does the child take from the experience?

There is a close link between shape and number and we should do our best to inter-relate the two.

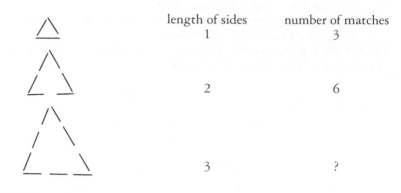

	length of sides	number of matches
	1	3
	2	6
	3	?

Figure 7.11

What pattern can you find here?
Use matches or drawings. How far can you take the pattern?
Use matches to make squares, increase size, find a pattern in the numbers of matches used. Investigate the growth of other shapes.

Use cubes

One cube   length = 1 faces = 6 edges = 12

Two cubes   ? Three cubes? Ten cubes?

What patterns can you find in the number of cubes, faces and edges? Investigate the patterns of bricks in walls, tiles on the floor of the kitchen. Look at chessboards – how many squares in 2 × 2, 3 × 3, 4 × 4 boards? There are patterns to be discovered in the shapes and measurements and, as Bertrand Russell said, in that patterning lies 'not only truth but supreme beauty'.

Measures

Children are not interested in maths for its own sake any more than they are interested in taxidermy for its own sake. They are interested in what relates to human purposes and principally what relates to their own concerns. They may not see much point in measuring the desk in handspans or in estimating the speed of a car on its journey to Oxford but they may be keen to find out how long they can hold their breath for, how quickly they can walk, how big to make the model doll's house or garage, how tall Goliath was, whether a table will go through a doorway or how hot or cold the drink is in the thermos.

Ways of infusing thinking into measuring activities include asking children first to estimate, second to test their estimate, then finally to review the margin of error and work out strategies for improving the accuracy of prediction and measurement.

This process is an application of the scientific method of investigation, one reason for calling maths 'the queen of the sciences'.

Data handling

Data handling is to do with statistics and probability. Children are growing up in a media environment rich in statistics, statistics that describe (how many died in the earthquake?), statistics that inform (how many people are unemployed?) and statistics that try to persuade (how much have the prices gone up?). Children's statistical judgement will develop through practical experience of collecting and analysing data from a variety of sources such as reference books, newspapers, magazines, computer databases, graphs, charts, radio and TV. They can look for evidence of bias and distortion and consider reasons for this.
Questions to consider:

Is the information sufficient?

Is the information sound?

What conclusions can we draw from it, or from the way it has been presented?

We live in an uncertain world and probability offers a means of measuring uncertainty. It provides the foundation for much statistical work. What is the probability that there will be a rainy day in June? What is the probability of tossed coins landing heads or tails? What is the probability in a bag of M&Ms that you will pick out an orange one?

Problem solving

'If it took two men two days to dig a hole 8 feet by 4 feet, what colour socks were they wearing?' This is the sort of question (slightly exaggerated) that used to appear in traditional maths books. You could get the right answer if you knew the trick or could guess the method. True mathematical problem solving is more than the ability to remember standard solutions to known problems. The true use of maths is seen in its application to real-life problems.

A mathematical problem has a starting point and a clear goal that needs to be reached. Can you make a box in which to put a particular toy? How much card would you need? What size would the box be? The need to add up numbers may not seem a significant problem for children but saving and budgeting their own pocket money provides real purpose for their mathematical thinking.

When the mathematician, Gauss, was a schoolboy his teacher told the class to add all the numbers from 1 to 20. Almost at once without any apparent calculation Gauss wrote down the answer. The teacher was amazed to read the correct answer, and it was not merely a guess. Most students when faced with the problem approach it by adding

$1 + 2 + 3 \dots 18 + 19 + 20$. Gauss noticed that $1 + 20 = 21$, $2 + 19 = 21$, $3 + 18 = 21$, therefore the answer to the question was $21 \times 10 = 210$. Many children without the genius of Gauss enjoy responding to the challenge of mathematical puzzles (some adults too share this passion). For example:

- Insert addition and subtraction signs to make this a true statement: 1 2 3 4 5 6 7 8 9 = 100 (there are several ways).
- Find change for £1 using 13 coins. (How many different ways? Try using different numbers of coins.)
- If five people meet and shake each others' hands, how many handshakes are there? (Try different numbers of people – any patterns?)
- In Farmer Jones's farmyard there were some hens and pigs. Farmer Jones counted all their legs. There were 34 legs. How many hens? How many pigs? (Adapt the problem – different animals, different numbers of legs.)
- A frog fell down a well 10 metres deep. He climbed up 1 metre each hour, then fell back ½ metre. How long did he take to reach the top? (A trick question – check the answer, vary the problem.)

Strategies for encouraging applied thinking to problems include sharing your real-life problems (do-it-yourself, recipes, planning a party, organising an outing), offering challenging puzzles (e.g. in a class puzzle or problem corner), clothing mathematical processes in realistic or imaginative stories (the hero of one teacher was Freddy Fly, who met many mathematical problems, like the day he walked round the rim of a glass of beer and fell in; fortunately Freddy could swim, so he escaped, leaving the children to investigate and measure the empty glass). Given suitable models, children can also create and share their own story problems.

Mathematical thinking is encouraged by talking about and talking through the process and strategies used. It is also encouraged by the child writing what she thinks in notepads or think books. Concepts can often get overlooked in the hurly-burly of maths activities. One teacher found some interesting replies when he asked his 8-year-olds 'What is a fraction?' Answers included 'Numbers in bits', 'One number above another', 'Colours in the rainbow', 'Number things', 'Eating bits of cake', 'It's when a tyre gets hot on the road' (friction?). The think book responses provided useful starting points for teaching and further discussion.[39] Think books give children a chance to play with ideas, to offer verbal reasoning on paper and to untangle the web of interwoven ideas and perceptions. In Figure 7.12 a child makes several drafts to move closer to the true meaning of a mathematical investigation.

Tiles

First attempt:

If I had 5 tiles I would have 5 tiles on the top 5 tiles on the bottom and 3 tiles down each side because you have to have 4 corner tiles.

Second attempt:

If I had a row of tiles, to find how many I need to surround the row, I need to times the number of tiles by 2 and add 6. I need to add 6 because there is four corner tiles and 1 tile on each side.

Third attempt:

If I had a row of tiles, to find how many I need to surround the row I first have to count the number of tiles, then I have to times the number by 2 and add 6. I need to add 6 because there is 4 corner tiles and 2 end tiles.

Fourth attempt:

If I had a row of tiles ▢•▢•▢•▢ to find how many I need to surround the row I first have to count the number of tiles ▢•▢•▢•▢. Then I have to times the number by two $5 \times 2 = 10$ and add 6. I need to add 6 because there are 4 corner tiles ▨ ▨ and two end tiles ▨•▢•▢•▨.

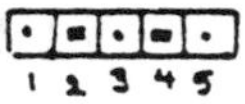

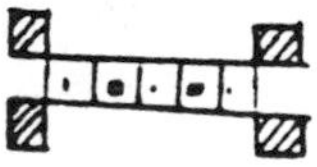

So the formula is $2OT + 2E + 4CT = ST$

OT is original tiles.
E is end tiles.
CT is corner tiles.
ST is surrounding tiles.

Figure 7.12

Other children find it helpful to develop their thinking through drawings and diagrams.

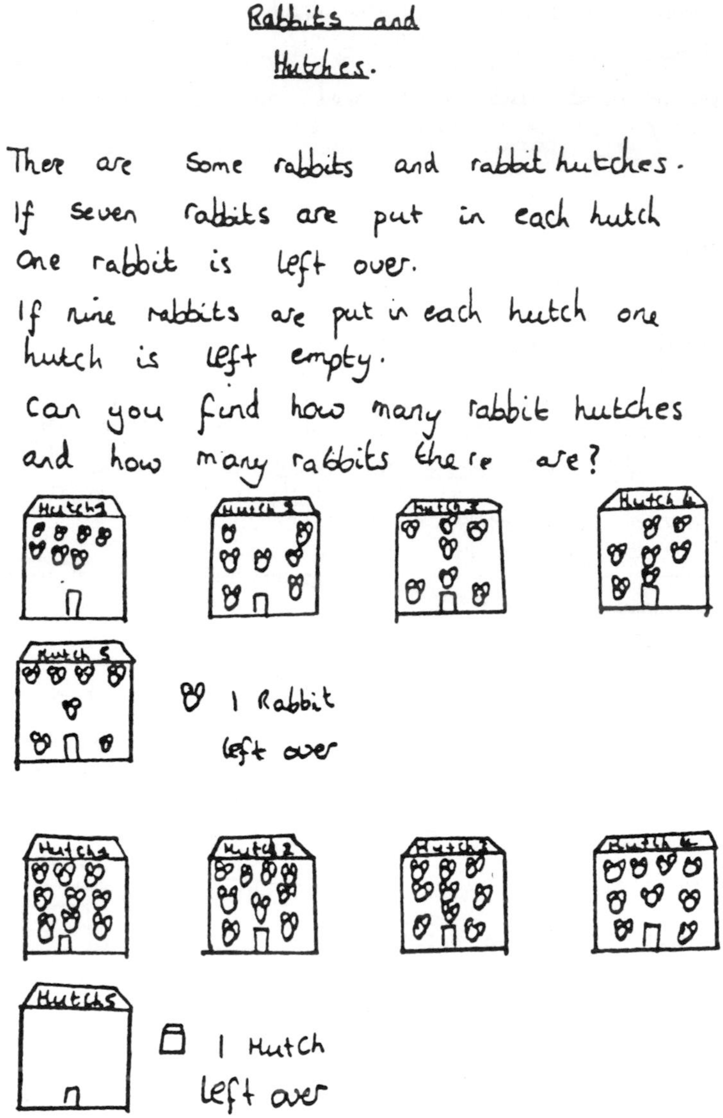
Rabbits and
Hutches.
There are Some rabbits and rabbit hutches.
If seven rabbits are put in each hutch
One rabbit is left over.
If nine rabbits are put in each hutch one
hutch is left empty.
Can you find how many rabbit hutches
and how many rabbits there are?
1 Rabbit
left over
1 Hutch
left over

Figure 7.13

Many children are helped by being able to model their thinking with apparatus. This applies not only to the young children that Piaget believed to be in the 'concrete operational stage'. Lord Hume, one-time Prime Minister, used to say he could never have understood economics without the use of matchsticks. Shakespeare wrote, 'I cannot do it without counters' (*The Winter's Tale*). The calculator and computer have replaced the abacus as the most powerful tools of mathematics but the challenge remains: we must in the end make our own way up the mountain of maths understanding, supported by others but relying mainly on our own native wit; and the personal path we take may well be better for us than having to follow a given way.

Summary

'Teaching for thinking' is a mode of teaching that values the child's own ideas. Teaching for thinking can be applied to all areas of a child's experience. Subject teaching in school should equip a child with transferable skills and expertise. Language and literacy begins through development of inner speech, talking and listening. Reading and writing are ways to make meaning, develop thinking and understanding. Maths and numeracy should engage all aspects of a child's intelligence. Mathematical thinking needs to be linked to real-life problems, stimulated by challenging children to create their own problems and developed through discussion of processes and strategies.

8 Teaching for thinking: across the curriculum

Science

Discovery teaching involves not so much the process of leading students to discover what is 'out there', but rather, their discovering what is in their own heads.
    Jerome Bruner, *The Relevance of Education*

Children watch intently as two balloons are blown up to the same size. The inflated balloons are hung carefully at either end of a balance. The children are asked 'If we let the air out of one of the balloons, which way will the other one move?' The correct answer is 'down'. Air has weight and is denser inside the balloon than outside because it is under pressure. Releasing the air will therefore make the first balloon lighter. What answer would children of different ages give to this problem?[1]

When the problem was put to groups of children aged 5, 8, 12 and 16, in different schools, researchers found some surprising results. All the 5 year olds gave the right answer, three out of four 8 year olds were correct, but none of the 12 year olds and only one in three of the 16 year olds. Similar results were produced over a range of simple scientific problems. Superficially this seemed to show that the height of scientific reasoning occurs at five and tails off to zero at 12 before slowly recovering. There must be something wrong somewhere. What could explain this strange pattern of results?

The youngest children were giving the right answers but they were giving them for the wrong and unscientific reasons. They could say what would or should happen but they couldn't say why. The older children brought a variety of scientific ideas to the problem, many of them intuitive but wrong. If a child's intuitive ideas remain unquestioned and unexamined they can hamper the development of understanding in science and other areas of a child's experience.

Science is both a method of enquiry and a set of ideas, a mix of attitudes, skills and knowledge. We need to feed the child's natural curiosity, the urge to explore, to try things out, to look more closely, to see what happens. We need to build on the child's disposition to explore and investigate, to satisfy the 'rage to know'. We need to be learners alongside the child, infecting the child with our enthusiasms and our curiosities. We too can share and communicate that longing to grasp the reality of things that is a characteristic of the great scientist. 'Out yonder was this huge world,' wrote Einstein, 'which exists independently of us human beings and which stands before us like a great, eternal riddle, at least partially accessible to our inspection and thinking.'

Children begin developing ideas about the world from an early age. These are based on casual observations, hearsay and a haphazard collection of everyday ideas. Most of these notions are unexamined and untested, many of them erroneous. When a 7-year-old boy was asked how the electric light worked, he replied:

Well it's electricity. It, er . . . goes along in the wires and makes the bulb light . . . you can't see it, it's in the wires . . . it's like water . . . you have to keep the bulb in otherwise it would all come out when you switch it on. That's why you have to switch it off. The glass (bulb) holds it in. It would just jump out otherwise and electrocute you.

Children develop their own intuitive ideas about the natural world well before being taught any science. Such thinking can be ingenious but it is not effective. Unquestioned, these ideas can hamper the development of truly scientific understanding. Children need to be told not that their ideas are wrong but to consider other possibilities and to test them against other theories, to engage in a scientific method of enquiry. Children need to learn how to work on their ideas if they are to think scientifically.

A major step in scientific thinking is to move from what is happening to why. Children under the age of 7 seem generally to be uninterested in why things happen. To the young child the world is something to be seen and described; it is primarily a visual world. They find it hard to relate what they observe to unseen causes. Puzzling processes of physical change tend to be consigned to the world of 'magic'. In focusing children's attention on the real causes of things we are not necessarily robbing them, as some have argued, of the rich imaginative resources of fantasy and fairyland. As Wittgenstein noted, 'The true mystery of the world is the visible, not the invisible. Every object in the natural world is in a process of change and can be an object of wonder, from the drifting snowflakes to the dust on the shelf.' Science is characterised by what Imre Lakatos called 'scientific research programmes'[2] in which groups of scientists work together on a variety of related theories, collaborating to produce their best joint efforts, which need to be tested, re-visited and re-assessed. Children too need to return to experiences time and time again, often re-arranging their ideas and unlearning certain notions in order to continue to learn. We need to create our own scientific research programmes with children, utilising other children, adults, teachers, relatives, library and museum staff in the process in creating an impetus for enquiry.

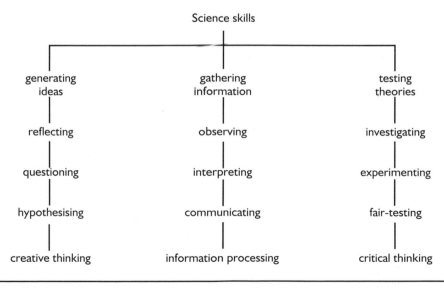

Figure 8.1

The scientific method can be seen as the basis for all kinds of learning about the world, a core subject in any curriculum. The following model of science skills begins and ends with exploring the ideas and thinking that children have about the world.

Children can come to appreciate the patterns of natural forms simply by being active, curious, playful and open minded. But in order to think in specifically scientific ways they will need to be involved in:

- reflecting on, questioning and hypothesising (creative thinking)
- gathering evidence, clues, information and knowledge (information processing)
- investigating, experimenting with and testing their ideas (critical thinking).

Scientific research needs starting points, for example the question: 'Where do all the puddles go?' Examples of questions for stimulating investigation could include:

How would you find out which grow faster, fingernails or toenails?

Does hot water freeze more quickly than cold water?

Which letters show more clearly: white on black, red on blue, black on white, etc.?

What is best to cover a teapot with to keep it warm?

Is a plastic bag stronger than a paper one?

Which design of paper aeroplane will fly the furthest?

What do seeds need to germinate and grow?

Scientific investigation needs the benefit of discussion. The more children can think aloud in informal discussions the more they become responsible for formulating and refining their own ideas in the struggle to create meaning and patterns from their experience.[3]

Notebooks, journals or think books can give permanence and stability to the child's thoughts. Written records can become extensions of mental activities, giving purpose and form to the enquiry. A notebook provides a paper memory and can become a storehouse for personally important information. Notebooks can contain such unsayable things as drawings or diagrams. All the great scientists, like the great artists, have kept their own notebooks, or sketchbooks. A characteristic of these notebooks, such as Darwin's (see p. 34) or Leonardo's, is that they are personal records. Just as we are interested in the child's own thinking so we are concerned to value the child's personal responses to the research programme. Notebooks should belong to the child and not be the test pads for teachers. They provide evidence of effort but not a public record. There may be exceptions to this when artists/scientists write up their notes in order to illustrate the process of discovery but generally the notebook is a tool for thinking, not an excuse for marking.

Young children have a natural urge to explore the world – the clouds in the sky (What keeps them up there? Where do they come from? Where do they go?), the birds in the bush (How do they make their nest, Can you do it?), the pebbles along the seashore (What kinds? What shapes?), the sound of a drum (What causes it?), the feel of fur (Is it real? How can you tell?). In gathering evidence about the world the senses can tell us a lot. They provide food for thought. But they are selective. They focus and they ignore, and what they do notice is influenced by ideas, expectations and previous experience. Like the men who fell into the gutter (one saw the mud, the other saw the stars), we all see different aspects of the same experience. Children's perception can be developed by encouraging them to observe details. One 11 year old looking at the yellow pointed flicker of a candle flame wrote:

*The flame is blue at the bottom, turns yellow higher up and tapers to a darker feathery tip.
Inside the whole there is a smaller darker flame the same shape. The shape is always
changing as the flame flickers.*[4]

Take any two like objects, for example leaves, stones, chairs, and challenge children to
spot the differences. Children's senses are acute and are able to observe and identify
similarities, for example between two chairs:

Figure 8.2 Similarities and differences.

The child's conceptual development relies on recognising similarities and differences.
Scientific analysis of properties and taxonomies of natural objects depend on the use of
these skills.

Children also need to observe change over time. When will it rot? How long will
mould take to develop? How fast does the snail travel? What changes are noted from
one day to the next? How has the sky changed, how has the plant grown, how long
until the ice melts, for the moisture to evaporate, for the puddle to dry? What patterns
can you see? Can you make any predictions? What connections can the child make
between two phenomena? How does water vapour from a boiling kettle relate to the
misting on the kitchen windows? How does a pencil looking distorted in a glass of
water relate to a magnifying glass?

What is needed is not for the child simply to look, but to look and think. What is happening? What has happened? What will happen? Which way does the water go down
the plughole? Is it the same with all plugholes? Can it be made to run away in a different direction? Children can be helped to observe by being asked to draw from real
life or from memory (compare the two). Always give children sufficient time. Help
them to notice details, to look from different angles to compare features, to look at
similarities and differences and to see what changes are wrought over time.

In moving children on from observing what an object or process is like, to thinking about why it is like it is, we often need to probe deeper than a child's initial reactions. Sometimes probing fails to move the child beyond a perceptual level of explanation, as in the following example:

Teacher	What makes things fall to the ground?
Child	When you let them go.
Teacher	What is it about letting them go that makes them fall to the ground?
Child	When you let them go they hit the ground. Sometimes the loud noise does it. The wind blows things to the ground too.
Teacher	Why do these things fall instead of going up?
Child	Because they can't float.[5]

The theories that children construct are often not so much wrong as incomplete. Here a follow-up question reveals a more thoughtful response than appears in a child's initial answer:

Teacher	What makes things fall to the ground?
Child	*(initial response)* You let them go. They hit the ground. They were too close to the edge.
Child	*(after probing question)* The weight of them. The heaviness pulls them down. The earth pulls them.

What helps children to extend their thinking and theorising about scientific processes is to see the principles being demonstrated with real objects. How can we test the theory? How can we show if it works? What would be a fair test?

Children need not only to see scientific principles in action but also to be introduced to terms and ideas. Two scientists-in-the-making on the way to a science museum were discussing the nature of atoms. The 9 year old wondered how one could walk through atoms without feeling them. Her 6 year old companion replied that atoms were only 'in things you can see' like tables or chairs. 'Atoms', she said, were just 'little pieces of sand glued together'. The development of scientific understanding in a child, like the history of scientific discovery, is built up gradually from fragments, new insights, linking ideas, constructing theories, experimenting, reviewing the same concepts time and again, responding to the challenges that others offer and relating known principles to a wide range of practical applications. Some of these applications will be making and doing things, applying principles to manufactures, using design and technology.

Design and technology

Technology is the application of science to doing and making. Every object made by people has a variety of technological aspects, which can be observed and evaluated. The following chart shows some major elements of technology.

A range of questions can be asked and a variety of observations made relating to the technological character of, for example, a teapot. How much does it hold? What is it made from? Why is it that shape? How does it retain heat? Is it a good design? Does it fit its purpose? Is it beautiful? How was it made? Is it good value? What do you think of it? Why? How could the design be improved?

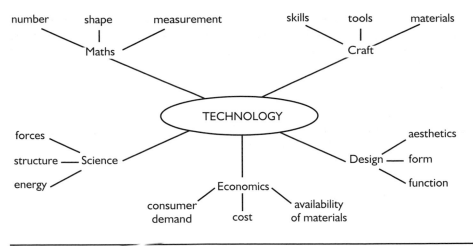

Figure 8.3

Stimulus for technological thinking can come from active reflection on everyday objects. How do the gadgets in the kitchen and garage work? What human needs do they meet? How successful are they in meeting those needs? How are they constructed? What scientific principles are involved? What materials do they use? Can the child communicate the elements of design in drawing or in words? Play the 'Mystery object' game (ask the child to describe an object hidden from view for others to identify) or the 'Twenty questions' game (others to quiz the child to guess the object, the child only able to answer Yes or No).

Stories and nursery rhymes can also provide starting points for technology.[6] For example 'The Three Little Pigs' is as much about construction – structures, forces and materials – as it is about the Big Bad Wolf. For example:

- *Why does a house need to be strong?* Protection, climate, thieves, wild animals.
- *What are houses made from?* Different sorts of building materials.
- *How are houses built?* Foundations, brick, patterns, types of roof.
- *Why do some fall down and not others?* Build houses of different materials, test them, consider what you find out.

Nursery rhymes are full of themes that can extend thinking. For example, use 'See Saw Marjory Daw' as a stimulus for investigating balances and levers, 'London Bridge is Falling Down' to look at different bridge structures, 'The Grand Old Duke of York' on ways of getting up a slope or 'Humpty Dumpty' for ways of balancing (and reassembling!) an egg.

Talk about the way things work. If a child asks a question he may be ready for a long answer, or a quick response. There is always a simpler or more complicated answer to every question. Find out what the child thinks first. To a child's question, 'Where do babies come from?' another nursery child answered, 'I know where they come from. They come from 'ospital. You go there and they give you a girl or boy. You can't say, they just give you one.' In the same nursery a 4 year old could explain in great detail the workings of an internal combustion engine. He was overheard saying to a bemused friend, 'Dad's having trouble with his sparking plugs again.' Through imagination and observation and being introduced to key concepts children fashion their view of the world. All children have a capacity for scientific thinking, for, in the words of T.H. Huxley, 'Science is nothing but trained and organised common sense.' Isaac Newton echoed the potential for discovery that is in every child when, shortly before his death in 1727, he wrote:

> *I seem to have been only like a boy playing on the sea shore, and diverting myself in now and then finding a smoother pebble or a prettier shell than ordinary, whilst the great ocean of truth lay all undiscovered before me.*

Geography

In the early years of life a child's awareness of his surroundings is vivid but undiscriminating. As Karl Popper says, 'observation ... needs a chosen object, a definite task, an interest, a point of view, a problem'.[7] One question that can be asked about any observed event is 'Where did it take place?', to the child as observer 'Where are we?', or traveller 'Where are we going to?' These are questions that can be answered with various degrees of geographical precision, and may pose problems relevant not only to children (for example, G.K. Chesterton's famous telegram to his wife, 'Am at Crewe. Where should I be?').

In thinking about places and locations we need the help of maps. Maps are a relatively new invention. In the fifteenth century hardly anyone could draw maps, partly because of limited means of surveying and partly because of a lack of a conventional code. Children, too, are in the position of the early map makers. They begin making maps by constructing simple codes, which are partly intuitive, partly modelled on the conventional representations of space picked up from observing maps. Maps are symbolic representations of space in which children can locate themselves, other people and places, and their capacity to create maps is developed by exposing them to maps of various kinds and showing them how to read or decode maps. At a simple level this kind of thinking about maps can begin in the nursery.

Researchers have identified six levels of mapmaking development in children (Figure 8.4).[8] Early mapmaking efforts reflect children's conceptual difficulties in representing space when they only have a hazy grasp of what a map is. In the early levels children present trees, houses and other features as elevations rather than plans. They demonstrate problems regarding scale and positioning of objects. Right up to the fifth level children use concrete symbols or words to represent mountains. Only at the final level do they use contours and an effective key. Developing children use increasingly sophisticated cultural codes in which to express their growing cognitive awareness of the environmental context in which they live. Only by exposing children to these symbolic resources and discussing their meanings is it possible for them to develop increasingly abstract concepts.

In drawing maps of the neighbourhood children, like adults, create their own cognitive maps. These reflect their interpersonal understanding, shared representations of places known by their particular social group, that are important in their own lives. Children can begin by mapping their own room – bedroom or classroom. Later they can map their houses, school and neighbourhood. They can extend their mapmaking

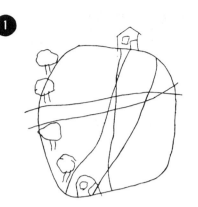

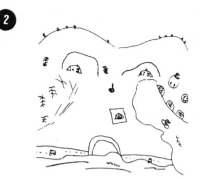

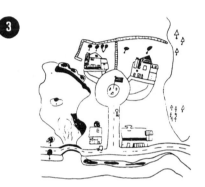

Figure 8.4 Stages in the representation of maps.

skills by inventing imaginary maps, desert islands (treasure maps), maps based on fairy stories (Hansel and Gretel, Sleeping Beauty, Red Riding Hood) or on their favourite reading book. Collect, study and discuss a variety of maps, plan journeys together. Let them navigate! Map their fantasy worlds, which may include underwater cities, space colonies or dolls' houses.

Extend your child's thinking by giving her first-hand experience of places near and far:

- Encourage your child to make a visual/verbal record of holiday visits to distant places in scrapbook or diary. Use the record to discuss, observe details, ask questions later.
- If you cannot go to distant places study pictures from colour magazines. Get the children to list all the details they notice. Ask them to make up questions about the picture. Find out or discuss possible answers.
- Discuss environmental problems. What is changing in the neighbourhood? Are amenities adequate? How are open spaces used? What is the public transport provision? Is there environmental pollution? What different approaches are there to these questions? Debate priorities, decide on action.
- Go on a thinking journey to explore the near environment. Have a focus for your thinking, for example prettiest sights, pleasantest smells, most interesting shapes, most interesting things – on the ground (surfaces, textures, grates, litter), looking upwards (roofs, chimneys, treetops, aerials), walls (materials, plaques, ornaments), street furniture (lamps, signs, litter-bins) and houses and shops (variations in designs, materials, architectural styles). What would be the best way of getting from one place to another, for example in a wheelchair, for a blind person, for speed, for secrecy, for best overview of surroundings?

History

'The past can only be lived forwards', said Kierkegaard, 'but it can only be understood backwards.' The past is an essential part of a child's cultural knowledge and experience. Only by reflecting on the past can meanings be found from it that will illuminate the present and help plan the future. Only by reference to the past can the present be fully understood. How do children come to a thoughtful understanding of history?

According to research[9] into ways that children learn, the concepts of time, like place, are 'constructed little by little, and involve the gradual elaboration of a system of relations'. Children learn by the gradual accumulation of facts and ideas but perhaps more importantly they learn by seeing situations as a whole, by seeing a pattern of relationships that helps to build up a structure of understanding. A parallel can be seen in the way children learn a story. They come to know a story by the repetition of detailed sequences, for example 'Who has been eating my porridge/sitting in my chair/sleeping in my bed?' but also by grasping the whole shape of the story, being able to fill in missing gaps and anticipate what's coming next. It takes time: few young children are able to tell a narrative story without leaving something out. Random facts (knowing

the good bits) are better than no facts at all. The task of the teacher is not only to facilitate the gathering of facts but also to foster the forging of connections in the child's
mind, to provide a scaffolding on which the child can build her own understanding.

Here are some ways through which children can be encouraged to think about the
structures, as well as the details, of history and to move on from what happened to why.

- *Encourage children to make time-lines* to record the important events in their
  lives, in book form or long roll-chart. What events are important? What evidence
  is there of these events? How did they relate to what came before and after?
- *Compile a calendar* for home or class to record everyday and important events;
  compare different calendars; what do they tell you/what don't they tell you?
- *Design a time capsule* for someone in the future to find: use a box, bag or bottle.
  What drawings or message would you leave for people in the future? What
  might people in the past have put in their time capsules?
- *Look for historical clues*, ponder and speculate about the evidence around you.
  For example 'How did it get its name?' Pick the name of a familiar street, town
  or river and try to find out where the names derive from.
- *Investigate old relics, antiques and byegones*. Test them with the senses, make up
  theories (stories) about their history and possible origins. What does the evidence suggest?
- *Study historical pictures* such as old paintings or prints. What clues are there
  about how people used to live? Find a story (asking children to tell a story from a
  picture is a challenging task, difficult for under-nines).
- *Think about the particular periods of history* that stories, TV programmes and films
  are set in. 'I Spy' for clues.
- *Interview a grandparent or another older person*. Ask what they did at school.
  Where did they go on holiday? What are their earliest memories? Prepare interview questions and tape a piece of real oral history.
- *Practise sequencing events*, such as the correct order of a story or historical narrative, put artefacts or pictures (such as postcards or photos) into historical
  order.[10] Encourage the calculated guess or hunch. Ask for reasons why a particular order was chosen.
- *Compare the present with the past*, for example 'What did early man need to
  survive/what do we need to survive?'
- *Visit places of historical interest*, look for clues to the past. 'How old is it? Who
  lived here? How can we tell?'
- *Reproduce the past* through modelling, drawing, painting, computer programmes,
  acting games – dressing up, role-play, play acting, mime, improvisation, re-enact-
  ment of historical events.
- *Ask why things happened when they did*, consider viewpoints; for example, in the
  murder of Thomas Becket, who was guilty of murder, Henry II or the knights
  who killed him?[11]

Interest in the past is frequently fired by an imaginative experience or story. Historical celebrations and anniversaries fill the media. Children are bombarded with adverts from TV, hoardings, food packets and comics. Many of these use historical characters to get over their message. You do not need to go to an archaeological site to find fragments of history, they are all around you. The real work of the historian, be it the academic, teacher or child, is in fitting the fragments together. Therein lies the fascination of history, filling in what we can of the tapestry of time and space.

Art – visual thinking

Art is a fundamental human process. It is a way of exploration, experiment and discovery, an expression of visual thinking. Picasso said 'I never do a painting as a work of art. All of them are researches. I search constantly and there is a logical sequence to all this research.' The process of visualising, drawing, painting or constructing is a complex one and involves many forms of research.

First there is the process of assimilation. The child assimilates through the senses a vast amount of information. Art can help this assimilation by developing perceptual sensitivity and discrimination through the study of form, colour, shape and texture. Of any experience we can ask 'What are the forms/shapes/colours/textures involved?' Through art we can add an important dimension to any research. Not just 'Tell me!' but 'Show me!'

Art can also help in the expression of a child's knowledge and experience. It can be the visual expression of her thinking and also a process through which thinking takes place. Art is a means of intellectual growth.[12] A child's artistic development is also a development of her thinking processes, the way she perceives the world and gives expression to that perception. Art also allows children to express feelings they cannot otherwise articulate, 'thoughts that lie too deep to know'.

Art is a problem-solving activity. It provides the opportunity to explore and solve problems in the visual field. In the search for answers the child discovers new ways to express what he sees, new ways to use materials and to refine methods. As they investigate and explore ideas children find there is no one right answer for every question. They need to organise ideas in personal ways, integrating their sensory information and striving to express it in ways thatthey find aesthetically pleasing. This involves decision making, assuming responsibility to deal with the choice of materials, methods and ways of visual presentation. Art activities present the child with a range of technical, physical and interpersonal demands, which challenge both thought and feeling. The following are some of the elements of aesthetic awareness developed through art activities.

Ways of encouraging the child's visual thinking include the following.

Visualisation

A famous story of scientific discovery in the nineteenth century illustrates the power of visualisation. The German chemist Kekule had been spending many months trying to unravel the mystery of the chemical structure of benzene. One summer evening he visualised the atoms dancing before his eyes. He carefully sketched the images. Later

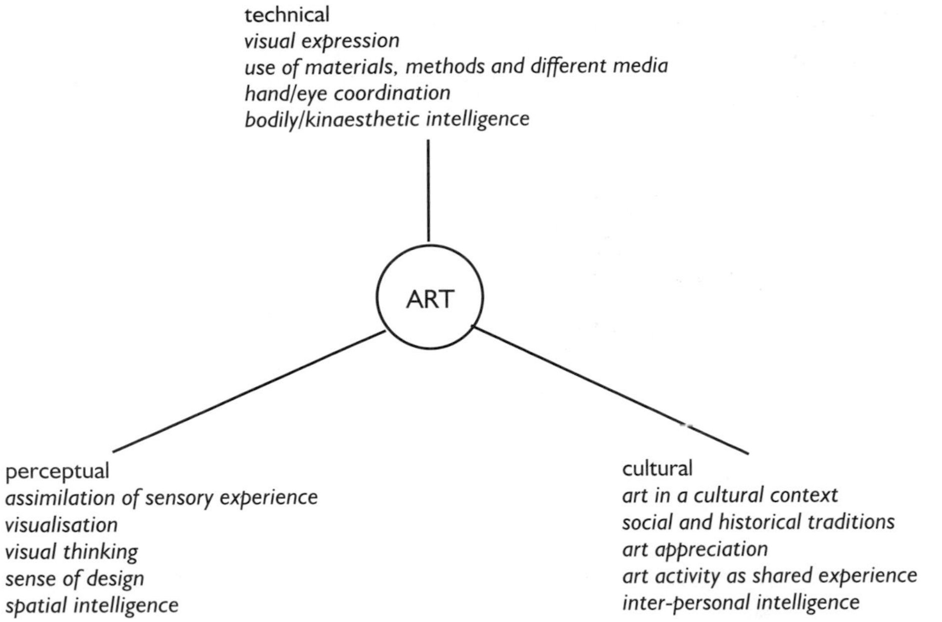

technical
visual expression
use of materials, methods and different media
hand/eye coordination
bodily/kinaesthetic intelligence

ART

perceptual   cultural
assimilation of sensory experience   *art in a cultural context*
visualisation   *social and historical traditions*
visual thinking   *art appreciation*
sense of design   *art activity as shared experience*
spatial intelligence   *inter-personal intelligence*

Figure 8.5

as he was relaxing by a fire he saw the atoms dancing before him again; like snakes they spun, chasing one another's tails. Suddenly he realised that benzene must also have a fundamental ring-like structure.

Thinking with images can be a powerful aid in all aspects of the school curriculum, in language work as a stimulus to imagination, in maths to reinforce spatial and geometric concepts, in design and technology as visual models, in science as metaphors for complex processes, and in art as the inner representation of creative experience. It is possible to create a 'memory' for children, for example a day at the beach, by walking them through the experience. If you decide the image is to be a hot summer day, ask them if they can feel the sun beating down on their bodies. Can they see the people in the water? And the cloudless sky? Can they feel the hot wet sand sliding between the toes? Smell the salt sea air? Hear the waves crashing against the beach? Such visualisation can provide a powerful stimulus for creative writing or artwork.

Various activities can help train children in thinking in images. While reading a story, stop from time to time and ask the children to envisage the scene in the story. Closing their eyes sometimes helps focus their minds on their 'inner eye'. They may describe the scenes they can see, or try to envisage what comes next in the story. Another approach is to ask them to study a complex object for about 20 seconds, then to shut their eyes and try to recreate the object as a clear mental image. Once the image is clear and steady see if the child can move it around in their mind's eye like a computer image or hologram, observing it from different angles. The next step is to imagine something without actually seeing it, like the growth, flowering and decay of a favourite flower. Then go on a mental journey – a shopping trip, a walk in the jungle or an aeroplane flight. Once children learn that images can help them understand and remember things, they can begin to create their own images, using the technique to become more effective learners.

Drawing

The developmental stages in children's drawings are closely related to the whole process of cognitive growth. The well-known Draw a Person Test (Figure 8.6) is a good indicator of cognitive maturity.

DRAWING TEST   (adapted from the Goodenough 'Draw a Person Test' of intelligence).
Say to the child: 'I want you to draw a picture of a man or woman.
Make the very best picture that you can.
Take your time and work very carefully.
See what a good picture of a man or woman you can make.'
Score one mark for each of the following items in the drawing:

1   Head present
2   Legs present
3   Arms present
4   Trunk present
5   Height of trunk more than breadth (not a mere line)
6   Shoulders shown
7   Arms and legs attached to trunk
8   Arms and legs attached at correct point
9   Neck present
10   Outlining of neck is continuous with head
11   Eyes present
12   Nose present
13   Mouth present
14   Nose and mouth in more than one single line each
15   Nostrils shown
16   Hair present
17   Hair on more than circumference and non-transparent
18   Clothing present
19   Two articles clothing, shown as cover
20   Sleeves and trousers or skirt non-transparent
21   Clothing complete for figure drawn
22   Hand distinct
23   Fingers shown on hand
24   Correct number (including thumb)
25   Fingers 2 dimensional, i.e. not single lines but with shape
26   Thumb position distinct
27   Arm joint, elbow – shoulder shown
28   Leg joint knee shown
29   Head in proportion
30   Arms in proportion
31   Legs in proportion
32   Feet in proportion
33   Arms and legs – 2 dimensions – not single lines
34   Heel shown
35   Motor co-ordination ordinary, i.e. standing still
36   Motor co-ordination extraordinary, i.e. moving head in appropriate position
37   Head outline, motor co-ordination
38   Trunk outline – co-ordination
39   Arms and legs co-ordination
40   Features co-ordination, i.e. showing appropriate expression
41   Ears shown
42   Ears correct position and proportion
43   Eye detail, brows and lashes
44   Pupils shown
45   Eye detail in proportion
46   Eye detail focus shown
47   Chin and forehead
48   Projection of chin shown
49   Profile: only one error
50   Correct profile

Score	2	6	10	14	18	22	26	30	34	38	42	46
Maturity level (age equivalent)	3	4	5	6	7	8	9	10	11	12	13	14

Figure 8.6

For the artist, drawing is discovery. It is not only recording what the artist has seen but is important for what it will lead the artist on to see. Sketching, cartoon drawing, doodling with ideas are all ways of making thinking visible. Other ways of using drawing for thinking include:

- *Squiggles* – draw a squiggle, see what the child can create through thinkdrawing in a time limit of say one minute.
- *Add-on pictures* – children sit in a circle with a variety of art materials, mark their piece of paper then pass these on to the right, and add something to the paper received. Keep passing the papers, adding to the original mark four or five times.
- *Dotted art* – ask the child to scatter 12 dots on their paper, then let them create a design or picture incorporating the dots. Encourage them to put a title to finished pictures.
- *Sound-pictures* – play music and see what images are stimulated in children's minds and on paper.

Art appreciation

- Visit an art gallery: choose one painting you like, list all the features you like about the painting, or don't like
- Take a closer look, cut a hole 6 cm across a square of paper to help focus on details of a reproduction. Compare and contrast two paintings.

Questions to ask:

What do you see when you look at this work of art?
What do you think the artist was trying to show/say?
How does the work of art make you feel?
What do you like about it? What don't you like?

Music

Every child is musical but not every child has a chance of discovering it. Like art, music educates the senses. Through music children develop spatial awareness, auditory discrimination, the understanding of whole–part relations and sequencing skills. Listening to music and learning to play an instrument are both problem-solving activities. Music is simply pattern making with sound. Part of the skill of problem solving and learning is the ability to notice and make coherent patterns out of given elements. Both listening to music and making music are patterning and problem-solving activities.

Music is often confined to a fringe activity because of economic pressures or the cry of 'back to the basics'. The basics for children should include music. It is a unique form of human intelligence, which can enhance all learning abilities. Music also provides many opportunities for creative thinking, for example:

- *Sound pictures* – Play a piece of music. What pictures does it evoke in the mind's eye (visualisation). Try drawing or painting them. What words, probably adjectives, might be used to describe the music (verbalisation)? Write a story, poem or title inspired by the music.
- *Movement* – What creative movements best express the mood of the music?
- *Inventing* – Design an instrument from a collection of junk.
- *Water music* – Fill glasses with different levels of water, experiment with pitch by varying the levels of water, compose your own water music!
- *Musical accompaniment* – Invent sound/music accompaniment to a story. Tape it, share the experience with others.

Movement

Children need physical exercise in order to ensure their health of mind and body. Through movement and physical education their bodily, kinaesthetic and spatial skills are developed. Through physical games children also acquire the skills necessary for cooperating with others, such as making friends, inventing games, and for asserting themselves in cooperation and in competition with others. Physical challenge encourages children to be alert, responsive and attentive and provides many opportunities for creative thinking and problem solving.

Routine physical activities such as washing up, doing exercises, running round a track, may require no cognitive effort. An effective physical education programme will, however, challenge both mind and body, providing opportunities to plan courses of action (such as a creative dance or gymnastic sequence) and consider strategies (as in traversing an obstacle course or approaching a team game). One strategy often overlooked in problem-solving activities is the value of rehearsing mentally the physical actions you are going to make. When presented with a physical problem the direction 'think it first' can make a big difference to performance. All physical activity can benefit from a mental warming up session, which may involve:

- talking through to oneself what one is going to do, being mentally prepared and being clear about the goal of the action
- visualising outcomes, the child seeing in the mind's eye what he intends to happen when climbing the rope, shooting the goal or performing the dive. Forming images of the complete physical performance successfully accomplished. Visualising a perfect result.

Physical activity that is not merely routine requires mental processing, if the participant is to perform at his best. The aim should be focused action, focusing the mind on what is to be achieved before the effort of achieving it. Questions to focus attention might include:

What are you intending to do?
What is the purpose?
What is your target?

The aim is not to analyse the component parts of action; often this results in a deficient model of teaching because it focuses on what might go wrong. As an anonymous poet once put it:

The centipede was happy quite
Until the toad in fun
Said 'Pray, which leg goes after which?'
And worked her mind to such a pitch
She lay distracted in the ditch
Considering how to run.

The body thinks best in terms of whole patterns of movement. Avoid overloading the instructions, concentrate on the results. The value of thinking first is that the child can then concentrate on the doing. Trying to think while doing impairs the doing. Trying to do while we're thinking prevents us from thinking clearly. Do not overburden the child with extraneous effort. The motions of a child who is too tense become inefficient. Overforcing generally results in poor performance. Think first, measure the challenge, concentrate the mind then enjoy the movement.[13]

Computers – thinking and artificial intelligence

Six-year-old Sally thumped the computer. 'This machine's dumb.' Her finger had slipped and she had pressed the wrong key. The computer did not, could not respond. Sally was right – compared with her everyday abilities, computers are dumb. They cannot perform the commonplace routines of daily life. Computers can only simulate thinking, they have no self-knowledge. The power of a computer is that it can process great quantities of information with great accuracy. Unlike the computer the human mind does not think with bits of information but with ideas that contain, generate and control information. When the human mind asks 'What does this mean?' it is not simply asking for the computerised response of a logical definition. Thinking in human terms includes knowing opinions, having thoughts, feelings, motivations, tolerating uncertainties, experiencing the capacity to choose, being unpredictable, thinking for ourselves. A computer has no emotions or human concerns. No computer can tell us what values to choose or whether one project is more worth pursuing than another. A computer is logical but it is not reasonable; it can help facilitate thinking but it cannot think for us.[14]

One question that can be asked of any learning activity is 'Who is doing the thinking?' When children are working with computers an added question should be 'Is there thinking going on here?' With many of the low-level task or games programs the answer is probably 'very little'. The interactive nature of computers, with their offer of immediate feedback in terms of tunes, bleeps, ticks and smiley faces to mark correct responses can be highly motivating for children, sharing much of the appeal of mechanical toys. But even with low level tasks like electronic flashcards it helps to have human intelligence at work and the interaction of teacher or peers to give access to ideas and to relate what is on the shimmering screen to the real world.

Adventure games offer a series of puzzles set in an enclosed fantasy environment. Simulations use facts about real circumstances, such as exploring Egyptian pyramids, following clues to locate objects on a map or grid. The best of these programs offer problem-solving opportunities that can be pursued away from the screen. Many computer programs, however, trap children into a small microworld, making them passive responders to illuminated messages that have little meaning or relevance outside the program. The best programs put the child in control and provide software through which the child can express her own thoughts and purposes.[15]

Perhaps one of our tasks as teachers is to help children see the limitations of computer intelligence, to show them what it cannot do, as well as what it can do, and that, although the computer may be 'dumb', we who are its creators need not be. (For more on computers and thinking, see p. 215.)

Factors that hinder thinking

I can't think now, my mind's too full.
       Jenny, aged 7

There are many factors that may serve as blocks to children's thinking. One of the most pervasive of these is the fear of failure. Some children take an optimistic view of the chances of success, gain confidence from past success and can take failure in their stride without being daunted. Other children take a pessimistic view. They draw little comfort from past success, tending to regard it as accidental. Failure is regarded as confirming their incompetence. As William Gordon[16] observed, 'All problems present themselves to the mind as threats of failure.' Failure for these children becomes a self-fulfilling prophecy. Ways need to be found to counter such attitude blocks, to bolster confidence, to provide guidance and to encourage effort.

Children are not helped by always being presented with books, pictures, songs and thoughts as finished products in polished form. They seldom have the chance of seeing the false starts, rough drafts and imperfect first efforts, the hours of practice and frustrating labour that goes into most products of creative endeavour. Alfred Butt's game of Scrabble was rejected as worthless when first presented to the major game companies. Dr Seuss's first book was turned down by so many publishers that he nearly burned it. Children need to see that success is more often a matter of fits and starts, of returning to an original idea and working on it, of overcoming initial failure. Historian L.L. White once remarked, 'Thought is born of failure.' Show how failure can become the spur of effort.

Various forms of stress such as anxiety and worry can block thinking. The thoughts of anxious children who feel under threat tend to turn away from their task and focus on their possible failure: 'I can't do this', 'I'm no good'. Arguments with parents or friends may also raise barriers and prevent thoughts from focusing on a given task. Children respond to anxiety with various coping mechanisms:

- *Avoidance* – If I keep quiet perhaps I won't be noticed.
- *Blaming others* – It's his fault, not mine.
- *Denying reality* – What does she know anyway?
- *Insulating self* – I just don't care.

Such coping mechanisms can soon become habits of mind, shields against criticism in a hostile environment. Ways need to be found to channel feelings of anger and frustration, to accentuate the positive and redirect the negative.

Fatigue can also impair cognitive functioning. It is not surprising that, in the first decade of life, children need long periods of sleep to cope with the efforts of learning. The nerve cells and synapses that are so active during the day need the period of sleep to recover. Without suitable periods of rest the energies needed for mental effort may not be sufficiently restored. Short bursts of activity are preferable for many children to long stretches of tiring effort. Thoughts are best when the child feels freshest.

Related to fatigue is the problem of overload. This may be the result of the child being asked to do too many things at once. In writing, for example, they may be expected to get their ideas right and in good order and at the same time to attend to punctuation, grammar, spelling and handwriting. Stimulus is necessary but it is counterproductive for a child to be over-challenged. 'Think one thing well' should be the watchword, rather than doing many things superficially. Beware of distractions that disturb concentration, such as high noise levels or attention-grabbing activity. Try to reduce conflicting demands on a child's attention, which may be external or internal.

One cause of conflict may be confusion in the child's mind about what he is being asked to do. Ambiguity can be stressful. 'What are we supposed to be doing?' 'How do we begin?' 'What's it all about?' There should be a clear focus on the process involved or the task to be achieved. Check that the child is clear about the purpose of the activity. Help the child to preview, overview and review the task in hand. Show how a large undertaking can be broken down into small steps. Beware spoon feeding. ('Spoon feeding in the long run teaches us nothing but the shape of the spoon' – E.M. Forster.) The child should be given the freedom to explore her own thoughts within the framework of support you have provided.

Various cultural disincentives may block thinking. There are always people around, peers and sometimes teachers, who are willing to do the child's thinking for him. Machines may offer the promise of relief from the burden of thought. Calculators and computers are teaching aids that can substitute for rather than stimulate thinking. The machine that most flatters to deceive in this respect is of course the television. It has been estimated that by the time they leave high school US children will have spent 11 000 hours in the classroom and 22 000 hours watching television. Much of the criticism of television focuses on its obvious effects, which include:

- keeping children away from books and reading, denying them the opportunities to develop skills and imagination
- depriving them of intellectual challenge by offering programmes appealing to the lowest common intellectual denominator
- retarding the use of language by exposing them to a diet of slang and clichés
- showing violence and physical conflict as acceptable everyday occurrences
- the manipulative effects of commercial advertising on attitudes and values.

More importantly TV invites passivity, it discourages the use of the critical faculties, it allows no time for reflection. Bruno Bettelheim says: 'being seduced into passivity and discouraged about facing life actively, on one's own, is the real danger of TV, much more than the often asinine or gruesome content of the shows'.[17]

Television has a tranquillising effect: it is pre-packed and pre-digested, it requires no effort. It has powerful appeal because we are visual animals. As Goethe said, long before the age of TV, 'Thinking is more interesting than knowing, but less interesting than looking.' The trouble with thinking is that it is not a performing art; it does not show well on television. We need to infuse some thinking into our children's viewing habits. Like all drugs, TV needs to be rationed and justified. Encourage your child to forward plan the viewing schedule, to think through and discuss the merits of pro-grammes. Help her to become a thoughtful and critical viewer. Children can absorb a great deal of information through television, mostly held in short-term memory. Rarely does this information come in attention-holding forms, but in flashing images that briefly leave their mark in the child's consciousness. The information comes in discrete forms, with many elements and key ideas missing so that the child is unable to make connections. For the child to benefit from TV it is up to others to help her make con-nections, create networks of ideas and to see significance. TV can stimulate the curiosity and interest of children, presenting class or family with starting points for discussion. Learning from the stimulus of TV or video occurs best if thinking is switched on when the set is switched off.

Lawrence Durrell once said television was like having a sick child in the house, you cannot take your eyes off it yet you wish all the time that it would get better. Other forms of environmental pollution can also block thinking and brain power. Many substances in the environment can damage the brain and the nervous system directly (neurotoxins). The effects may be indirect, for example by damaging the circulation of blood to the brain. These substances can affect not only the growing child but also the brains of unborn children from the moment of conception. For example:

- lead in the atmosphere may damage the intelligence of children
- smoke from cigarettes and exhaust fumes contain poisons that may damage the immune system
- alcohol, when excessively consumed, can cause brain damage and, in pregnant women, may retard foetal growth
- chemical additives used in agriculture as pesticides, herbicides and fungicides and in food additives, such as food dyes, may be toxic to the brain or nervous system.

Other possible pollutants in the environment include aluminium deposits, which may occur in the water supply, and mercury in dental fillings. There is much controversy about these and other possible neurotoxins. More research is needed into these and other possible environmental pollutants. One area in which research has yielded interesting results has related to the influence of children's diet on behaviour and aca-demic performance.

For years the health food lobby has claimed that we don't get enough goodness from modern processed food and that extra vitamins and minerals are needed to remain at optimal health. Established medical opinion tended to scoff at this view, arguing that excess nutrients are excreted from the body and that they simply provide vitamin-rich sewage. Many teachers have, however, become worried at the lack of concentration and behaviour problems being increasingly shown by children. At the same time, surveys of the eating habits of British children, being increasingly fed on junk foods, showed that many had significant nutritional deficiencies in their diet. One teacher, Gwilym Roberts, read up on the biochemistry of nutrition and found what seemed to be a clue.[18] Many of the vitamins and minerals missing from the diet of his pupils were involved in the enzymes essential for optimum brain function. He decided to test whether dietary deficiencies could affect brain functioning. In September 1986 he gave his second formers a battery of mental tests. Then for the rest of the year he gave half his pupils a vitamin and mineral pill and the other half an identical dummy pill. The experiment was checked and overseen by David Benton, a research psychologist from University College, Swansea. In the following July the children were tested again. Benton was not surprised that on tests of memory, concentration and verbal IQ there was no significant difference between the two groups. What amazed him was the significant improvement in non-verbal IQ recorded (on average 9 points up) in the vitamin-taking group. It was known that severe malnutrition affected intellectual functioning. What was not known was that vitamins and minerals might influence the brain's chemistry to boost innate forms of intelligence. The health food industry has been quick to follow up these findings with offers of vitamin and mineral supplements as possible brain-boosters for children. More research is urgently needed in this vital field.

Factors that foster thinking

I'm quite good at thinking. I just need someone to start me up.
   Barry, aged 8

For two days after the murder of Martin Luther King, Jane Elliott, a third-grade (first-year junior) teacher from Iowa, conducted a unique experiment in how discrimination can affect a child's self-concept. During the first day, brown-eyed children were declared superior. They were given special privileges and were expected to live up to their label in class. They were also encouraged to discriminate against their blue-eyed classmates, who were labelled inferior. Next day the roles were reversed, the blue-eyed children were labelled as superior, given special privileges and encouraged to discriminate against the brown-eyed boys and girls. The results amazed both children and teacher.

On both days the children labelled inferior took on the look, behaviour and work habits of genuinely inferior students. The children labelled superior excelled in their work and relished discriminating against the inferior group. Jane Elliott repeated the experiment with succeeding classes, with similar results. When, many years later, some of the children returned as adults for a reunion with the teacher they spoke of the profound and enduring effect that this long ago lesson had on their understanding of what discrimination is and what it can do.[19]

There is a growing body of research into the factors that foster thinking and learning. Key elements include the child's concept of himself as a learner, the teaching style of the teacher and the environment in which learning and teaching take place. These three elements are closely interrelated.

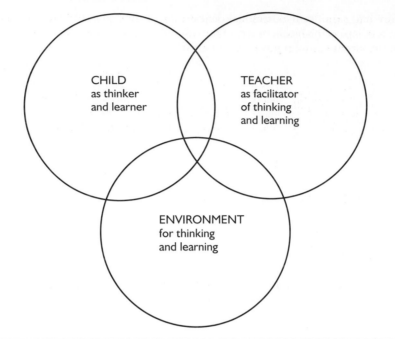

Figure 8.7 The child as thinker and learner.

Success comes in cans not can'ts.
> Sign seen on classroom wall

There is now a generally held view that self esteem is an important factor in the pro-motion of a child's academic achievement and ability. Studies[20] have shown how the way a child sees and feels about himself is related to how he responds in the classroom. Self esteem cannot be said to be a sufficient condition for promoting academic achieve-ment but there is ample evidence to suggest that it is a necessary condition if children are to achieve their best in a learning situation.

Some children never develop a positive self-image. They may not be encouraged to participate in family or class discussion and decision making, they may not receive the feedback they need for efforts made. Their thinking may not be invited and may not be valued. Treated with indifference, they become indifferent. 'Don't know' becomes 'Don't care' and 'Can't do'. Not being trusted to do things or allowed to make mistakes, they may be treated or come to see themselves as incapable. Lack of self-confidence induces failure-avoiding behaviour. They use excuses to discount failure, 'Nobody told me what to do.' They may seek to avoid failure and achieve minimal success through low aspirations, 'I did as I was told, what more do you want?' To chil-dren who have learned over a length of time to regard themselves as stupid, failure can be deeply satisfying – 'Told you so!'

The search for personal significance and identity in the face of continuous internal and external pressures seems a basic human drive. Research shows that persons with high self-esteem tend to be more independent, more consistent in their efforts because of the expectation that they will be well received. Children who regard themselves as effective thinkers will not be slow to offer their thoughts. Those with negative self regard will develop a sense of worthlessness about their thinking.

Although self concept is consistent and tenacious in its hold, there is a flexibility in human personality, particularly in children, which allows for change. The work of Feuerstein in fostering the idea of the child as a thinker, Lipman's child as a philosopher, the notion of the child as problem solver,[21] and the various thinking skills programmes that have emerged from these works all aim to build up the self-esteem of the child.

The teacher: inviting thinking

The good teacher invites you to like yourself, to take pride in your work and expects a great deal from you. The importance of teacher expectations has been confirmed by extensive research.[22]

> *When teachers had high expectations, they actually produced higher achievement in those students than in students for whom they had lower expectations.*[23]

Many studies have shown that success in student performance can be achieved by giving teachers favourable (though false) information about the superior abilities of selected students.[24] However researchers have found that prophecy is not automatically fulfilled. It is a necessary but not sufficient condition for enhancing student progress. The quality of the invitations to think and learn are also key factors. Parents and teachers are the prime sources of these invitations and will see possibilities in children that others miss, will value what others ignore and will create opportunities for children to exercise thought and choice in their learning. The way children respond to these opportunities will depend in large measure on the attitudes and strategies that the teacher adopts. Factors that foster the thinking child include the following.

I Building self-esteem

I didn't know I could do it until I did it!
    Nursery child on making a bridge of bricks

Invite the child to be responsible, for example for equipment, younger children or planning and reporting on tasks that need to be done. Offer choices and respect the choices the child makes. Allow the child to do something unaided and to be trusted when no adult is present. Value the child's suggestions, be enthusiastic about specific abilities. Remember Montessori's motto, 'Never do for a child what he can do unaided', but make an effort to help when needed. Encourage the child to like herself and take pride in who she is and what she can do. Show approval and love for the child as a person.

2 Reaching each child

> *I try to talk at least once to each child in my class as if they were the only child in the world.*
>   Student teacher

Research shows that teachers tend to communicate much more with some children than with others. Good teachers make an effort to invite each class member to contribute rather than relying on patterns of random interaction. It is difficult to over-estimate the importance of offering some one-to-one contacts with each child. This can be achieved through squeezing in a few moments of personal chat with individual children. Open systems of written communication (journals, logs, think books, etc.) can encourage children who rarely speak in class to express their thoughts and feelings.

3 Listening with care

When I talk no one listens. When I listen everyone talks!
Comment overheard in an infant classroom

What the teacher says in the classroom is important. One way of finding out what thinking is going on is to ask the child and then listen with care. Aesop has a fable about a fox who succeeded in crossing the thin ice when other animals, even smaller ones, had fallen through and drowned. The fox was the only animal to listen out for the sound of the ice cracking. Teachers too can fail to listen out for their children. A factor often mentioned by children in describing what good teachers are like is that they listen and care about what the children say. Such teachers demonstrate their care by active listening, for example by paying attention to what the child is saying, pre-venting others from interrupting, allowing the child to finish, facing the child and maintaining eye contact.

4 Being genuine

I like Miss X . . . she thinks what she says.
Mandy aged 7

Most teachers enjoy praising and rewarding children. But to be effective praise needs to be realistic and relevant. Indiscriminate praise devalues both the language of praise and children's real efforts. It needs to be sincere and it needs to be focused. Is it for the quantity or the quality of the work? What criteria are you judging by? What criteria would the child judge by?

Being genuine means sharing feelings with children: 'What you do upsets me because....' In a genuine response the non-verbal language – tone of voice, body stance, eye contact, facial expression and physical gesture – supports the verbal message. Being genuine means also being aware of possible prejudices, being aware of our weaknesses and being prepared to share these with others.

5 Being positive

You can do it Tom, you just need to take a deep breath.
Older child encouraging a younger one to tackle a maths problem

Being positive works both ways, it means rewarding others and rewarding ourselves for what we do well. Be interactive, offer challenges that demand a response from the child. Expect some rejection. Children are not so much against teachers as for themselves. Change takes time; there will be setbacks as well as successes. Every creative act, even baking a loaf of bread, can be seen to change the world in some small way.

6 Being clear

> *I can't understand, there's too many words.*
>
>   Child trying to summarise a difficult passage in a reading book

Communicating what you mean and reaching each child relies on the clearness of the message. Use clear, direct invitations to think rather than vague indirect ones. 'You must think!' is less likely to produce a required response than 'Try to think of . . . .' with some specific aspect given. What is clear for one child, of course, is not clear for another. There is a need to vary the message to suit the needs of the hearer. There are many ways of being clear – actions, diagrams, keywords written in prominent places can all help to reinforce the message. If you have told the child a thousand times and the child still does not respond, it is probably not the child who is the slow learner. Seek feedback: you know what you are saying but what message is the child hearing? Put the message in different ways, be stimulating and novel, elaborate your ideas. Your model will in turn influence the ways in which your children will express what they are trying to say.

7 Being a learner too

Try out your own teaching methods on yourself. Invite the children to share your own learning, hobbies and interests. Passion for a subject can be catching. If you want your children to be readers then let them see you reading. Let them see you writing and share its problems. Learn a musical instrument (or brush up your skills); try painting or a new creative hobby.

The classroom where thinking is fostered is one where enquiry and investigation are values. It's an 'I wonder why?', a 'Let's find out' and a 'What do you think?' environment. The teacher admits uncertainty: 'We are not quite sure about that – people have different ideas' and welcomes challenge, 'That's an interesting question, I shall have to think about that.' The teacher conveys her belief in the value of thinking, and emphasises that education is as much about exploring the unknown as it is about repeating the known. In the enquiring classroom the teacher is also a learner alongside the child.

The environment for thinking

Some teachers enrich the intellectual atmosphere of their classrooms by setting up a special thinking area, for example displays with questions related to national issues (with newspaper clippings) or local environmental issues. Problem corners can have problem-of-the-day (or week) with a box in which to post solutions or for children to pose their own problems. There can be a class museum of changing exhibits prompting investigation, science experiments, a graffiti board or a class think book for jokes, riddles, puzzles, odd quotations, reflections, queries or complaints. Advice on thinking and learning strategies can be displayed on charts for all to see, devised by teacher or children. This could be a one-line reminder like 'Think before you ink', or a chart like the one in Figure 8.8.[25]

Thinking about our thinking

- Did I stop and think?

- Did I ask any good questions?

- Did I use my senses (see, hear or touch) to get information?

- Did I listen well?

- Did I make a plan?

- Did I give good reasons for what I thought?

- Did I have any new thoughts or ideas?

- Did I take care and check my work?

- Did I work well on my own?

- Did I think for myself?

- Did I work well with others?

- Did I make use of the thinking of others?

- Did I persevere and keep trying?

- Did I solve any problem(s)?

- Do I know how I solved my problem(s)?

- Did I show or tell what I thought and did?

- Did I learn anything?

- Do I know how I learnt it?

- Do I know what would help improve my thinking and learning?

- Do I know what I need to remember in the future?

The air should be fresh. Remember the brain needs plentiful supplies of oxygen to function well. Stay cool, dress in warm clothes and let the air circulate. Avoid the soporific effects of a warm, stuffy atmosphere. Let there be light and as much space as possible for working, thinking and movement. Dull, cramped spaces tend to produce dull cramped minds.

An emphasis on problem solving. In a thinking-centred classroom the teacher encourages a problem-finding attitude by encouraging children to ask questions as well as answer them. For example with any found object of interest the teacher asks not only 'What is it?' or 'What is it made from?' but also 'What questions could we ask?' 'What problems does it pose?' (look for *objets trouvés*, things that can be taken apart and put together again, like old clocks, typewriters, machines or gadgets – that can be manipulated, observed, drawn, explored and questioned). With any topic, project or centre of interest children can be encouraged to find problems, to wonder and to speculate. 'We'll be studying *x*... what questions would you like to have answered?'

A more reflective pace. Some teachers tend to encourage impulsiveness. When they ask a question they expect an immediate answer, often calling on the first child who waves a hand. If an answer is not immediately forthcoming the teacher will repeat or rephrase the question, ask a different question or another child, reacting too soon with praise, an additional question or another interjection. The quick reaction can cut off the child's effort to answer or elaborate. Rapid-fire question-and-answer sessions can stimulate quick thinking, help check and reinforce knowledge, and maintain attention, but can be counterproductive when children need time to deliberate, to reflect on alternatives, to weigh the evidence, choose the right words and express their view fully. One useful way to achieve a more reflective pace is to wait until all children who wish to answer have raised their hands. Then call for say three answers, and discuss the differences between those answers. Another way is simply to extend waiting time. Silence can be more inviting than words. In the Paired Reading Project the 'thinking time' recommended for recall of words is up to 5 seconds. In some classrooms the waiting time of teachers tended to be about 1 second. When waiting time is extended the length of pupil responses is usually increased.

In teaching for thinking the child becomes an active participant not a passive observer in school learning. The subjects of the school curriculum provide the knowledge base necessary for thinking and become in a dynamic sense 'food for thought'. The strategies used in teaching for thinking (brainstorming, visualising, inner-speech, networking, feedback, waiting time, open questioning, modelling, drawing, problem finding and theorising) can improve both general thinking skills and mastery of subject content. Teaching for thinking can therefore make the school a more interesting and challenging place for the child. It has the advantage for the teacher of being free in the sense that no expensive teaching aids are necessary. It also makes teaching not less difficult but more of a shared adventure, an intellectual adventure. We offer children the adventure of physical play and exploration; we also need to introduce them to the adventure of ideas. This lifelong journey can begin in the child's earliest years, given the right help. It will enrich school learning and help the child to face more confidently the problems of her own life. Personal survival may also depend on the developing ability to think for oneself, as the following true story illustrates.[26]

Four small girls were walking home one afternoon from their infant school when a car drew up beside them. The man inside the car called to the girls and said to them, 'Your father says you're to come with me at once. He sent me to fetch you.' The man held the back door open and three of the girls got in. They had always been taught to do as their father said. But the fourth girl did not get in. She had been taught to think for herself. So she did. And ran.

The car drove off, while the fourth girl ran as fast as she could to a nearby police station. She told her story to the policeman, describing the colour of the car and direction it was going. At once a call went out to all patrol cars in the area. Within a short while the car in which the man and girls were travelling was stopped, and the girls were soon brought back safely.

The girl who raised the alarm was questioned by the police. 'What made you run off instead of going too?' 'I don't know, but Mummy and Daddy are always saying, "Think!" They say, "You've got a mind of your own, use it." So I thinked. I thinked that if Daddy really wanted us he'd have come himself, and I thinked that the man only said one Daddy and we've got three Daddies, all of us I mean. So I ran.'

The future survival of the human race will depend on the preservation of the world's physical resources. Even more it will depend on the development of its mental resources. People are perhaps only a shadow of what they might be. A UNESCO report on education claimed, 'The human brain has a very large unused potential, which some authorities – more or less arbitrarily – have assessed at 90%.' The job of education is to realise this potential. 'Man is but a reed,' wrote Pascal, 'the feeblest thing in nature, but he is a thinking reed .... All our dignity lies in thought ... let us endeavour then to think well; therein lies the principle of morality.' In teaching children to think well we are aiming high. Let us aim high, for their sakes and for ours.

Summary

Teaching for thinking should take place across the curriculum. Scientific thinking develops through asking questions about the natural world, gathering evidence and information, generating and testing hypotheses. Technological thinking involves applying scientific thinking and design to doing and making. Geographical thinking is about place, expressed, for example, through mapmaking. Historical thinking is about time, expressed though, for example, constructing timelines. Art involves developing visual thinking, expressed through, for example, visualisation, drawing and discussing art. Music and movement provide opportunities for creative thinking. Computers can facilitate thinking, but should not be a substitute for thinking. Teachers need to be aware of the factors that hinder and foster thinking and seek to create an environment for thinking.

9 Thinking schools

If one learns from others but does not think, one will be bewildered. If, on the other hand, one thinks but does not learn from others, one will be in peril.
  Confucius

You get a bigger brain by adding to it what others think that you would never have thought.
  Sarah, aged 8

Research in the latter half of the twentieth century laid the foundations for new directions in teaching thinking and learning in the twenty-first century.[1] In recent years there has been growing interest across the world in ways of developing children's thinking and learning skills. This interest has been fed by new knowledge about how the brain works and how people learn, and evidence that specific interventions can improve children's thinking and intelligence.

Almost every new curriculum report and guideline now emphasises the importance of promoting thinking and reasoning, as well as knowledge about the world, as essential foundations for successful learning. If it is by thinking that we learn, then improving pupils' thinking skills will help them to make more sense of their learning and their lives. Thinking skills enable pupils to turn their experience into learning. They focus on 'knowing how' rather than 'knowing that', not just gaining knowledge but learning how to learn. Teachers and researchers have demonstrated that thinking and learning can be developed using a variety of approaches. This chapter looks at the implications of research in developing thinking children, thinking classrooms and thinking schools.

What does research tell us about thinking?

Research in neuroscience and psychology is providing a clearer picture of the brain and the processes associated with thinking. These have some important implications for teachers. Key principles that emerge from this research include the need for teachers and carers to provide:

- *cognitive challenge*, challenging children's thinking from the earliest years
- *social construction of learning*, extending their thinking through working with others
- *metacognitive discussion*, reviewing what they think and how they learn.

We know that most of the growth in the human brain occurs in early childhood: by the age of six, the brain in most children is approximately 90% of its adult size. This implies that intervention while the brain is still growing may be more effective than waiting until the brain is fully developed. Cognitive challenge is important at all stages, but especially in the early years of education.[2]

Cognitive psychology and educational philosophy have both done much to clarify our understanding of the term 'thinking' and the importance of dispositions, such as attention and motivation, commonly associated with thinking.[3] This has prompted a move away from a simple model of 'thinking skills' as isolated cognitive capacities to a view of thinking as inextricably connected to emotions and dispositions, including our ability to learn with and through others ('emotional intelligence').[4]

There is a growing realisation that we need not only to teach cognitive skills and strategies but also to develop the higher 'metacognitive' functions that are involved in metacognition. This involves making learners aware of themselves as thinkers and how they process/create knowledge by 'learning how to learn' (metacognition).

The notion of inborn intelligence that dominated educational practice until the mid-twentieth century was challenged by Vygotsky (1962) and others who developed a constructivist psychology predicated on learners as active creators of their own knowledge. Continuing this attack on the concept of a fixed general intelligence, Howard Gardner's theory of multiple intelligence has had a growing influence in recent years on educational theory and practice, although not all are convinced of its claims.[5]

This research and the pioneering work of Feuerstein and Lipman, as well as other leading figures such as Edward de Bono, have inspired a wide range of curriculum and programme developments. These have introduced a number of approaches to teaching and learning, including 'cognitive acceleration', 'brain-based' approaches (such as 'accelerated learning') and 'philosophical' approaches aimed at developing the moral and emotional as well as intellectual aspects of thinking – caring and collaborative as well as critical and creative thinking. These are discussed below.

By the end of the twentieth century there was a widespread realisation that 'key' or 'core' skills of thinking, creativity and problem solving lay at the heart of successful learning and should be embedded in primary and secondary school curricula. In 1998 the Department for Education and Employment commissioned Carol McGuinness to review and evaluate research into thinking skills and related areas.[6] Key points that emerged from her study of research were that:

- pupils benefited from being coached in thinking
- not one model, but many approaches proved effective
- success was due to pedagogy (teaching strategies), not specific materials
- strategies were needed to enable pupils to transfer thinking to other contexts
- teachers needed professional support and coaching to sustain success.

McGuinness points out that the most successful interventions are associated with a 'strong theoretical underpinning, well-designed and contextualised materials, explicit pedagogy and teacher support'.

In England and Wales the revised National Curriculum (1999) included thinking skills in its rationale, stating that thinking skills are essential in 'learning how to learn'.[7] The list of thinking skills identified in the National Curriculum is similar to many such lists: information processing, reasoning, enquiry, creative thinking and evaluation. The curriculum was no longer to be seen simply as subject knowledge but as being underpinned by the skills of lifelong learning. Since the review and the explicit inclusion of thinking skills in the National Curriculum, interest in the teaching of thinking has burgeoned in the UK. Teaching for thinking in schools has been strongly influenced by the work of certain leading individuals and programmes. Research showed that interventions seem to work, if they had a strong theoretical base and if teachers were enthusiastic and well trained in the use of a programme or strategy. Teachers using these approaches are developing them in new directions, integrating them into everyday teaching to create 'thinking classrooms', and developing whole school policies to create 'thinking schools'.

Thinking classrooms

We saw in Chapters 4 and 5 how both Feuerstein and Lipman, though coming from different starting-points, hold similar beliefs about the possibility of transforming children's abilities. Research findings vindicate their claims.[8] Another well researched programme, developed in the UK, that, like the work of Feuerstein and Lipman seeks to raise intelligence through the explicit teaching of thinking, is Cognitive Acceleration through Science Education (CASE).[9]

Cognitive acceleration approaches

CASE

Of particular note is the work of Philip Adey and Michael Shayer at Kings College in London. Through the original CASE project, which was developed in the 1980s and early 1990s for Key Stage 3 Science, their work now extends into other subjects and age groups and has perhaps the best research and most robust evidence of the impact of thinking skills in the UK.[10]

The following is a typical format of a CASE lesson for thinking that builds in time for cognitive and metacognitive discussion:

1 *Concrete preparation* – stimulus to thinking, introducing the terms of the problem.
2 *Cognitive conflict* – creates a challenge for the mind.
3 *Social construction* – dialogue with others, discussion that extends thinking.
4 *Metacognition* – reflection on how we tackled the problem.
5 *Bridging* – reviewing where else we can use this thinking and learning.

CASE lessons for young children and related courses in Thinking Maths (CAME) and Thinking Technology (CATE) have been developed. CASE lessons have also been developed for young children. 'Let's Think!' aims to raise achievement by developing Year 1 pupils' general thinking patterns and by developing teachers' understanding of children's thinking.

During 'Let's Think' lessons young children work with a teacher in groups of six and each activity takes about 30 minutes. The session is completely oral, with discussion based on a range of objects. At the beginning of the session the teacher helps agree a common language to describe the objects being used. Having established the vocabulary and the concepts involved, the teacher sets the challenge of the activity. One popular activity in this schema is called the 'hoop game' when children are required to put orange toy dinosaurs in one hoop and *Tyrannosaurus rex* dinosaurs in another hoop. The challenge is that one of the dinosaurs is an orange *T. rex*. This is very perplexing for our preoperational children because they have to utilise two pieces of information about the dinosaur and find a solution to the problem. The children work together as a group to come to a solution or a number of possible solutions to solve the task. They discuss their ideas and make suggestions. The teacher guides them, without being obvious, towards the idea of overlapping the hoops and putting the wayward dinosaur in the intersection.

The children are encouraged to state whether they agree or disagree with each other by giving a reason. For example, they can be heard to say, 'I think ... because' or 'I disagree with you because...'. The activities are designed as problems to be solved, thus creating a context for developing thinking. Children are required to work collaboratively; to plan and evaluate their own and others' thinking strategies, which enables the teacher to get children to think about their thinking (metacognition) through asking such questions as 'What do you think we are going to have to think about?' and 'How did you get your answer?', rather than 'Is your answer correct?'

'Let's Think!' aims to accelerate the transition between two types of thought process. The first type of thought is what Piaget called 'preoperational', when children still find it difficult to engage in what adults perceive as rational thought. The next stage, which Piaget described as 'concrete operational', involves manipulating at least two ideas in order to produce a third, new idea, which is what the sessions encourage the children to do. 'Let's Think' aims to accelerate the transition between the two types of thought in order to help pupils make better sense of their learning and improve general achievement. It is too early for independent evaluations of the project but, as in other programmes, teachers involved have reported positive improvements in their professional practice.

CAME

The name CAME stands for Cognitive Acceleration of Mathematics Education.[11] Its aim is to use discussion-based tasks where children have the opportunity to make rapid development. The tasks are aimed at developing children's conceptual thinking rather than the mechanics of doing the maths. They differ from open-ended investigations in that each lesson has a specific concept to develop. The activities generate group and whole-class discussion, which is an alternative to written individual work with a big emphasis on 'How did you get your answer?' rather than 'What is the answer?' The emphasis on 'How did you get your answer' is far more conducive to learning than 'Is your answer correct?'

Thinking through geography

This programme was designed by David Leat in partnership with geography teachers.[12] They identify a list of 'big concepts' that the authors claim are necessary for an understanding of geography. These include: cause and effect, classification, planning, decision making, location, inequality, development, systems. Twenty-four exemplar lessons were developed, each of which targets a concept. The lessons encourage development of geographical concepts, the development of children's vocabulary for talking about thinking and the use of talk and group work for generating and evaluating alternative solutions.

Brain-based approaches

Accelerated learning

Many educationalists are influenced by recent research into how the human brain works and draw on some of the implications of this research for teachers and schools. Edward de Bono and Eric Jensen have long argued that teaching approaches in schools have not developed in accord with this research. Accelerated Learning and Multiple Intelligence approaches all draw on these broad ideas, together with research into learning styles. The common feature is the reliance on brain research to inspire teaching techniques in the classroom.[13]

There are many theories of learning styles. They are rooted in a classification of psychological types and the fact that individuals tend to process information differently. Different researchers propose different sets of learning style characteristics but many remain unconvinced by their claims that children learn best through using one preferred style.[14]

'Accelerated learning' includes applying VAK (visual, auditory and kinaesthetic) learning styles in approaches to teaching:

- *visual* – learning best through pictures, charts, diagrams, video, ICT etc.
- *auditory* – learning best through listening
- *kinaesthetic* – learning best through being physically engaged in a task.

For example, in teaching children to spell a word a teacher might show them how to chunk the word into three pieces, emphasising this by using different colours for each section of the word, and to visualise it in their heads. She might also ask them to write the word in the air with their fingers.

There is still much scope for research into the effectiveness of 'accelerated learning' and other 'brain-based' teaching strategies, such as 'BrainGym'.

De Bono

According to de Bono we tend to think in restricted and predictable ways. To become better thinkers we need to learn new habits. His teaching strategy, known as 'Thinking hats', helps learners try different approaches to thinking.[15] Each 'thinking hat' represents a different way to think about a problem or issue. Children are encouraged to try on the different 'hats' or approaches to a problem to go beyond their usual thinking habits. The 'hats' or approaches to thinking are as follows:

- White hat = *information* – what do we know?
- Red hat = *feelings* – what do we feel?
- Purple hat = *problems* – what are the drawbacks?
- Yellow hat = *positives* – what are the benefits?
- Green hat = *creativity* – what ideas have we got?
- Blue hat = *control* – what are our aims?

De Bono claims that the technique is widely used in management, but little research has been published to date on its use in education.

Philosophical approaches

Many resources have been developed in recent years to adapt Lipman's approach to philosophy for children to the needs of children and teachers in the UK, using stories and other kinds of stimulus to create a community of enquiry in the classroom.[16]

Stories for Thinking

In a typical Stories for Thinking lesson the teacher shares a 'thinking story' with the children. They have 'thinking time' when they are asked to think about anything in the story that they thought was strange, interesting or puzzling. After some quiet thinking time the teacher asks for their comments or questions and writes each child's questions on the board, adding her name after her question. The children then choose from the list of questions which one they would like to discuss. The teacher then invites the children to comment and to say who agrees or disagrees with particular comments made. If children do not give reasons or evidence from the story for their opinions, the teacher asks, 'Why do you think that?' or 'Have you got a reason for that?'

When asked the value of a Stories for Thinking lesson, one child said, 'You have to ask questions and think hard about the answers.' Another said, 'Sometimes you change your mind and sometimes you don't.' A third reply was, 'It is better than just doing reading or writing because you have to say what you really think.' Teachers note that in Stories for Thinking lessons, in which they may also uses poems, pictures or other texts for thinking, the children have become more thoughtful, better at speaking and listening to each other, better at asking questioning and using the language of reasoning, more confident in posing creative ideas and in judging what they and others think and do, and more confident about applying thinking when answering written comprehension questions – skills that underpin success in the National Curriculum and success in life.

Teaching strategies across the curriculum

Researchers have identified a number of teaching strategies that can help stimulate children's thinking in different subject areas.[17] For example, teachers can use Odd One Out as a teaching technique to identify pupils' understanding of key concepts in different subjects. In a numeracy lesson a teacher might put three numbers on the board, such as 9, 5 and 10; or in science three materials; or in English three characters to compare and contrast – then ask the children to choose the 'odd one out' and to give a reason. Teachers who use this strategy claim it can reveal gaps in the knowledge that they have taught and the knowledge and vocabulary that the children are then able to use. The children think of it as a game and are used to thinking up examples and ideas thatshow their thinking in different curriculum subjects. This approach also encourages creative thinking.

Concept mapping

Concept mapping is an information-processing technique with a long history. Tony Buzan developed this technique into a version he calls Mind Mapping.[18] Concept maps are tools that help you think and learn – and involve writing down, or more commonly drawing, a central idea and thinking up new and related ideas that radiate out from the centre. By focussing on key ideas written down in children's own words, and then looking for branches out and connections between the ideas, they are mapping know-ledge in a manner that will help them understand and remember new information. A simple concept map might be used to map out the connections between characters in a story. Children might also draw maps from memory to test what they remember or know. Teachers have found concept maps helpful in finding out or revising what chil-dren know and the technique is especially popular when used in pairs or groups. Children can learn from the technique from an early age and many find it motivating. As one young child put it, 'Concept mapping gets you to think and try more.' There is no evidence that it transforms thinking or intelligence but it is a useful teaching and revision technique for extending thinking and making it visually memorable.

Activating Children's Thinking Skills (ACTS)

This project aimed to promote the development of thinking skills in ordinary classrooms in Northern Ireland at Key Stage 2.[19] Thinking diagrams or 'graphic organ-isers', for instance for decision making, were produced as an aid to making the steps in thinking explicit to learners. Evaluation of ACTs, like other approaches, has been positive but inconclusive. It is very difficult, in evaluating the success of particular interventions, to control the influence of the many variables involved in the teaching situation. There is still much scope for further research.

Computers and thinking

There is evidence that the use of computers can lead to improved learning of some basic skills, but do they develop thinking?.

Research shows that there are several ways in which the use of ICT could particularly enhance the teaching and learning of thinking skills.[20] First, thinking skills can be developed by supporting multiple and complex representations of information, allow-ing learners, for example, to think with a richer knowledge base. As James, aged 8, said, 'I didn't know there was so much to know!'

Educational software can act like a teacher to prompt and direct enquiry through asking questions, giving clues and suggesting avenues of investigation. It can also act as a resource while learners discuss and explore ideas, prompting reflection around a simulation, for example.

Networks via the Internet and including video conferencing can allow students to engage directly in collaborative learning and knowledge sharing with others who are not physically present.

The main criticism of the computer as a tutor model is that directed computer teach-ing does not allow children to be creative learners, able to think and make connections for themselves, and so is unlikely to support the development of higher order think-ing. This can be transformed, however, by collaboration around ICT activities, which has been shown to have the potential to enhance the learning of transferable thinking skills.[20]

Effective collaborative learning still needs to be structured. Learners should be taught how to reason and learn together before they are asked to work collaboratively with ICT, because having to articulate and explain strategies to others is more likely to lead to transfer than just doing things without thinking or talking them through.[21] For example, working with LOGO is not just manipulating a screen turtle. It is about reasoning and developing effective problem-solving strategies, which can be achieved much better with a learning partner or small group through discussion. In the lesson plenary, by reflecting on the process of collaborative problem solving, the teacher can help children to 'bridge' their thinking to different areas of the curriculum.

Computers can promote children's thinking skills when used as part of a larger dialogue about thinking and learning.

Thinking Schools

Schools and parents need to prepare their children for a rapidly changing world. Children need more than knowledge. Schools and parents need to teach children how to think, to reason and to make wise and informed choices. They need to teach the skills that will enable children to respond creatively to the challenges and opportunities of the future and continue learning throughout life. As James, aged 10, put it, 'We should be learning not just for today but for every day of our lives.'

Research shows that children do best in classrooms where the work is intellectually challenging – 'Work that makes your brain hurt,' as Jody, aged 6, put it. Such work will involve the child exercising both creative and critical thinking skills, learning to think for himself and learning how to benefit from the thinking of others. So how do schools help pupils develop these skills? In recent years there has been a growing awareness of the need to develop whole school policies to create 'thinking schools'.[22]

Techniques for teaching thinking are a key focus in England's new Primary and Key Stage 3 Strategies designed to raise achievement in primary and secondary schools. A growing number of primary schools have introduced teaching strategies drawn from recent research into teaching thinking and accelerated learning. One of these – the Queen's School – has developed a unique whole-school approach focused on developing a number of strategies for intellectually challenging teaching in a whole-school approach that puts thinking at the heart of the curriculum.[23]

Case study 1: The Queen's School Thinking Skills Project

After a three-year thinking skills project a Year 6 class produced the best SATs results ever achieved at Queen's Primary School. But the success of the project is not best measured by SATs results. It is best measured by the impact it has had on the children, the teachers and the school.

Initially the school was seeking a range of teaching strategies to challenge their able children. However they soon realised that a research project on thinking skills might enhance the curriculum and raise standards of achievement for all children. What they developed was a unique whole-school approach focused on developing the thinking of all pupils.

Through the Thinking School project the school wanted to achieve:

- a thinking curriculum to enhance the daily prescribed national strategies
- infusion of higher order thinking skills across the curriculum
- improved quality in teaching for thinking and learning
- a teaching and learning policy for a thinking school.

The project was generated by a group of inspirational teachers who were keen to integrate philosophy for children, theories of multiple intelligence, a broad range of thinking skills and accelerated learning into their teaching. The project began with one new thinking skills approach – philosophy for children – using my 'Stories for Thinking' materials. Gradually, staff began to create communities of enquiry in their classrooms where children were challenged to question texts and deepen their thinking through dialogue. Resources were developed, a coordinator was appointed and all teachers became involved in the training. As the project found, it takes time, vision, energy and organisation for new strategies to permeate a school.

The key principle of the project was that effective learning is underpinned by cognitive talk. Reading and writing, as well as maths and science, float on a sea of talk. Teachers found that the community of enquiry approach created a space for questioning and discussion and gave cognitive pace to their lessons. The community of enquiry was not a 'bolt-on' addition to lessons but was seen to underpin the whole approach to creating an enquiring classroom and a thinking school. The classroom became a place of possibilities, a place of order and of serendipity – of adventures in ideas. The community of enquiry and other thinking techniques were not seen as 'how to' recipes but as sources of creative inspiration, a set of possibilities to be adapted and developed by each teacher.

Once the community of enquiry is established in the classroom – and it takes time to establish and internalise the rules and habits of intelligent discussion – its strategies can be applied to any lesson. This helped to create what one visitor described as a 'hugely energised and happy school'. Parents and governors were invited to training sessions and conferences with local schools followed. After one conference on the thinking skills project a teacher reports an old man muttering, 'That is what we were taught *not* to do when I was a boy.'

The Thinking School project was very much a whole-school commitment. In the classrooms teachers have become learners and researchers, collaborating on planning, developing new materials together and trying out strategies designed to improve teaching and learning. Teaching strategies included:

- planning for effective questioning
- modelling thinking processes
- evaluating thinking teaching and learning.

The headteacher reports that 'the outcomes have given us renewed insight into what makes an effective teacher and learner, feeding into our school self-evaluation'. Teachers were encouraged to innovate and experiment. They observed each other's lessons and shared their lesson planning. Staff who initially stood back – young and older – were gradually drawn in. As one teacher put it, 'I've developed what I do and I know why I'm doing it.'

The process of monitoring and evaluation has become more firmly embedded into practice and is seen as an essential prerequisite to improvement. Self-evaluation extends into the classrooms through peer observation, and for pupils through reviews/questionnaires and the use of thinking logs. They are part of an impetus, as one teacher put it, 'to know the world from the child's point of view'. One way of achieving this was through the introduction of children's learning logs. For one teacher, thinking logs are valuable because they provide children with 'a special time for thinking and reflecting in their own words on their own thinking'.

Other thinking skills strategies used in the project included the use in all classes of concept mapping (rather than just brainstorming), encouraging children to make their thinking explicit through both verbal and visual means, and the use of metacognitive questioning. Teachers were encouraged to display some metacognitive prompts to thinking in every class. The questions teachers chose to display varied in each class. Questions on display included:

- What have you learnt today?
- What have you found hard today?
- How can you apply what you have learnt?
- What could you have done better?
- What do you want to learn tomorrow?

The project's principle that there was 'no one model' meant that teachers chose, or discussed with children, their own best questions for display. They hoped that these questions would be internalised by children as habits of reflection, become a focus for end-of-day plenaries and prompt children's 'think writing' in their logs (or, for young children, in the class thinking log scribed by the teacher). Teachers were encouraged to identify their own key question(s) in every lesson, and to show evidence of pupil questioning in every classroom. A child's interest in life is wider than any curriculum, and teachers found a focus on questioning provided children with opportunities to explore issues outside prescribed topics as well as to explore more deeply key concepts within topics. Questioning can have other purposes too. When a class was asked, 'Why do we ask questions?' one boy replied 'To annoy our parents.'

Teachers found that a benefit of including more cognitive talk is the greater emphasis it gives on the processes of thinking, and with less emphasis on written outcomes there was less marking. One drawback they found was that lessons tended to run over. An implication of this was to do less but to try to do it more deeply, spending more time on extended discussion, extended writing, extended cross-curricular projects.

One such a mini project undertaken in Year 6 was on Educating for Sustainable Development, which offered opportunities for cross-curricular work. Such extended research projects provide opportunities for concept mapping, creative thinking, reasoning, evaluation and sustained thinking about matters of importance. Pupils worked in pairs to create short presentations on different countries for the rest of the year group. Techniques for these presentations included TV interviews, game shows, plays, posters and persuasive speeches. The presentations reflected the development of the children's ideas about sustainable development at personal, local and global levels – all examples of ways the project teachers are seeking to create the 'caring, critical and creative citizens of the future'. Some of the activities in this topic were filmed and appear in the project video – *Thinking Allowed* – which allowed teachers to share and discuss the teaching and learning in the project.

Findings from the project indicated that it had a positive effect on:

- teachers' professional confidence and self-esteem
- pupils' achievements across a range of curriculum measures, including SATs results
- children's self-esteem and self-concept as thinkers and learners
- the fluency and quality of children's questioning
- the quality of their thinking evidenced in their writing
- their ability to listen to others and engage effectively in class discussion
- evaluation and assessment via self-evaluating pupils, teachers and school.

The project included the development of whole-school policies, including teaching and learning, curriculum policies and a behaviour policy emphasising the 3Rs: Respect, Responsibility and Reflection.

Case study 2: Westbury Park Primary School

This school found that a focus on thinking skills could have a dramatic effect on the way the school worked to maximise the learning of children. They decided that the children in this school needed 'HOTS not MOTS – Higher-Order Thinking Skills, not More Of The Same'.

Initiatives aimed at using thinking skills approaches to transform learning included:

- sharing a vision and communicating these in agreed policies
- developing the thinking environment of every classroom
- introducing philosophy for children
- developing thinking science
- encouraging greater creativity in literacy and numeracy teaching
- sharing teaching for thinking strategies across a network of schools
- developing creative partnerships with local institutions and businesses.

Evidence of a thinking school is to be found in thinking classrooms. The staff believe that children need to feel they are working within a thinking classroom. There are daily thinking challenges put on the whiteboard for children to respond to at the start of each day. A thinking challenge might be a verbal, mathematical or visual puzzle, a problem, investigation or challenge such as working out the similarities and differences between ketchup and blood. The children tackle the daily task in their A4 size thinking books, and the results are then shared in class but not marked. Children find these 'thinking starters' to the day a good preparation for the lessons ahead. 'Our brains feel so ready after these,' said one child. Another said, 'We keep thinking about them all day.'

There are displays showing key words about learning styles and thinking skills. Evidence of specific techniques is displayed, such as 'Mind Mapping' (tree diagrams showing connections between ideas), 'PMI' (listing the Plus, Minus and Interesting points of a topic) or 'concept cartoons' created by the children. A table of 'thinking books' and resources is available for children to consult.

Thinking time is built in before lessons, when they think about and describe the learning objective (TLP or 'Today's Learning Point'), during lessons, when the teacher tries to include a thinking skills enrichment task intended to motivate the children to apply in a different context or explain a key concept to a partner, and at the end, when children think about and add a TIL (Today I Learnt) point to their work. Children are also encouraged to think about their thinking (metacognition). Kate, aged 10, for example, wrote that for her 'thinking skills' was just 'a different word for creativity'.

What is a thinking school?

These case studies illustrate some key elements of a thinking school. These can be summarised as developing the quality of thinking and learning in the school through:

- *a vision of the school* as a thinking and learning organisation expressed in a shared mission and policy guidelines
- *an environment for thinking*, with stimulating resources and displays of work showing high quality thinking and learning
- *teaching for thinking*, using teaching strategies that explicitly model, scaffold, motivate and help students to transfer what they learn to new contexts
- *assessment for learning*, with self-evaluating pupils engaged in self-assessment and setting their own targets for learning
- *community values,* where respect, responsibility and reflection are developed through group discussion in communities of enquiry
- *teachers as learners*, engaged in self-evaluation, classroom research, staff development in sharing ideas and practice, towards
- *creative partnerships*, within and beyond the school community, expanding individual and organisational intelligence by linking with a wide range of creative partners.

The challenge for schools is to develop educational programmes so that all, not just an elite, can become effective thinkers. The challenge for teachers is to make every lesson a thinking lesson – not only about the curriculum but also the skills of thinking and learning. The challenge for children is to develop the skills and strategies of effective thinking and so develop habits of intelligent behaviour. As Paul, aged 10, put it: 'We need to think better if we are going to become better people.'

Recent test results show that standards in schools are rising – but slowly. Could the teaching of thinking be the key to raising achievement? The work in this book shows that, when pupils are taught the habits of effective thinking they grow in confidence, their learning is accelerated and they are better prepared to face the challenge of the future. As Tom, aged 10, said, 'We don't know what's going to happen in the future, so we need all the brains we can get – because we'll need them.'

Summary

Recent years have seen growing interest in teaching for thinking and in approaches that focus not only on cognitive skills but also metacognitive functions and dispositions. Thinking skills are seen to underpin learning in the English National Curriculum and National Primary Strategy. Success is claimed for approaches aimed at 'cognitive acceleration', 'brain-based' learning, philosophical approaches and various teaching for thinking strategies. There is growing research into ways of developing schools as learning organisations ('thinking schools'). Success in the future will depend on developing thinking children in thinking homes, thinking classrooms and thinking schools.

Notes

Introduction

1 M. Lipman (1984) The cultivation of reasoning through philosophy. *Educational Leadership*, September, 51–56.
2 Recent books on the teaching of thinking skills include:
P. Costello (2000) *Thinking Skills in Early Childhood Education*, London: David Fulton.
R. Fisher (2003) *Teaching Thinking: Philosophical discussion in the classroom*, 2nd edn, London: Continuum.
S. Higgins, V. Baumfield and D. Leat (2001) *Thinking Through Primary Teaching*, Cambridge: Chris Kington Publishing.
D. Moseley, V. Baumfield, S. Higgins, M. Lin, J. Miller, D. Newton *et al.* (2004) *Thinking Skill Frameworks for Post-16 Learners: An evaluation*, London: Learning and Skills Research Centre.
M. Lipman (2003) *Thinking in Education*, 2nd edn, Cambridge: Cambridge University Press.
M. Rockett and S. Simon (2002) *Thinking for Learning*, Stafford: Network Education Press.
M. Shayer and P. Adey (2002) *Learning Intelligence*, Buckingham: Open University Press.

1 What is thinking?

1 Francis Galton's *Hereditary Genius* (1869) singled out ability as a measurable entity and founded psychometrics (the study of mental testing). Galton was a cousin of Charles Darwin and he used Darwin's theory of evolution to support the idea of higher/lower classes and superior/inferior races. A summary of Galton's *Hereditary Genius* by M.I. Stein and S.J. Heinze (1960) can be found in P.E. Vernon (ed.) (1970) *Creativity*, Harmondsworth: Penguin.
2 Quoted in W. Mays (1985) Thinking skills programmes: an analysis. *New Ideas in Psychology*, 3, 149–163. See also A.L. Brown (1985) Mental orthopedics: the training of cognitive skills. An interview with Alfred Binet, in J.W. Segal, S.E. Chipman and R. Glaser (eds) *Thinking and Learning Skills*, vol. 1. Hillsdale, NJ: Lawrence Erlbaum.
3 Charles Spearman was a student of Galton. He believed that all intellectual activities shared a common characteristic, which he called the G factor, which stood for 'general intelligence' or 'general intellectual energy'. Thurstone later called this factor 'reasoning'.
4 See S. Modgil and C. Modgil (1986) *Hans Eysenck: Consensus and Controversy*, London: Falmer Press.
5 Jensen argues that 'intelligence is what intelligence tests measure'. See S. Modgil and C. Modgil (1987) *Arthur Jensen: Consensus and controversy*, London: Falmer Press.
6 See L. Kamin (1987) *The Science and Politics of IQ*, Hillsdale, NJ: Lawrence Erlbaum. For debate between Eysenck and Kamin see their *Intelligence: The battle for the mind, H.J. Eysenck versus Leon Kamin* (1981), London: Macmillan.

7   See J. Wertsch (1985) *Vygotsky and the Social Formation of Mind*, Cambridge, MA: Harvard University Press.

8   M. Donaldson (1978) *Children's Minds*, London: Fontana. See also P. Bryant (1974) *Perception and Understanding in Young Children*, London: Methuen.

9   See P. Mortimore *et al.* (1988) *School Matters*, Wells: Open Books.

10 See R.J. Sternberg (ed.) (1984) *Advances in the Psychology of Human Intelligence*, Hillsdale NJ: Lawrence Erlbaum; R.J. Sternberg (ed.) (1985) *Beyond IQ: A triarchic theory of human intelligence*, Cambridge: Cambridge University Press; R.J. Sternberg (ed.) (1985) *Human Abilities: An information processing approach*, New York: Foreman.

11 P. Chance (1986) *Thinking in the Classroom: A survey of programs*, New York: Teacher's College Press. See also P. Chance (1984) Thinking skills in the curriculum. *Educational Leadership*, 42(1).

12 H. Gardner (1983) *Frames of Mind: The theory of multiple intelligences*, New York: Basic Books.

13 L.L. Thurstone (1938) *Primary Mental Abilities*, Chicago: University of Chicago Press; P.E. Vernon (1971) *The Structure of Human Abilities*, London: Methuen. For a general discussion see R.K. Wagner and R.J. Sternberg (1984) Alternative conceptions of intelligence and their implications for education. *Review of Educational Research*, 54, 179–223.

14 M. Minsky (1987) *The Society of Mind*, London: Heinemann.

15 For Paul Hirst's 'forms of knowledge' see P. Hirst and J. Peters (1970) *The Logic of Education*, London: Routledge & Kegan Paul.

16 J.A. Fodor (1983) *The Modularity of Mind*, Cambridge, MA: MIT Press.

17 For an introduction to the theories of Chomsky see J. Lyons (1970) *Chomsky*, London: Fontana. See also S. Modgil and C. Modgil (1986) *Noam Chomsky: Consensus and controversy*, London: Falmer Press.

18 Piaget's story is quoted in S. Meadows (ed.) (1986) *Understanding Child Development*, London: Hutchinson, p. 33.

19 For examples of children using language for abstract reasoning see G. Matthews (1986) *Dialogues with Children*, Cambridge, MA: Harvard University Press. For studies of young children using abstract reasoning with numbers see R. Gelman and C.R. Gallistel (1978) *The Child's Understanding of Number*, Cambridge, MA: Harvard University Press.

20 For variations on this and other mathematical investigations see R. Fisher and A. Vince *Investigating Maths* (photocopiable resources), Books 1–4, Hemel Hempstead: Simon & Schuster.

21 From Leonardo da Vinci's *Treatise on Painting*, quoted in E.H. Gombrich (1962) *Art and Illusion*, London: Phaidon Press.

22 J. Piaget and B. Inhelder (1956) *The Child's Conception of Space*, London: Routledge. See also M.I. Smith (1964) *Spatial Ability*, London University Press and P.N. Johnson-Laird (1983) *Mental Models*, Cambridge, MA: Harvard University Press.

23 For a refutation of what he calls 'the myth of Descartes' see G. Ryle (1949) *The Concept of Mind*, London: Hutchinson.

24 For a review of research on the development of pro-social behaviour see Meadows S. (1986) *Understanding Child Development*. London: Hutchinson, pp. 155–158.

25 For more on the physical make-up of the brain see Brierley, J. (1987). *Give Me a Child Until he is Seven: Brain studies and early childhood education*. London: Falmer Press; Smith, A. (2002) *The Brain's Behind It*, Stafford: Network Education Press.

26 R. Ornstein (1986) *The Psychology of Consciousness*, 2nd edn, Harmondsworth: Penguin.
27 A. Binet (1908) *L'année psychologique*, quoted in the Hadow Report (1931), London: HMSO.
For more on ways to develop children's thinking see Bibliography.

2 Creative thinking

1 One of the reasons for the historic decline of British industry is that it has been stuck in the reproductive mould, focusing on reproduction of goods and services rather than on new design and innovation. Industrial stagnation over the past century has a direct parallel with traditional approaches to learning, which is divided between theoretical (pure) and applied subjects and between public and private education.
2 For research into school effectiveness see J. Goodlad (1984) *A Place Called School: Prospects for the future*, New York: McGraw-Hill; P. Mortimore (1988) *Schools Count*, Wells: Open Books.
3 L.L. Thurstone, in *The Nature of Intelligence* (1924), argued that many specific abilities made up intelligence.
4 A.H. Maslow (1971) *The Farther Reaches of Human Nature*, New York: Viking Press.
5 K. Popper (1968) *The Logic of Scientific Discovery*, London: Hutchinson, p. 32.
6 C.R. Rogers (1961) *On Becoming a Person*, Boston, MA: Houghton Mifflin; C.R. Rogers (1954) *Towards a Theory of Creativity*, quoted in P.E. Vernon (ed.) (1970) *Creativity*, Harmondsworth: Penguin Books.
7 For research on teacher expectations and their effects on children see the classic study by R. Rosenthal and L. Jacobson (1968) *Pygmalion in the Classroom*, New York: Holt, Rinehart & Winston; also J.B. Dusek (ed.) (1985) *Teacher Expectancies*, Hillsdale, NJ: Lawrence Erlbaum.
8 P.E. Torrance (1973) *Creativity*, San Rafael, CA: Dimensions Publishers.
9 M.M. Hunt (1982) *The Universe Within*, New York: Simon & Schuster.
10 J. Bruner (1966) *Studies in Cognitive Growth*, New York: John Wiley & Sons.
11 J. Huizinga (1949) *Homo Ludens*, London: Routledge.
12 J.P. Guilford (1950) Creativity. *American Psychologist*, 5, 444–454, in which he identified fluency, novelty, flexibility and complexity, which later became characterised as fluency, flexibility, originality and elaboration. E.P. Torrance used these four aspects of creativity as the basis of the Torrance Test of Creative Thinking (1969). See also E.P. Torrance (1977) *What Research Says to the Teacher: Creativity in the Classroom*, Washington, DC: National Education Association.
13 A.F. Osborn (1953) *Applied Imagination: Principles and procedures of creative problem solving*, New York: Charles Scribner's Sons.
14 E. De Bono (1993) *Teach Your Child How to Think*, Harmondsworth: Penguin.
15 Quoted in P. Chance (1986) *Thinking in the Classroom: A survey of programs*, New York: Teacher's College Press.
16 For more on the use of stories for thinking see R. Fisher (1997) *Stories for Thinking*, Oxford: Nash Pollock.
17 E. de Bono (1970) *Children Solve Problems* and *The Dog-Exercising Machine*, London: Jonathan Cape.
18 See S. McCosh (1976) *Children's Humour*, London: Granada, a fascinating field study of the modern folklore of children's humour.

19 Quoted from J.A. Paulos (1985) *I Think, Therefore I Laugh*, New York: Columbia University Press.
20 J. Bronowski (1965) *Science and Human Values*, New York: Harper & Row.
21 W.J.J. Gordon (1961) *Synectics: The development of creative capacity*, New York: Harper & Row.
22 Alfred North Whitehead, quoted in A.F. Osborn (1953) *Applied Imagination: Principles and procedures of creative problem solving*, New York: Charles Scribner's Sons. For more information on creativity see:
    Craft, A. (2000), *Creativity Across the Primary Curriculum*, London: Routledge.
    Cropley, A. J. (2001) *Creativity in education and learning: a guide for teachers and educators*, London: Kogan Page.
    Csikzentmihihalyi, M. (1996) *Creativity*, New York: HarperCollins.
    Fisher R. and Williams M. (eds) (2004) *Unlocking Creativity*, London: David Fulton.
    Gardner, H. (1993) *Creating Minds*, New York· Basic Books.
    Heppell, S. (1999) *Computers, Creativity, Curriculum and Children*, Cambridge: Anglia Polytechnic University Ultralab Website.
    Robinson, K. (2001) *Out of Our Minds: Learning to be creative*, Oxford: Capstone.
    Sternberg, R.J. (ed.) (1999) *Handbook of Creativity*, Cambridge: Cambridge University Press.

3 Critical thinking

1   From Jean Piaget's study for UNESCO on the causes of war.
2   From Lewis Carroll's *The Hunting of the Snark*.
3   J.S. Mill's *Autobiography* was published posthumously in 1873.
4   R.H. Ennis (1962) A concept of critical thinking. *Harvard Educational Review*, **32**, 83–111, quoted in J.E. McPeck (1981) *Critical Thinking and Education*, Oxford: Martin Robertson.
5   B.S. Bloom *et al.* (1956) *Taxonomy of Educational Goals: Handbook 1: Cognitive Domain*, New York: David McKay.
6   See the HMI Report (1985) *The Curriculum 5–16* (DES/HMSO).
7   R. Paul, A.J.A. Binker and M. Charbonneau (1986) *Critical Thinking Handbook: K-3* and *Critical Thinking Handbook: 4th–6th Grades*, Center for Critical Thinking and Moral Critique, Sonoma State University, Rohnert Park, CA.
8   See D.N. Perkins (1986) *Knowledge by Design*, Cambridge: Cambridge University Press.
9   This lesson is described in Marilyn Burns's article (1985) The Role of Questioning. *Arithmetic Teacher*, March, 14–16.
10 For ways of answering these and other penetrating questions that children ask see J. Hughes (1981) *Questions Children Ask*, Tring: Lion Publishing.
11 See T.L. Good and J.E. Brophy (1973) *Looking in Classrooms*, New York: Harper & Row, also M.B. Rowe (1974) Wait time and rewards as instructional variables: their influence on language, logic and fate control. *Journal of Research in Science Teaching*, 11, 81–94.
12 Reported in D. Cohen (1979) *All in the Head*, Harmondsworth: Kestrel/Penguin.
13 See P.N. Johnson-Laird (1983) *Mental Models*, Cambridge, MA: Harvard University Press, who argues that people think in terms of models rather than rules. Thinking involves constructing an internal model of the way things appear to the thinker. Good thinkers are able to construct alternative models, or alter a model

to explore what the consequences might be.

14 R.M. Smullyan (1978) *What is the name of this book? – the riddle of Dracula and other logical puzzles*, Englewood Cliffs, NJ: Prentice Hall.
15 For a description of the High Scope programme see M. Hohmann, B. Banet and D.P. Weikart (1979) *Young Children in Action*, Ypsilanti, MI: High Scope Press.
16 A. Korzybski (1933) *Science and Sanity*, Lancaster, PA: International Non-Aristotelian Library Publishing Co. Korzybski's three laws ran counter to the three laws of Aristotle on which traditional logic had been founded. The laws can be compared as follows:

Aristotle's law	*Korzybski's law*
1 Law of Identity (A = A)	Law of Non-Identity (A is not A)
2 Law of Excluded Middle (All is either A or not-A)	Law of Non-Allness (A is not all A)
3 Law of Non-Contradiction (Something cannot be both A and not -A)	Law of Self-reflexiveness (A can be both A and not-A)

Korzybski's ideas were popularised by S.I. Hayakawa (1964) *Language in Thought and Action*, New York: Harcourt Brace Jovanovich.
17 See R. Fisher and A. Vince (1989) *Investigating Maths*, books 1–4 for ways of investigating probability with children.
18 John Stuart Mill, *On Liberty* (1858).
     For more on the nature of critical thinking see:
     Ennis R.H. (1996) *Critical Thinking*, New York: Prentice Hall.
     Fisher A. (2001) *Critical Thinking: An introduction*, Cambridge: Cambridge University Press.
     Paul R. (1993) *Critical Thinking*, Center for Critical Thinking, Sonoma State University, Rohnert Park, CA.
     Quinn, V. (1997) *Critical Thinking in Young Minds*, London: David Fulton.
     Thomson A (1996) *Critical Reasoning: A practical introduction*, London: Routledge.

4 Problem solving

 1 This case study was contributed by Margaret Mears of St Luke's CE Primary School in Oldham. Further information on the teaching of problem solving can be found in R. Fisher (ed.) (1987) *Problem Solving in Primary Schools*, Hemel Hempstead: Simon & Schuster.
 2 Planning is an essential part of the curriculum of the pre-school programme called High Scope. See M. Hohmann, B. Banet and D.P. Weikart (1979) *Young Children in Action*, Ypsilanti, MI: High Scope Press.
 3 This problem may be more than 3500 years old. For the Egyptian original see D. Wells (1986) *The Penguin Dictionary of Curious and Interesting Numbers*, Harmondsworth: Penguin, p. 8.
 4 G. Polya (1957) *How to Solve It*, New York: Doubleday.
 5 Thomas (1974) An analysis of behaviour in the Hobbit–Orcs problem. *Cognitive Psychology*, 6, 257–269.
 6 J. Dewey (1933) *How We Think*, New York: Heath.
 7 Adapted from R. Charles and F. Lester (1982) *Teaching Problem Solving*, Pala Alto, CA: Dale Seymour.
 8 See J.G. Greeno (1980) *Trends in the Theory of Knowledge for Problem Solving* in D.T. Tuma and F. Reif (1980) *Problem Solving and Education: Issues in teaching and research*, Hillsdale, NJ: Lawrence Erlbaum.

9   See W.G. Chase and H.A. Simon (1973) Perception in chess. *Cognitive Psychology*, 4, 55–81 and The mind's eye in chess, in W.G. Chase (ed.) *Visual Information Processing*, London: Academic Press. Also H.A. Simon (1980) in D.T. Tuma and F. Reif (1980) *Problem Solving and Education: Issues in teaching and research*, Hillsdale, NJ: Lawrence Erlbaum.
10 See G. Cohen, M.W. Eysenck and M. Le Voi (1986) *Memory: A cognitive approach*, Milton Keynes: Open University.
11 See E. Tulving (1972) Episodic and semantic memory, in E. Tulving and W. Donaldson (eds) *The Organisation of Memory*, New York: Academic Press.
12 G.A. Miller (1956) The magical number seven, plus or minus two: some limits on our capacity for processing information. *Psychological Review*, 63, 81–97.
13 See M. Donaldson (1978) *Children's Minds*, London: Fontana.
14 This may be where we get the expressions 'in the first place' and 'in the second place' to mark stages of an argument – and also the term 'topics' for the major points in a presentation (*topos* is the Greek word for place).
15 For more on metacognition see pp. 9 and 20.
16 Whitehead wrote 'In training a child to activity of thought, above all things beware of what I will call "inert ideas" – that is to say, ideas that are merely received into the mind without being utilised, or tested, or thrown into fresh combinations' – A.N. Whitehead (1932) *The Aims of Education*, London: Williams & Norgate.
17 The concept of problem-posing education is expounded in Paulo Freire's (1972) *Pedagogy of the Oppressed*, London: Sheed & Ward. Practical ways of teaching problem posing are explored in S. Brown and M. Walter (1983) *The Art of Problem Posing*, Philadelphia, PA: Franklin Institute Press.
18 E.L. Thorndike (1924) Mental discipline in high school studies. *Journal of Educational Psychology*, 15, 1–22, 83–98.
19 See H. Simon (1980) *Problem Solving and Education*, in D.T. Tuma and F. Reif (1980) *Problem Solving and Education: Issues in teaching and research*, Hillsdale, NJ: Lawrence Erlbaum.
20 For a review of this research see Kahney H. (1986) *Problem Solving – A cognitive approach*, Milton Keynes: Open University Press.
     For more on problem solving see Robertson S.I (2001) *Problem Solving*, Hove: Psychology Press.

5 Instrumental enrichment

1   H. Sharron (1994) *Changing Children's Minds: Feuerstein's revolution in the teaching of intelligence*, London: Souvenir Press.
2   *Ibid.*
3   R. Feuerstein and M.R. Jensen (1980) Instrumental enrichment: theoretical basis, goals and instruments. *Education Forum*, 401–423.
4   Quoted in R. Feuerstein (1980) *Instrumental Enrichment: An intervention program for cognitive modifiability*, Baltimore, MD: University Park Press, p. 21.
5   H. Sharron (1994) *Changing Children's Minds: Feuerstein's revolution in the teaching of intelligence*, London: Souvenir Press.
6   R. Feuerstein (1980) *Instrumental Enrichment: An intervention program for cognitive modifiability*, Baltimore, MD: University Park Press, p. 21 describes 21 of these cognitive deficiencies. These include lack of verbal skills, failure to use spatial concepts, to orient oneself, to make comparisons, to appreciate the need for logical evidence, to recognise and define problems, and so on.

7 L.S. Vygotsky (1978) *Mind in Society: The development of higher psychological processes*, Cambridge MA: Harvard University Press.

8 *Ibid*.

9 H. Haste (1987) Growing into rules, in J. Bruner and H. Haste (eds) (1987) *Making Sense*, London: Methuen.

10 See W. Doise and G. Mugny (1984) *The Social Development of the Intellect*, Oxford: Pergamon Press.

11 Quoted in J. Nisbet and J. Shucksmith (1986) *Learning Strategies*, London: Routledge & Kegan Paul.

12 See also p. lll.

13 For more on Input, Elaboration and Output see R. Feuerstein (1980) *Instrumental Enrichment: An intervention program for cognitive modifiability*, Baltimore, MD: University Park Press, p. 21.

14 *Ibid*, p. 194.

15 Answers to the Family Puzzles: 1 The two people were husband and wife. 2 At the Family Party there were two sisters and their brother, father and mother and two paternal grandparents.

16 R. Feuerstein (1978) *Just a Minute ... Let Me Think*, Baltimore, MD: University Park Press, p. 7.

17 *Ibid*, p. 13.

18 Children's own cartoon drawing can help serve their cognitive development. See R. Fisher (ed.) (1987) *Problem Solving in Primary Schools*, Hemel Hempstead: Simon & Schuster, pp. 179–185.

19 R. Feuerstein (1978) *Just a Minute ... Let Me Think*, Baltimore, MD: University Park Press, p. 6.

20 *Ibid*, p. 13.

21 M. Shayer and E. Beasley (1987) Does Instrumental Enrichment work? *British Educational Research Journal*, 13, 101–117; D.M. Romney and M.T. Samuels (2001) A meta-analytic evaluation of Feuerstein's Instrumental Enrichment program. *Educational and Child Psychology*, 18, 19–34; N. Blagg (1991) *Can we Teach Intelligence? A comprehensive evaluation of Feuerstein's Instrumental Enrichment*, Hillsdale, NJ: Lawrence Erlbaum.

22 T. Bailey (1987) *Instrumental Enrichment and Cross Curricular Bridging – A handbook of suggestions*, London: London Borough of Enfield.

23 M. Shayer and E. Beasley (1987) Does Instrumental Enrichment work? *British Educational Research Journal*, 13, 114.

24 N. Blagg, M. Ballinger and R. Gardner (1988) *Somerset Thinking Skills Course*, Hemel Hempstead: Simon & Schuster.

25 The Oxfordshire Skills Programme is a whole-school approach to problem solving and critical awareness.

26 A.R. Luria (1976) *Cognitive Development: Its cultural and social foundations* (ed. M. Cole), Cambridge, MA, Harvard University Press.

27 Quoted in W. Mays (1985) Thinking skills programmes: an analysis. *New Ideas in Psychology*, 3, 149–163.

For more on instrumental enrichment see:

Romney, D.M. and Samuels, M.T. (2001) A meta-analytic evaluation of Feuerstein's Instrumental Enrichment program. *Education and Child Psychology*, 18, 19–34.

Instrumental Enrichment web site: www.icelp.org.

6 Philosophy for children

1 Quoted in P. Chance (1986) *Thinking in the Classroom*, New York: Teacher's College Press, p. 41.
2 M. Lipman (1982) Philosophy for children. *Thinking: the Journal of Philosophy for Children*, 3, 35–44.
3 M. Lipman, A.M. Sharp and F.S. Oscanyon (1980) *Philosophy in the Classroom*, Philadelphia, PA: Temple University Press.
4 L.S. Vygotsky (1962) *Thought and Language*, New York: John Wiley & Sons.
5 M. Lipman (1974) *Harry Stottlemeier's Discovery*, Upper Montclair, NJ: Institute for the Advancement of Philosophy for Children.
6 *Ibid*, p. 10ff.
7 M. Lipman, A.M. Sharp and F.S. Oscanyon (1980) *Philosophy in the Classroom*, Philadelphia, PA: Temple University Press, p. 84.
8 Plato *The Republic*, Book 8 (357), Harmondsworth: Penguin (1973), p. 307. In *The Republic* Plato argues that dialectic (philosophy) should only be introduced to those who have undergone many years of training and study and who have reached the age of 30. (*Republic*, Book 7, 537d.)
9 *Ibid*, p. 309.
10 *Ibid*, p. 309.
11 Reported in A. Brandt (1982) Teaching kids to think. *Ladies Home Journal*, September, 104.
12 M. Coles (1987) Critical children: philosophy for the young. *Cogito*, 1(2).
13 A. Brandt (1982) Teaching kids to think. *Ladies Home Journal*, September, 105.
14 M. Whalley (1982) Some factors influencing the success of philosophical discussion in the classroom. *Analytic Teaching*, 3, 6–8, reprinted in *Thinking*, 4, 2–5.
15 S. Tann and M. Armitage (1987) The power of speech: primary children discussing their discussions. *Times Educational Supplement*, 30 October, 38.
16 See also A. McIlvain (1987) Now listen carefully, *Child Education*, September, 37.
17 C. Rogers (1967) *On Becoming a Person*, London: Constable.
18 See J. Tough (1976) *Talk for Teaching and Learning*, London: Ward Lock.
19 For more starting-points for discussion see R. Fisher (ed.) (1987) *Problem Solving in Primary Schools*, Hemel Hempstead: Simon & Schuster, pp. 34–57.
20 Further information about IAPC materials is available from the Institute for the Advancement of Philosophy for Children, Montclair State College, Upper Montclair, NJ 07043, USA.
21 L. Stenhouse (1970) *Humanities Curriculum Project*, London: HMSO. The question of the teacher's neutrality may give rise to some misunderstanding. It is not quite the notion suggested by Stenhouse in his ill-fated Humanities Project (School's Council). The teacher is not being expected to relinquish management control nor quality control over classroom discussion.
22 N.R. Lane and S.A. Lane (1986) Rationality, self-esteem and autonomy through collaborative enquiry. *Oxford Review of Education*, 12, 263–275.
23 J. Piaget (1932) *The Moral Judgement of the Child*, London: Routledge.
24 L. Kohlberg (1984) *The Psychology of Moral Development: The nature and validity of moral stages*, New York: Harper & Row; S. Modgil and C. Modgil (eds.) (1986) *Lawrence Kohlberg: Consensus and controversy*, London: Falmer Press.
25 J. Rawls (1971) *A Theory of Justice*, Cambridge, MA: Belknap Press of Harvard University Press.
26 St Augustine *Exposition of the Psalms*, 26, 7.

27   Adapted from Rules, a remodelled lesson plan, in R. Paul, A.J.A. Binker and M. Charbonneau *Critical Thinking Handbook K-3*, Center for Critical Thinking and Moral Critique, Sonoma State University, Rohnert Park, CA.

28   See Moral problems, in R. Fisher (ed.) (1987) *Problem Solving in Primary Schools*, Hemel Hempstead: Simon & Schuster, pp. 186–201.

29   Adapted from M. Lipman and A.M. Sharp (1984) *Pixie: Looking for Meaning*, IAPC, Montclair College, Upper Montclair, NJ.

30   From A. M. Sharp (1986) *Is there an Essence in Education?*, IAPC, Montclair College, Upper Montclair, NJ.

31   G.B. Matthews (1984) *Dialogues with Children*, Cambridge, MA: Harvard University Press.

32   G.B. Matthews (1980) *Philosophy and the Young Child*, Cambridge, MA: Harvard University Press.

33   P.J.M. Costello (1988) Akrasia and animal rights: philosophy in the British primary school. *Thinking: The Journal of Philosophy for Children*, 8(1).

34   O. Stevens (1982) *Children Talking Politics*, Oxford: Martin Robertson. An investigation of ways in which children between 7 and 11 are able to think about the problems of politics.

35   *Ibid*, p. 28.

36   Quoted in M. Lipman (1974) Philosophy is also for the young – at least possibly. *New York Times*, 20 October.

37   M. Lipman, A.M. Sharp and F.S. Oscanyon (1980) *Philosophy in the Classroom*, Philadelphia, PA: Temple University Press.
For more on philosophy for children see www.sapere.net. Books on philosophical enquiry in education include:
Cam, P. (1995) *Thinking Together: Philosophical Inquiry for the Classroom*, Sydney: Hale & Iremonger.
De Haan C., MacColl, S. and McCutcheon L. (1995) *Philosophy with Kids*, Books 1–4, Melbourne: Longman.
Fisher, R (1996) *Stories for Thinking*, Oxford: Nash Pollock.
Fisher, R (1997) *Games for Thinking*, Oxford: Nash Pollock.
Fisher, R (1997) *Poems for Thinking*, Oxford: Nash Pollock.
Fisher, R. (2003), *Teaching Thinking: Philosophical Enquiry in the Classroom*, London: Continuum.
Haynes J. (2000) *Children as Philosophers*, London: Routledge Falmer.
Lipman, M. (1988) *Philosophy Goes to School*, Philadelphia, PA: Temple University Press.
Lipman, M. (ed) (1993) *Thinking Children and Education*, Dubuque, IA: Kendall/ Hunt.
Lipman, M. (2001) *Thinking in Education*. Cambridge: Cambridge University Press.
Lipman, M., Sharp, A.M. *et al. Philosophy for Children Program: children's novels and teacher's manuals for teaching philosophy with students aged 5–16+ years*, IAPC, Montclair University, Upper Montclair, NJ, USA.
Matthews, G.B. (1994) *The Philosophy of Childhood*, Cambridge, MA: Harvard University Press.
Murris, K. (1992) *Teaching Philosophy with Picture Books,* London: Infonet Publications.
Murris, K. and Haynes, J. (2000) *Storywise: Thinking through picture books*, Newport: Dialogue Works.

Splitter, L. and Sharp, A. M. (1995) *Teaching for Better Thinking: Community of enquiry*, Melbourne: ACER.
Sprod, T. (1993) *Books Into Ideas: A community of enquiry,* Highett, Victoria: Hawker Brownlow.
Sutcliffe, R. and Williams, S. *Newswise: Thinking through the news*, Newport: Dialogue Works.
Sutcliffe, R. and Williams, S. *The Philosophy Club: An adventure in thinking*, Newport: Dialogue Works.
Wilks, S. (1995) *Critical and Creative Thinking: Strategies for classroom inquiry*, Armadale: Eleanor Curtain.
Journals with articles on philosophical enquiry with children include:
Teaching Thinking and Creativity (Questions Publishing)
Thinking: The Journal of Philosophy for Children (IAPC, USA)
Critical and Creative Thinking: the Australasian Journal of Philosophy for Children
Analytic Teaching: The Community of Enquiry Journal (USA).

7 Teaching for thinking: language and maths

1 J. Moffet (1968) *Teaching the Universe of Discourse*, Boston, MA: Houghton-Mifflin.
2 The idea of the 'apprentice' reader is expounded in L. Waterland (1985) *Read With Me*, Stroud: Thimble Press. See also note 5 below.
3 See M. Donaldson (1978) *Children's Minds*, London: Fontana, pp. 17–31 for discussion on the ability to 'decentre'.
4 'Elaborate' refers both to developing an elaborated code of language (the linguistic conventions needed to understand and explain things) and to elaboration of ideas (extending the network of concepts and associations).
5 D. Meichenbaum (1977) *Cognitive Behaviour Modification*, New York: Plenum Press.
6 T. Gallwey (1981) *Inner Game of Golf*, New York: Random House; T. Gallwey (1981) *Inner Game of Tennis*, New York: Bantam Press; T. Gallwey (1982) *Inner Skiing*, New York: Bantam Books
7 This process of thinking aloud in pairs is advocated in A. Whimbey and J. Lochead (1979) *Problem Solving and Comprehension*, Philadelphia, PA: Franklin Institute Press.
   The evidence is reviewed in A.L. Costa (1985) *Teaching for Intelligent Behaviours*, Sacramento, CA: California State University.
9 *Ibid*, pp.44ff.
10 M. Hughes and R. Grieve (1983) On asking children bizarre questions, in M. Donaldson, R. Grieve and C. Platt (1983) *Early Childhood Development and Education*, Oxford: Basil Blackwell.
11 For research on 'wait-time' see T.L. Good and J.E. Brophy (1973) *Looking in Classrooms*, New York: Harper & Row; M.B. Rowe (1974) Wait-time and rewards as instructional variables, their influence on language, logic and fate-control. *Journal of Research in Science Teaching*, 11, 81–94; J.N. Swift and C.T. Gooding (1983) Interaction of wait-time, feedback and questioning instruction in middle school science teaching. *Journal of Research in Science Teaching*, 20, 721–730.
12 T. Gorman *et al.* (1988) *Language Performance in Schools: A review of language monitoring*, London: HMSO.
13 Research quoted in R. Glaser (1988) Cognitive science and education. *Cognitive Science*, 115.

14   M.D. Vernon (1957) *Backwardness in Reading*, London: Cambridge University Press.

15   J. Downing (1979) *Reading and Reasoning*, Edinburgh: W. & R. Chambers.

16   L.S. Vygotsky (1962) *Thought and Language*, Cambridge, MA: MIT Press.

17   J.F. Reid (1966) Learning to think about reading. *Educational Research*, 9, 56–62; J. Downing (1970) Children's concepts of language in learning to read. *Educational Research*, 12, 106–112.

18   B. Raban (1986) *Children's Thinking About Reading and Writing*, Reading: Reading Centre, University of Reading School of Education.

19   See V. Southgate *et al.* (1981) *Extending Beginning Reading*, London: Heinemann Educational. This research suggests that teachers should spend more time talking to children, particularly 7–9-year-olds, about their reading rather than simply listening to them read, in order to encourage comprehension and higher order reading skills.

20   H. Arnold (1982) *Listening to Children Reading*, Sevenoaks: Hodder & Stoughton.

21   T.M. Amabile (1983) *The Social Psychology of Creativity*, New York: Springer-Verlag.

22   F. Smith (1985) *Writing and the Writer*, London: Heinemann.

23   D. Ausubel (1963) *The Psychology of Meaningful Verbal Learning*, New York: Grune & Stratton.

24   G. Jacobs (1970) *When Children Think: Using journals to encourage creative thinking*, New York: Columbia University, Teacher's College Press.

25   D. Graves (1981) *Writing: Teachers and children at work*, London: Heinemann.

26   From L. Bradley, *Think Books with Infants*, a Somerset/Wiltshire Write to Learn Project booklet.

27   M. Wallen (1986) Journals five to thirteen, in *About Writing*, the SCDC National Writing Project Newsletter, 3, Summer.

28   J.P. Sartre (1964) *The Words: The autobiography of Jean Paul Sartre*, New York: George Braziller.

29   D. Murray (1978) Internal revision: a process of discovery, in D. Murray (1982) *Learning by Teaching: Articles on writing and teaching*, London: Heinemann/Boynton Cook.

30   I owe the concept of the writing journey to the work of Pat D'Arcy and the Wiltshire Writing Project (Write to Learn).

31   See G. Kress (1982) *Learning to Write*, London: Routledge.

32   See R. Fisher (ed.) (1987) *Problem Solving in Primary Schools*, Hemel Hempstead: Simon & Schuster, p. 7.

33   R. Skemp (1971) *The Psychology of Learning Mathematics*, Harmondsworth: Penguin.

34   See T.P. Carpenter (1985) Research on the role of structure in thinking. *Arithmetic Teacher*, February.

35   Quoted in M. Pritchard (1985) *Philosophical Adventures with Children*, Lanham, MD: University Press of America.

36   S. Plunkett (1979) Decomposition and all that rot. *Mathematics in School*, 18(3).

37   L. Buxton (1981) *Do you panic about maths?* London: Heinemann.

38   See R. Fisher and A. Vince (1989) *Investigating Maths*, Oxford: Blackwell Education, for ways of sharing various number-patterning investigations with children.

39   See N. Griffiths *Ssh, Children! It's a Maths Lesson*, a Wiltshire Write to Learn booklet.

8 Teaching for thinking: across the curriculum

1 From research undertaken by the Children's Learning in Science (CLIS) project at Leeds University, reported by Ian Nash (1988) Weighing up the theories of science. *Times Educational Supplement*, 20 May.

2 I. Lakatos (1978) *The Methodology of Scientific Research Programmes* (ed. J. Worral and G. Currie), London: Cambridge University Press.

3 See D. Barnes (1976) *From Communication to Curriculum*, Harmondsworth: Penguin.

4 W. Harlen (1985) *Primary Science: Taking the plunge*, London: Heinemann, p. 23.

5 M.P. Krupa, R.L. Selman and D.S. Jaquette (1985) The development of science explanations in children and adolescents: a structural approach, in S. Chipman, J.W. Segal and R. Glaser *Thinking and Learning Skills*, vol. 11. Hillsdale, NJ: Lawrence Erlbaum, pp. 427ff.

6 See Stories for Thinking, in R. Fisher (ed.) (1987) *Problem Solving in Primary Schools*, Hemel Hempstead: Simon & Schuster Education, pp.42–57.

7 K. Popper (1972) *Conjectures and Refutations: The growth of scientific knowledge*, London: Routledge, p. 46.

8 D.H. Feldman (1980) *Beyond Universals in Cognitive Development*, Norwood, NJ: Ablex.

9 See C. Modgil and S. Modgil (1984) The development of thinking and reasoning, in D. Fontana (ed.) (1984) *The Education of the Young Child*, Oxford: Blackwell.

10 J. West (1986) *Time Line*, Walton-on-Thames: Nelson, provides useful commercially produced picture materials for historical sequencing.

11 For research on how children of 7+, 9+ and 11+ years approached this problem see H. Cooper (1988) A research project investigating young children's thinking in history, in J. Blyth (1988) *History 5–9*, Sevenoaks: Hodder & Stoughton.

12 E. Eisner (1979) The contribution of painting to children's cognitive development. *Journal of Curriculum Studies*, 11, 109–116; E. Eisner (1982) *Cognition and Curriculum*, Harlow: Longman. Eisner argues that, far from being a 'fringe' activity or trivial hobby, visual representation makes a unique contribution to the process of education and the child's cognitive development.

13 See L.E. Morehouse and L. Gross (1977) *Maximum Performance*, London: Granada. A guide on training for peak performance in all physical activities.

14 T. Roszak (1986) *The Cult of Information*, Cambridge: Lutterworth Press.

15 See A. Straker (1988) *Computers in Primary Schools*, Oxford: Blackwell.

16 W.J.J. Gordon (1961) *Synectics: The development of creative capacity*, New York: Harper & Row.

17 For an alternative view see M.M. Davies (1989) *Television is Good for Your Kids*, London, H. Shipman.

18 See T. Edwards (1988) The right food means brighter children. *The Listener*, 21 January, who describes this experiment and others in America that show that nutritional supplements may help improve aspects of cognitive functioning and also behaviour in juvenile delinquents.

19 See W. Peters (1987) *A Class Divided: Then and now*, New Haven, CT: Yale University Press.

20 B.S. Bloom (1976) *Human Characteristics and School Learning,* New York: McGraw-Hill; W.W. Purkey (1970) *Self Concept and School Achievement*, New York: Prentice-Hall; P. Gammage (1982) *Children and Schooling: Issues in Childhood Socialisation*, London: Allen & Unwin: D. Lawrence (1988) *Self Esteem in the Classroom*, London: Paul Chapman.

21 R. Fisher (ed.) (1987) *Problem Solving in Primary Schools*, Hemel Hempstead: Simon & Schuster.
22 See W.W Purkey (1978) *Inviting School Success*, Belmont, CA: Wadsworth.
23 J.E. Brophy and T.L. Good (1974) *Teacher–Student Relationships: Causes and consequences*, New York: Holt, Rinehart & Winston.
24 R. Rosenthal and L. Jacobsen (1968) *Pygmalion in the Classroom. Teacher expectations and pupils' intellectual development*, New York: Holt, Rinehart & Winston.
25 Questions like these could be discussed, displayed or used for self-review.
26 R. Fisher (1983) *Together Today: Themes and stories for assembly*, London: Unwin Hyman.

9 Thinking schools

1 For a reviews of programmes see J.H.M. Hamers and M.T. Overtoom (1997) *Teaching Thinking in Europe: Inventory of European programmes,* Utrecht: Sardes; A. Costa (ed.) (2001) *Developing Minds: A resource book for teaching thinking*, Alexandria, VA: ASCD Publications.
2 For more on developing thinking with young children see P. Costello (2000) *Thinking Skills in Early Childhood Education*. London: David Fulton; R. Fisher (1999) *Head Start: How to develop your child's mind*, London: Souvenir Press.
3 For more on the effects of beliefs and dispositions on learning see G. Claxton (1999) *Wise Up: The challenge of lifelong learning*, London: Bloomsbury; G. Claxton (2002) *Building Learning Power: helping young people become better learners*, TLO, Bristol.
4 For more on emotional intelligence see D. Goleman (1995) *Emotional Intelligence*, New York: Bantam; on emotional intelligence for leaders see D. Goleman (2002) *The New Leaders: Transforming the art of leadership*, London: Time-Warner; on developing emotional intelligence in schools see K. Weare (2004) *Developing the Emotionally Literate School*, London: Paul Chapman.
5 For more on multiple intelligence theory see H. Gardner (1993) *Multiple Intelligences: The theory in practice*, New York: Basic Books; H. Gardner (1999) *Intelligence Reframed*, New York: Basic Books; for a critique of Gardner's theory see J. White (1998) *Do Howard Gardner's Multiple Intelligences Add Up?* London: Institute of Education, University of London.
6 See C. McGuinness (1999) *From Thinking Skills to Thinking Classrooms: a review and evaluation of approaches for developing pupils' thinking*, Research Report RR115, London: Department for Education and Employment.
7 Teaching thinking and learning skills in the National Curriculum have been supported by a range of initiatives, including the Key Stage 3 strategy and Primary Strategy (currently available from www.standards.dfes.gov.uk).
8 See, for example H. Sharron and M. Coulter (1994) *Changing Children's Minds*, Birmingham: Imaginative Minds, or D.M. Romney and M.T. Samuels (2001) A meta-analytic evaluation of Feuerstein's Instrumental Enrichment program. *Educational and Child Psychology*, **18**, 19–34, for results of projects using IE, and IAPC's literature, which quote results of a validation project carried out by an independent testing agency on over 2000 children. Compared with control children they made large gains, after a year, for maths, larger gains for English and even larger ones for reasoning. The results for Philosophy for Children have been replicated in studies across the world and in the UK. (R. Fisher (2003) *Teaching Thinking: Philosophical Enquiry in the Classroom*, London: Continuum, and S. Trickey (2002), *Evaluation of Clackmannanshire Thinking Skills Initiative*.)

9   See P. Adey and M. Shayer (1994) *Really Raising Standards: Cognitive intervention and academic achievement*, London: Routledge; M. Shayer and P. Adey (2002) *Learning Intelligence*, Buckingham: Open University Press.

10 For a summary, see M. Shayer and P. Adey (2002) *Learning Intelligence*, Buckingham: Open University Press.

11 See M. Adhami, D.C. Johnson and M. Shayer (1998) *Thinking Maths: The programme for accelerated learning in mathematics*, Oxford: Heinemann.

12 For more on research into strategies for teaching thinking see S. Higgins (2001) *Thinking Through Primary Teaching*, Cambridge: Chris Kington Publishing; M. Rockett and S. Simon (2002) *Thinking for Learning*, Stafford: Network Education Press.

13 For the theory behind 'accelerated learning' techniques see A. Smith (2002) *The Brain's Behind It*, Stafford: Network Education Press.

14 See, for example, F. Coffield *et al.* (2004) *Should we be Using Learning Styles? What research has to say to practice*, London: Learning Skills and Development Agency.

15 See E. de Bono (1999) *Six Thinking Hats*, Harmondsworth: Penguin; E. de Bono (1992) *Teach Your Child to Think*, Harmondsworth: Penguin.

16 See K. Murris and J. Haynes (2000) Storywise: thinking through picture books. Newport: Dialogue Works; L. Dawes N. Mercer and R. Wegerif (2000) *Thinking Together: A programme of activities for developing thinking skills at kS2*, Birmingham: Questions Publishing; R. Fisher (1996) *Stories for Thinking*; (1997) *Games for Thinking*; (1997) *Poems for Thinking*; (1999) *First Stories for Thinking*; (2000) *First Poems for Thinking*; (2001) *Values for Thinking*, Oxford: Nash Pollock.

17 See D. Leat (1998) *Thinking Through Geography*, Cambridge: Chris Kington Publishing.

18 T. Buzan (1974/1993) *Use Your Head*, London: BBC Publications. See also www.mind-map.com.

19 C. McGuinness *et al.* (1997) *Final Report on the ACTS Project: Phase 2*, Belfast: Northern Ireland Council for Curriculum, Examinations and Assessment.

20 R. Wegerif (2002) *Literature Review in Thinking Skills, Technology and Learning*. Available on line at: www.nestafuturelab.org.

21 See L. Dawes, N. Mercer and R. Wegerif (2000) *Thinking Together: A Programme of activities for developing thinking skills at KS2*, Birmingham: Questions Publishing.

22 See D. Perkins (1992) *Smart Schools: Better Thinking and learning for every child*, New York: Free Press.

23 For more on the Queen's School project see R. Fisher (2003) Thinking allowed. *Teaching Thinking*, **Summer**, 54–58. For more on Westbury Park school see M. Staricoff and A. Rees (2003) Thinking skills transform our days. *Teaching Thinking*, Spring, 40–43.

Glossary

accelerated learning – An approach to learning based on research into learning styles and how the brain works. Draws particularly on ideas from multiple intelligences and brain-based research.

analytic – Focusing on the parts of a whole or on underlying basic principles.

Bloom's taxonomy – Popular instructional model developed by the prominent educator Benjamin Bloom. It categorises thinking skills from the concrete to the abstract – knowledge, comprehension, application, analysis, synthesis, evaluation. The last three are considered **higher order** skills.

brain-based learning – A range of techniques and approaches to teaching and learning, which is inspired by research into how the brain works.

brainstorm – A technique for rapid production of ideas without critical examination, evaluation or elaboration, also called 'thought shower'.

bridging – A teaching strategy where explicit links are drawn from what has been learned to other related contexts to help transfer.

community of enquiry – Collaborative discussion with a class or group, a teaching technique used in Philosophy for Children.

concept mapping – Representing information in diagram form where key words are linked by lines. Also called 'mind mapping'.

concrete preparation – An introductory phase in some teaching thinking approaches where new words are introduced and learners become familiar with what the task is about.

constructivism – A view of learning in which learners are seen as building or developing their own understanding of how the world works from their experience and interaction with people around them.

creative thinking – Producing new ideas or thoughts; 'imaginative activity fashioned so as to produce outcomes that are both original and of value' (NACCE, 1999). Also called divergent or lateral thinking.

cognition – The mental operations involved in thinking; the biological/neurological processes of the brain that facilitate thought.

critical thinking – The process of determining the truth, accuracy, or value of something; characterised by reasoning and the evaluation of evidence. Also referred to as 'reasoning', 'inference and deduction', 'logical' thinking or 'analytical' thinking.

dialogue – Shared enquiry between two or more people.

dialogic – Communication informed by more than one voice or perspective.

disposition – A habit of mind or attitude.

emotional intelligence – How we understand and manage our emotions and our relationships with others, sometimes called emotional literacy.

enquiry – A systematic or scientific process for answering questions and solving problems based on gathering evidence through observation, analysis and reflection.

graphic organisers – Diagrams which help learners to organize information such as by comparing and contrasting using a grid of similarities and differences.

heuristics – General or widely applicable problem-solving strategies.

higher order thinking – Evaluation, synthesis and analysis, the higher levels of Bloom's taxonomy.

infusion – integrating teaching for thinking into the regular curriculum.

intelligence quotient (IQ) – A measurement of general ability obtained by multiplying the ratio of a child's mental age to chronological age by 100 and comparing the score with comparable groups of people.

mediation – Teaching that supports the development of a learner's understanding.

metacognition – Awareness of the processes of one's own thinking. Thinking about thinking in order to develop understanding and self-regulation.

mindmapping – A way of representing ideas and information visually where links between ideas are represented by branching lines. See also concept mapping.

multiple intelligences – A theory developed by Howard Gardner that IQ does not measure aspects of intelligence sufficiently and that people have strengths in different areas.

pedagogy – Knowledge or study of ways of teaching and learning.

reasoning – Drawing conclusions or inferences from observations, facts, experiences; either deductive: inferring conclusions from premises; or inductive: inferring provisional conclusions from information.

scaffolding – The support that teachers or carers need to provide for children to enable them to learn.

self-regulation – The process of setting goals for oneself, monitoring and evaluating progress.

Socratic questioning – Asking a series of probing questions that uncover meaning, truth, understanding or beliefs; moving in stages from literal to conceptual questions.

taxonomy – A classification of the elements of a field of study.

thinking skills – Capacities involved in effective thinking; practical ability in the processes of thinking; mental processes that underpin intelligent behaviour. Thinking skills identified in the English National Curriculum are: information processing, reasoning, enquiry, creative thinking and evaluation.

transfer – Taking something, an idea or skill, that has been learnt in one context and applying it in a different context.

zone of proximal development – The potential we have to learn and develop given assistance from others.

Bibliography

A select bibliography of books about teaching children to think.

Adey, P. and Shayer, M. (1994) *Really Raising Standards: Cognitive intervention and academic achievement*, London: Routledge.

Baron, J.B. and Sternberg, R.J. (eds) (1987) *Teaching Thinking Skills: Theory and practice*, New York: Freeman.

Blagg, N. (1991) *Can We Teach Intelligence? A comprehensive evaluation of Feuerstein's Instrumental Enrichment*, Hillsdale, NJ: Lawrence Erlbaum.

Brown, A.L. (1987) Metacognition, executive control, self-regulation and other more mysterious mechanisms, in Kluwe, R. and Weinert, F. (eds) *Metacognition, Motivation and Understanding*, Hillsdale, NJ: Lawrence Erlbaum, p. 65ff.

Buzan, T. (1974/1993) *Use Your Head*, London: BBC Publications.

Claxton, G. (1999) *Wise Up: The challenge of lifelong learning*, London: Bloomsbury.

Claxton, G. (2002) *Building Learning Power: Helping young people become better learners*, Bristol: TLO.

Coffield, F. *et al.* (2004) *Should We be Using Learning Styles? What research has to say to practice*, London: Learning Skills and Development Agency.

Coles, M.J. and Robinson, W. (1989) *Teaching Thinking*, Bristol: Bristol Press.

Collins, C. and Mangieri, J.N. (1992) *Teaching Thinking: An agenda for the twenty-first century*, Hillsdale, NJ: Lawrence Erlbaum.

Costa, A. (ed.) (2001) *Developing Minds: A resource book for teaching thinking*, Alexandria, VA: ASCD Publications.

Costa, A. and Kallick, B. (2000) *Habits of Mind*, Alexandria, VA: ASCD Publications.

Costello, P. (2000) *Thinking Skills in Early Childhood Education*, London: David Fulton.

Dawes, L., Mercer, N. and Wegerif, R. (2000) *Thinking Together: A programme of activities for developing thinking skills at KS2*, Birmingham: Questions Publishing.

De Bono, E. (1992) *Teach Your Child to Think*, Harmondsworth: Penguin.

De Bono, E. (1999) *Six Thinking Hats*, Harmondsworth: Penguin.

Dillon, J.T. (1994) *Using Discussion in Classrooms*, Buckingham: Open University Press.

Donaldson, M. (1978) *Children's Minds*, London: Fontana.

Feuerstein, R., Rand, Y., Hoffman, M.B. and Miller, R. (1980) *Instrumental Enrichment: An intervention programme for cognitive modifiability*, Baltimore, MD: University Park Press.

Fisher, A. (2001) *Critical Thinking: An introduction*, Cambridge: Cambridge University Press.

Fisher, P. (ed.) (2001) *Thinking Through History*, Cambridge: Chris Kington.

Fisher, R. (1996) *Stories for Thinking*, Oxford: Nash Pollock.

Fisher, R. (1997 *Games for Thinking*, Oxford: Nash Pollock.

Fisher, R. (1997) *Poems for Thinking*, Oxford: Nash Pollock.

Fisher, R. (1999) *First Stories for Thinking*, Oxford: Nash Pollock.

Fisher, R. (1999) *Head Start: How to develop your child's mind,* London: Souvenir Press.

Fisher, R. (2000) *First Poems for Thinking*, Oxford: Nash Pollock.

Fisher, R. (2000) *Thinking Skills: adding challenge to the curriculum. A guide for teachers of able children*, Glasgow: University of Glasgow, Scottish Network for Able Pupils.

Fisher, R. (2001) *Values for Thinking*, Oxford: Nash Pollock.

Fisher, R. (2003) *Teaching Thinking: Philosophical enquiry in the classroom*, 2nd edn, London: Continuum.

Fisher, R. (2005) *Teaching Children to Learn*, 2nd edn, Cheltenham: Nelson Thornes Ltd.

Gardner, H. (1983) *Frames of Mind: The theory of multiple intelligences*, New York: Basic Books.

Gardner, H. (1988) *The Unschooled Mind: How children think and how schools should teach*, New York: Basic Books.

Gardner, H. (1993) *Multiple Intelligences: The theory in practice*, New York: Basic Books.

Gardner, H. (1999) *Intelligence Reframed*, New York: Basic Books.

Goleman, D. (1995) *Emotional Intelligence*, New York: Bantam.

Goleman, D. (2002) *The New Leaders: Transforming the art of leadership*, London: Time-Warner.

Hamers, J.H.M. and Overtoom, M.T. (1997) *Teaching Thinking in Europe: Inventory of European programmes*, Utrecht: Sardes.

Higgins, S. (2001) *Thinking Through Primary Teaching*, Cambridge: Chris Kington.

Johnson, D.W. and Johnson, R.T. (1999) *Learning Together and Alone: Cooperative, competitive, and individualistic learning*, 5th edn, Boston, MA: Allyn & Bacon.

Leat, D. (1998) *Thinking Through Geography*, Cambridge: Chris Kington.

Lipman, M. (1988) *Philosophy Goes to School*, Philadelphia, PA: Temple University Press.

Lipman, M. (2003) *Thinking in Education*, 2nd edn, Cambridge: Cambridge University Press.

Lipman, M., Sharp, A. and Oscanyan, F. (1980) *Philosophy in the Classroom*, 2nd edn, Philadelphia, PA: Temple University Press.

McGuinness, C. (1999) *From Thinking Skills to Thinking Classrooms: A review and evaluation of approaches for developing pupils' thinking*, Research Report RR115, London: Department for Education and Employment. Available on line at: www.dfes.gov.uk/research/data/uploadfiles/RB115.doc.

McGuinness, C. et al. (1997) *Final Report on the ACTS Project: Phase 2*, Belfast: Northern Ireland Council for Curriculum, Examinations and Assessment.

Marzano, R., Pickering, D.J. and Pollock, J.E. (2001) *Classroom Instruction that Works: Research-based strategies for increasing student achievement*, Alexandria, VA: ASCD Publications.

Mercer, N. (2000) *Words and Minds: How we use language to think together*, London: Routledge.

Mercer, N., Wegerif, R., Dawes, L., Sams, C. and Higgins, S. (2002) *Language, Thinking and ICT in the Primary Curriculum: Final project report to the Nuffield Foundation*, Buckingham: Open University Press.

Moseley, D., Baumfield, V., Higgins, S., Lin, M., Miller, J., Newton, D. et al. (2004) *Thinking Skill Frameworks for Post-16 Learners: An evaluation*, London: Learning and Skills Research Centre.

Murris, K. and Haynes, J. (2000) *Storywise: Thinking through picture books*, Newport: Dialogue Works.

Novak, J.D. (1998) *Learning, Creating and Using Knowledge*, Hillsdale, NJ: Lawrence Erlbaum.

Novak, J.D. and Gowin, D.B. (1994) *Learning How to Learn*, New York: Cambridge University Press.

Paul, R. (1993) *Critical Thinking*, Rohnert Park, CA: Center for Critical Thinking, Sonoma State University.

Quinn, V. (1997) *Critical Thinking in Young Minds*, London: David Fulton.

Resnick, L.B. and Klopfer, L.E. (eds) (1989) *Toward the Thinking Curriculum: Current cognitive research*, Alexandria, VA: ASCD Publications.

Rockett, M. and Simon, S. (2002) *Thinking for Learning*, Stafford: Network Education Press.

Ryle, G. (1962) *The Concept of Mind*, London: Hutchinson.

Sharron, H. and Coulter, M. (1994) *Changing Children's Minds: Feuerstein's revolution in the teaching of intelligence*, Birmingham: Questions Publishing.

Shayer, M. and Adey, P. (2002) *Learning Intelligence: Cognitive acceleration across the curriculum*, Buckingham: Open University Press.

Smith, A. (2002) *The Brain's Behind It*, Stafford: Network Education Press.

Splitter, L. and Sharp, A.M. (1995) *Teaching for Better Thinking: The classroom community of enquiry*, Melbourne: Australian Council for Educational Research.

Sternberg, R.J. and Berg, C.A. (1992) *Intellectual Development*, Cambridge: Cambridge University Press.

Swartz, R.J. and Parks, S. (1993) *Infusing Critical and Creative Thinking into the Curriculum*, Pacific Grove, CA: Critical Thinking Press & Software.

Swartz, R.J. and Perkins, D.N. (1989) *Teaching Thinking: Issues and approaches*, Pacific Grove, CA: Midwest.

Vygotsky, L.S. (1962) *Thought and Language*, New York: John Wiley & Sons.

Wallace, B., Adams, H.B., Maltby, F. and Mathfield, J. (1993) *TASC: Thinking actively in a social context*, Bicester: A.B. Academic Publishers.

Wegerif, R. (2002) *Literature Review in Thinking Skills, Technology and Learning*. Available on line at: www.nestafuturelab.org.

Wilson, V. (2000) *Can Thinking Skills Be Taught? A paper for discussion*, Edinburgh: Scottish Council for Research in Education.

Index